IMAGES
of America

WARREN COUNTY

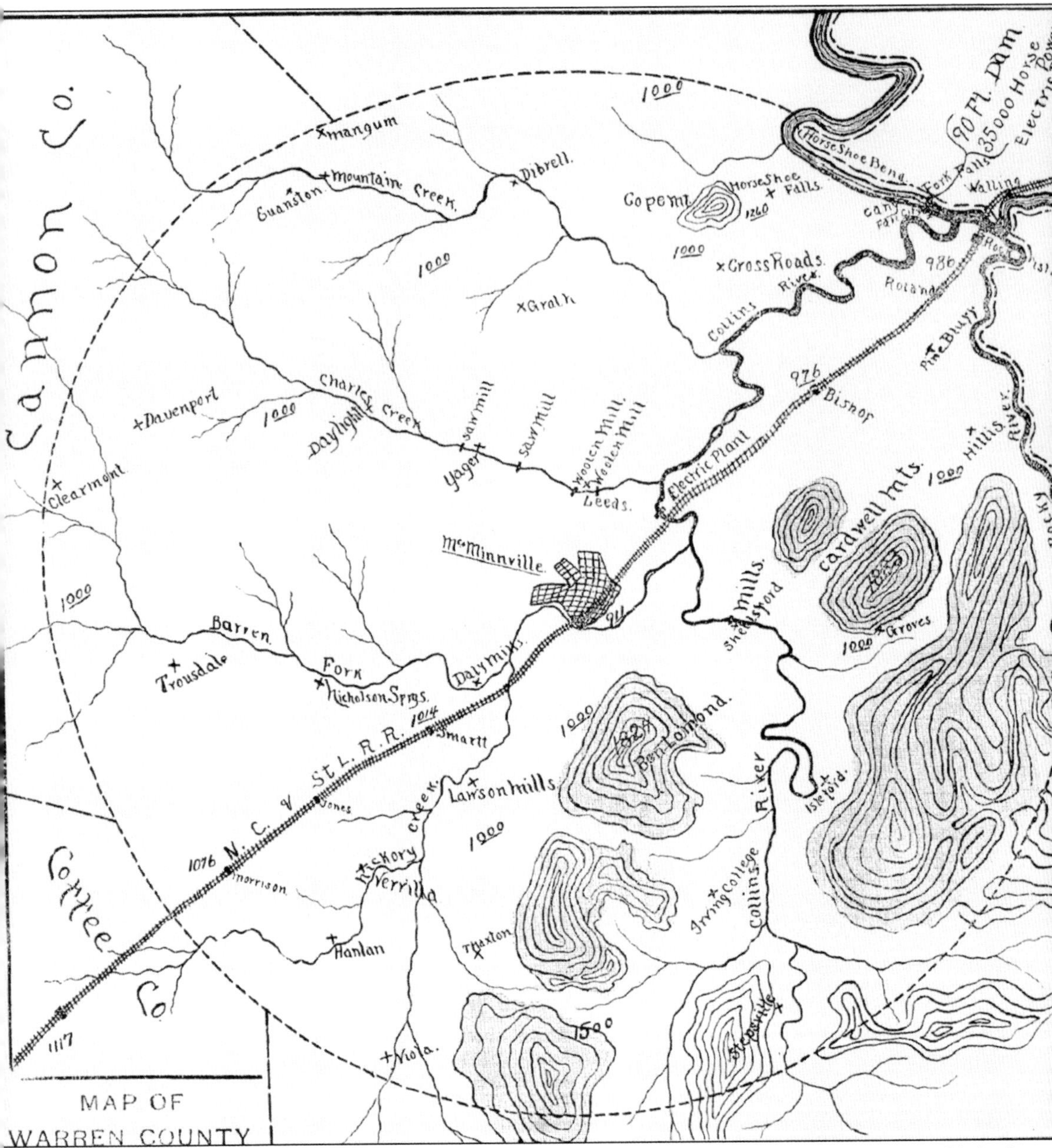

Warren County is the most perfectly round county in the state of Tennessee. This map, published in 1910, elucidates that fact and depicts the locations of early communities, most of which had post offices. Cardwell and Ben Lomond Mountain ranges are shown, as well as railroad lines. The county had numerous water-powered mills scattered throughout its boundaries, which are also designated on this important, early map.

ON THE COVER: Typical of such shops of the 1940s and 1950s, Cantrell's Shoe Shop was located in the Brown Hotel, on the north side of Main Street, near the corner of Sparta Street in downtown McMinnville. This photograph, taken in 1950, depicts an unidentified customer standing at the counter, with brothers Franklin "Brackett" Cantrell (left) and Cecil Cantrell (right) behind the counter.

IMAGES
of America

WARREN COUNTY

Monty Wanamaker and Chris Keathley

ARCADIA
PUBLISHING

ISBN 978-0-7385-4370-3

Published by Arcadia Publishing
Charleston SC, Chicago IL, Portsmouth NH, San Francisco CA

Printed in the United States of America

Library of Congress Catalog Card Number: 2006931762

For all general information contact Arcadia Publishing at:
Telephone 843-853-2070
Fax 843-853-0044
E-mail sales@arcadiapublishing.com
For customer service and orders:
Toll-Free 1-888-313-2665

Visit us on the Internet at www.arcadiapublishing.com

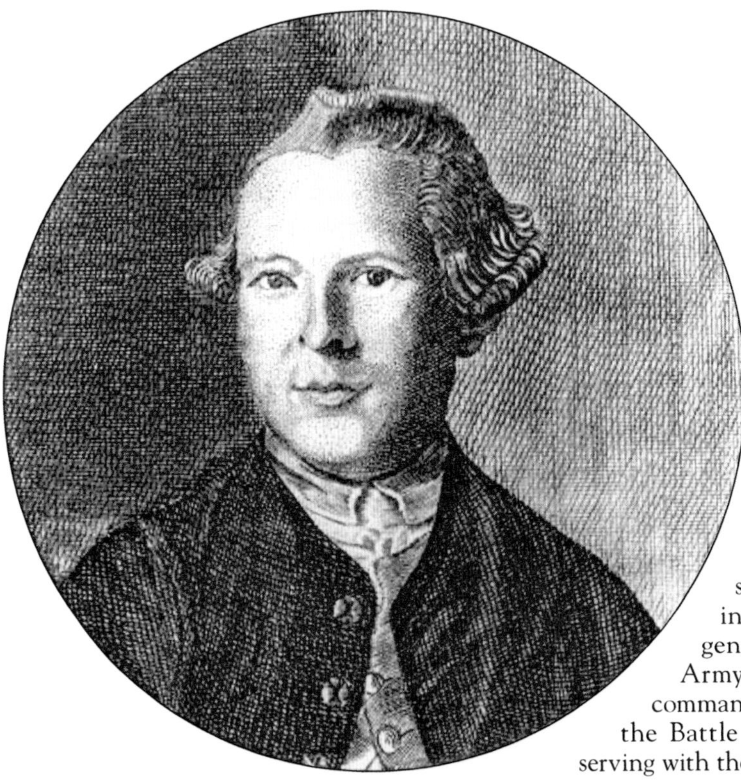

In 1807, the Tennessee Legislature named the new political district of Warren County in memory of Maj. Gen. Joseph Warren, patriot of the American Revolution. Born in Roxbury, Massachusetts, in 1741, he proved himself to be a successful politician, who, in 1775, became a major general in the American Army, in which he declined command and was killed during the Battle of Bunker Hill while serving with the troops.

CONTENTS

Acknowledgments

Since the Southern Museum and Galleries of Photography, Culture, and History was founded in 2001, numerous individuals have graciously shared their images and information of family, and Warren County history, with us. Were it not for their generosity and interest, this book as it stands could have never been produced. Some individuals and local citizens have gone out of their way to foster the cause and be helpful since our official opening in November 2001. It is impossible here to list each and every person who has contributed to the treasure trove of photographs, but we wish to acknowledge the following who have, from the beginning, been especially helpful: Curtis and Jane Coleman, Lucia Cordell Getsi, Charles Bostick, the late Connie Mullican, Helen Martin, Dorothy Roscinski, Kenneth "Peanut" Cantrell, Betty Higginbotham, Harold and Mazel Pendergraph, Wayne Wolford, Raleigh Miller, Lewis and Thetis Keel, the late Betty Bryan Haslam, Jeanette Lowery, Joan and Sewell Rhea, and Steve Wilsher. Many individuals have helped pave the way for this book through their dedicated research and passion for local history, which they shared with us. Specifically we wish to thank Billy and Betty Lively, Howard Locke, Martha Holt, Brenda Muncey, Ladye Jane Hunter, Almetia Cunningham, Mary Barnes, Doris Cantrell, Khyva Starkey, Glenda Cantrell, Bethany Hall, Robbie Beaver, George and Charlien McGlothin, Jaceine Denton, Dean Brewer, Bill Jakes, Marion Kelley, Frances G. Oliver, First Baptist Church, T. L. Coppinger, William "Bill" Byrd, Betty Borth, Donna Vaughn, and Warren County Historian James A. Dillon Jr.

We wish to express our deepest gratitude to G. B. Green and the Womack Printing Company in McMinnville, whose historical publications proved to be invaluable sources of information. The *Southern Standard* newspaper, which has been in operation for more than 100 years, has been an important reference. The Tennessee State Library and Archives in Nashville, the New York Public Library, and the Library of Congress in Washington, D.C., have contributed to our archives.

We also wish to acknowledge our editor at Arcadia Publishing, Maggie Bullwinkel, who has been from the beginning warmly responsive and inspirational in her encouragement and assistance.

INTRODUCTION

Located about midway between the northern and southern boundaries of the state of Tennessee and rimmed by the majestic Cumberland Mountain, Warren County was established in 1807 and named for Gen. Joseph Warren, a Revolutionary War patriot. Within 10 years of its first settlements, the county's population numbered almost 20,000. The 2000 Census recorded over 38,000 people within its 431 square miles.

In prehistoric times, the wilderness area that encompasses Warren County was inhabited by a mysterious race of people about which little is still known today. Referred to by archeologists as the Mound Builders, they predated the Cherokees and Chickasaws, and other modern races by several thousand years. Before its first white settlers, the area was an important hunting ground for the Cherokee and Chickasaw Indians, and, in 1838, the infamous Cherokee Trail of Tears meandered through the county and at the edge of the county seat of McMinnville.

Within the past 100 years, the area's moderate Southern climate and fertile agricultural diversity have helped make the county the "Nursery Capital of the World," presently home to over 600 productive, certified plant nurseries which for many years have supplied their products to customers throughout the United States and several foreign countries. In 1940, the county had over 2,500 farms and approximately 226,000 acres of productive farmlands.

Tennessee's largest cave, Cumberland Caverns, is located in the county at the base of Harrison Ferry Mountain, which brings thousands of tourists to the area each year. The magnificent scenic beauty of the area is encompassed in the richly wooded Rock Island State Park, situated at the confluence of the Collins and Caney Fork Rivers, where the waters flow through imposing limestone gorges, creating waterfalls of great beauty. The 883-acre park has a natural sand beach on the Center Hill Reservoir, home of one of Tennessee's early hydroelectric power plants. The area was the earliest in the county to be settled, and was home to an important 19th-century textile mill. It has long been one of the county's leading tourist attractions and recreational destinations.

McMinnville, founded in 1810 as the county seat of government, was named for Joseph McMinn, a transplanted Pennsylvania Quaker who was speaker of the Tennessee Senate at the time of its establishment and later became governor of the state.

The great, natural beauty of the Cumberland region was an important drawing card to the new town. Within a few years of its establishment, McMinnville overflowed its original boundaries and was soon a bustling metropolis, with a great variety of first-class stores and shops serving its community. It drew high-quality lawyers, doctors, and ministers from across the country who built fine, spacious homes and established academies, and churches. It gained a reputation in its early days as an important center of learning. The Edmondson Academy was built in 1820. The Cumberland Female College, established in 1850, brought great prestige to the town and continued to flourish for some 50 years. The Southern School of Photography, which officially opened its doors in 1904—the second of only two of its kind in the country—lent an ever-wider and greater prestige to the town for over 25 years.

During the half century after the Civil War, McMinnville was one of the state's most noted summer resorts, claiming one of the nation's finest hotels. Few institutions in the town have had a longer and more noted existence than the old Sedberry Hotel. During its heyday in the 1920s and 1930s, many persons of national and international fame came to McMinnville and experienced its hospitality. After visiting every American and Canadian city in 1927 with populations over 10,000, an official of the American Automobile Association termed the Sedberry, "The best little hotel on the North American Continent." The era of World War II brought a substantial decline in patrons and revenue from which the hotel never fully recovered. Therefore, Erby Sedberry, who had been largely responsible for its national recognition, made the decision to close the venerable establishment, which had become a legend it its own time by the time it served it final meal in November 1954.

Through the years, Warren County has been basically an agricultural community. Notwithstanding the early farm economy, its plant nursery industry had flourished from the beginning of the industry in the horse-and-buggy days when Jonathan Henry Boyd in 1887 discovered the value of the seeds of *Calycanthus floridus*, or sweet shrub, and settled in the Irving College Community where his first nursery was established in about 1913: the Forest Nursery and Seed Company. His business quickly grew to unimaginable proportions, as this self-taught and noted botanist exploited the greatest potential in the vast numbers of varieties of native trees and plants growing in the surrounding mountains. Daniel Porter Henegar, past president of the Tennessee Nurseryman's Association, coined the phrase "cradle of the plant kingdom." Warren County is nestled in the cradle of the plant kingdom, the Highland Rim area of some 9,300 square miles, and on the slopes of the Cumberlands extending onward to the Great Smokies. There are a greater variety of plants growing in their natural state than in any other area in America or in all Europe. After a 1993 nursery and floriculture survey in Tennessee conducted by the Tennessee Agricultural Statistics Service revealed that Warren County is undoubtedly the Nursery Capital of the World, the label has continued to dignify the county and its inhabitants, and remains factual to the present day. In December 1931, then governor of New York, Franklin Delano Roosevelt, ordered a large number of tulip poplar trees from Fernando C. Boyd of Boyd Nursery Company, in McMinnville, and later, when he was president, Roosevelt ordered trees from the nursery. Jimmy Carter actually visited McMinnville Nurseries to purchase trees while he was president.

This book is not meant to be a concise, progressive narrative of the history of Warren County, so much as it is a patchwork quilt of various and sundry events, landmarks, people, and communities down through its intriguing history. It is meant to give some general picture of the various colors and textures of Warren County as a whole, as it celebrates its official 200th birthday anniversary in November 2007.

One

Early Days

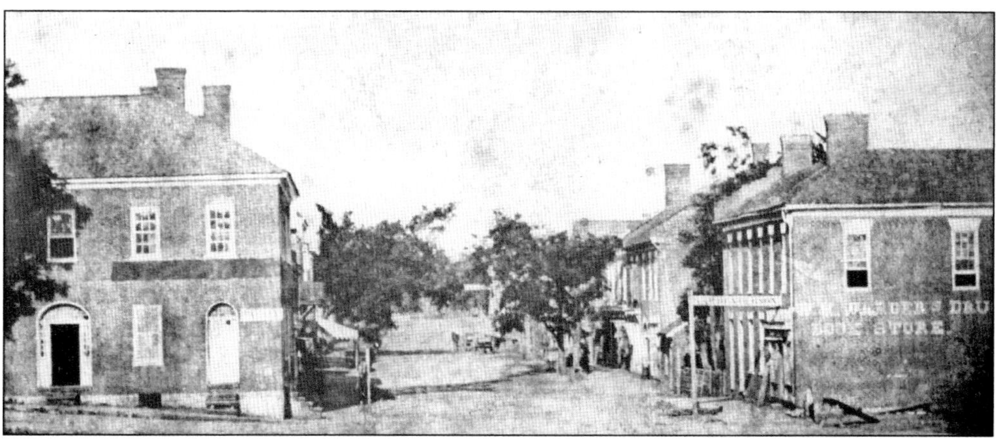

One of the earliest extant images of a McMinnville street scene is this view of Main Street looking east that shows the Mountain City Hotel, at left, dating to about 1820, the site of City Bank and Trust Company building decades later. At right in the distance is the Livingston Building, and the small building next to it, erected about 1830, is the law office of Andrew J. Marchbanks, who figured eventually as one of the town's and state's most important lawyers and judges.

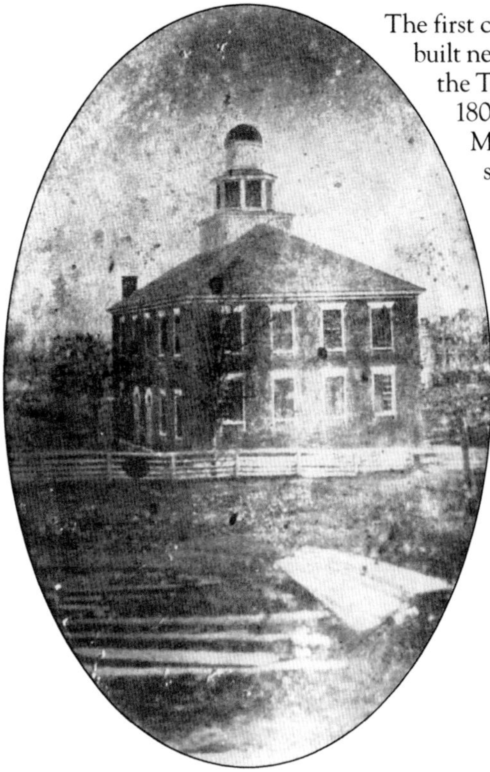

The first courts of Warren County were held in a log cabin built near the home of pioneer Joseph Westmoreland, in the Tanyard Springs community, during the summer of 1808, which served its purpose until after the town of McMinnville was officially formed in 1810. In the spring of 1811, Capt. William White came to the new town with workers and built a new, two-story, brick courthouse in the city park. This second courthouse, pictured, stood until 1858.

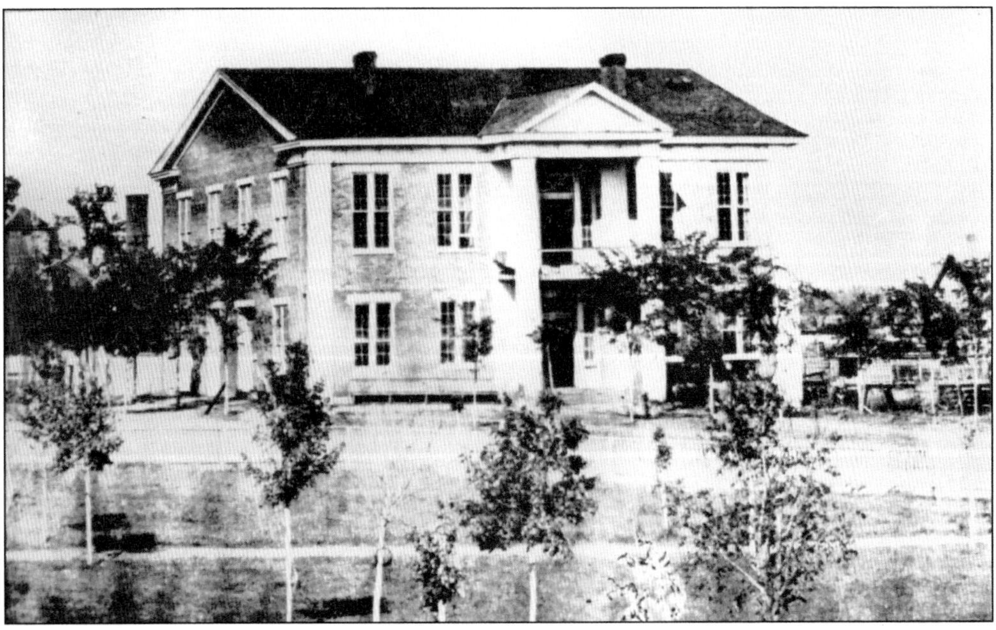

Judge Smith J. Walling supervised the construction in 1858 of the new, much larger courthouse, which the court had agreed to build. Designed by John E. Goodney, the building also accommodated on the second floor a printing office and Warren Lodge No. 125. This third Warren County Courthouse served until the county court made the decision in 1896 to discard the old building and erect a new, more stable one.

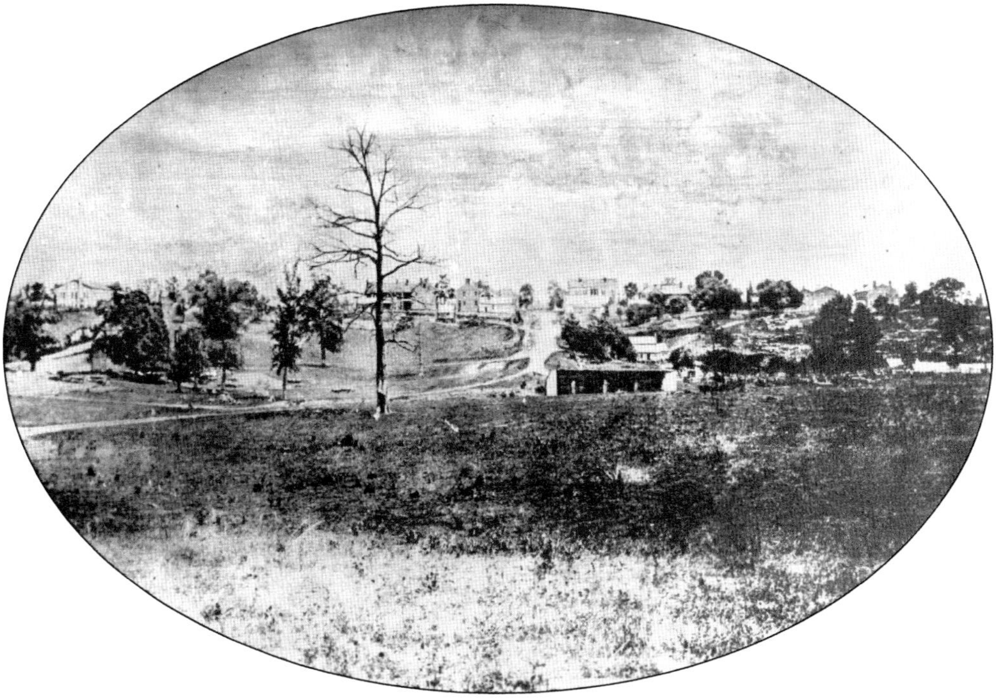

This 1863 J. Fletch Woodward photograph of the center of the town of McMinnville looking north was taken from the Depot Bottom area, which had recently been burned by Federal troops. Among the prominent landmarks that can be identified in this photograph is the third Warren County Courthouse, built in 1858, visible to the right of Depot Street, in the center of the photograph.

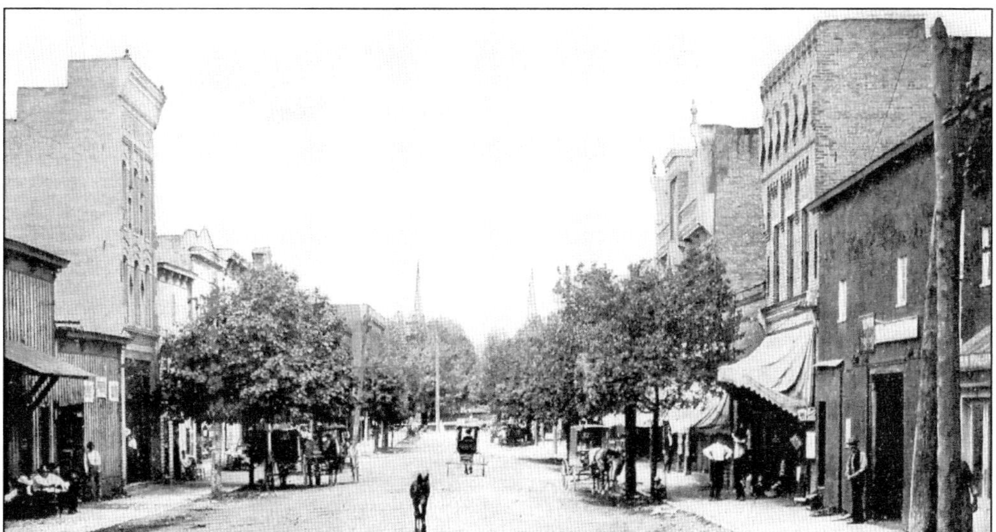

This c. 1898 McMinnville Street scene depicts a view from East Main looking west, with the spires of First Presbyterian Church and First Methodist Church rising in the far distance. The tall building at far left is the J. R. Brinkley Building, erected in the late 1890s as a saloon. Partially hidden by the tree at right is Houchin's Opera House, built in 1888. At extreme right is the Biles and Smith store, dealers in hardware and groceries.

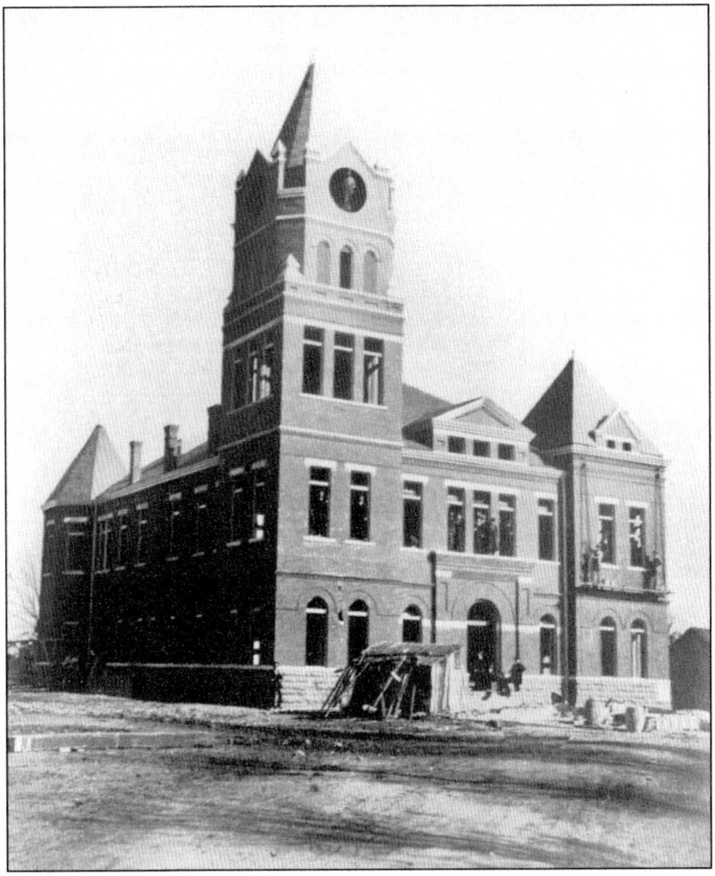

With R. H. Hunt as architect and B. M. Nelson as builder, work began in 1896 on the new Warren County Courthouse, near the site of the former building. In December 1897, the impressive structure was all but completed. A handsome brick structure of modified Roman architecture, the plans called for a four-story clock tower, which was later removed. The building was expanded and remodeled in 1978. This photograph, at left, shows men at work on the building, and a man standing in the face of the clock tower.

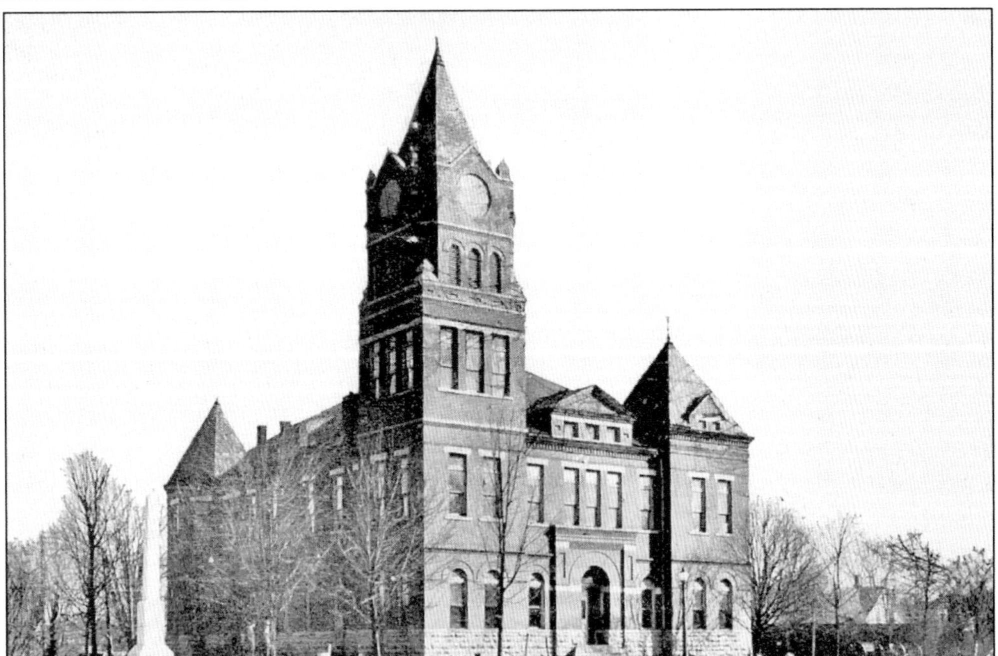

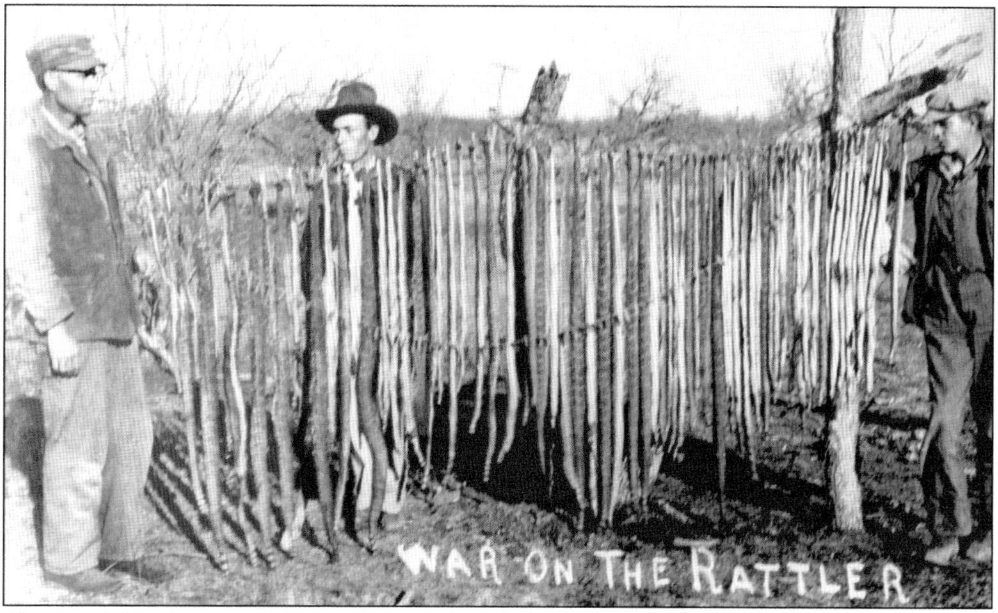

This late-1800s photograph depicts three unidentified men proudly displaying their bounty of timber rattlesnakes. Much of Middle Tennessee at that time was still vast wilderness, blanketed with virgin timber and untamed forests. As pioneer settlements increased, the poisonous snakes—namely copperheads and rattlesnakes—were killed in great numbers, greatly reducing the population in the following decades.

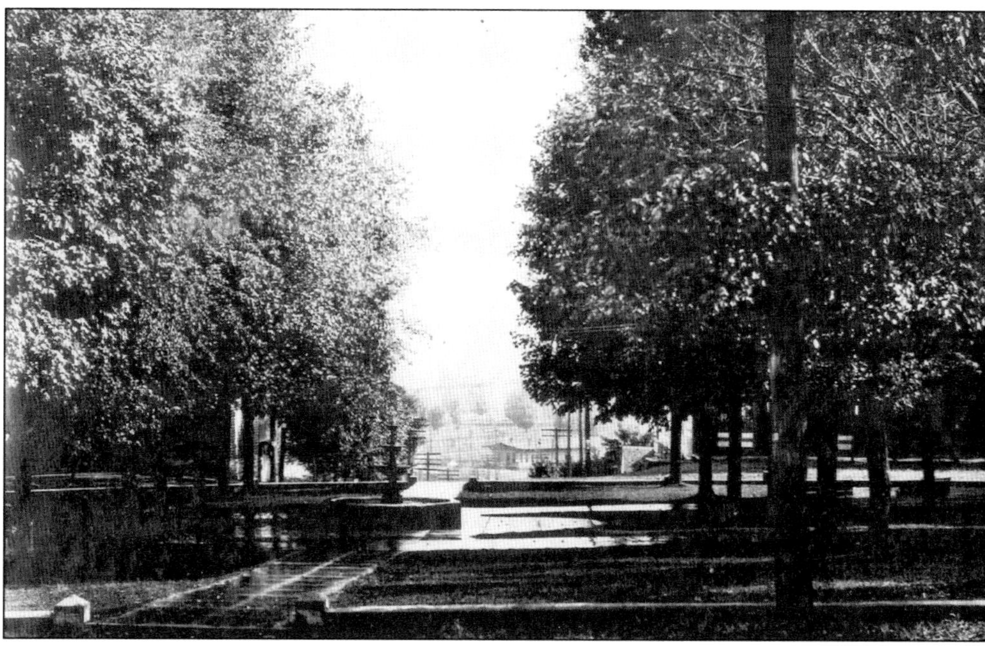

This late-1800s photograph, looking south to Depot Bottom through the city park, shows the railway station in the distance. In 1855, the McMinnville and Manchester Railroad began to run trains to connect with the Nashville and Chattanooga Railroad, which had been completed to Chattanooga the year before. In the history of McMinnville, the coming of the railroad marked a very important milestone for the town.

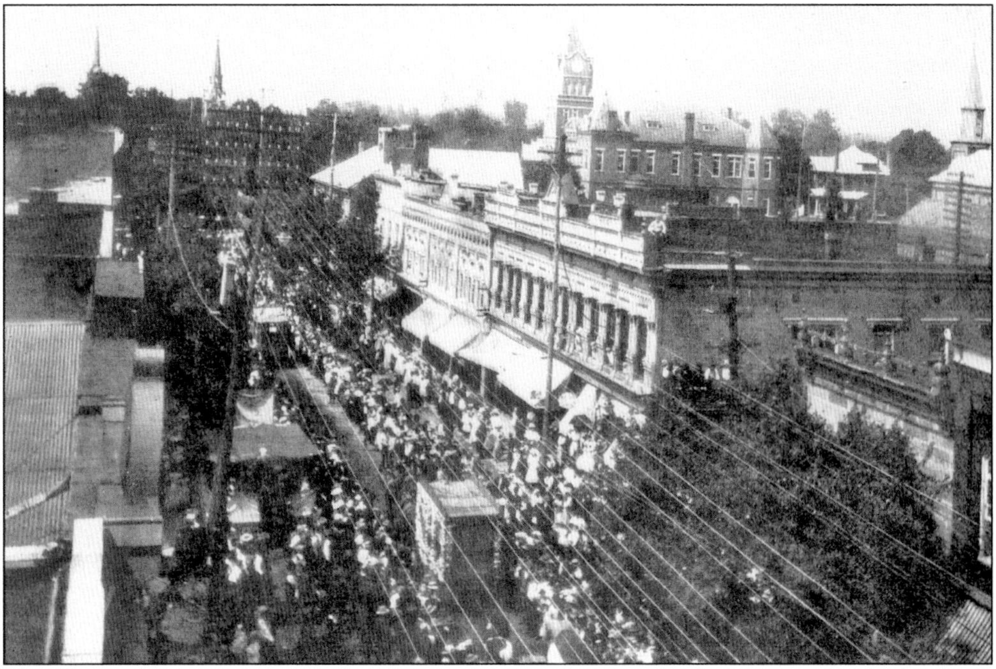

This late-1800s photograph of a bird's-eye view of McMinnville shows a parade making its way down Main Street with a massive crowd gathered along the thoroughfare. The old McMinnville Mercantile building is visible on the corner of Main and Spring Streets. The town was a bustling center of commerce and industry, with telegraph wires lining the streets. The Makay-Bennit Telegraph Company had opened an office in the town in 1890.

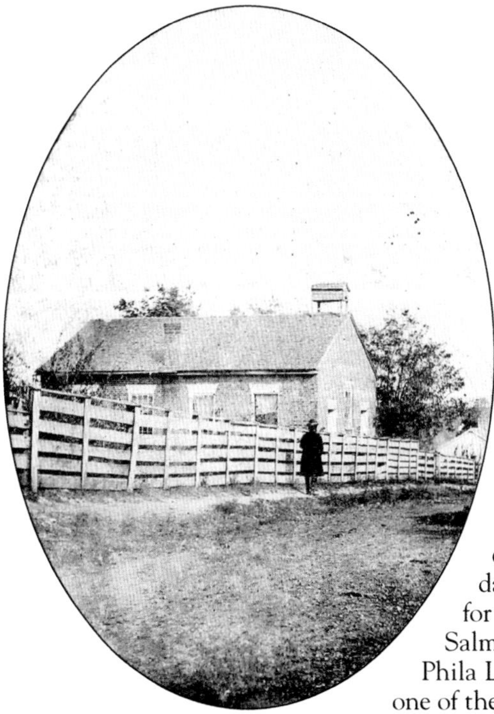

This small Baptist church stood on Lyon Street, established about 1838 by Phila Lyon and her daughter, "Grandma" Mitchell, on land donated for that purpose by the Lyon Family, and built by Salmon J. Mitchell, pioneer McMinnville contractor. Phila Lyon had earlier established the Lyon Institute, one of the earliest schools, where she taught.

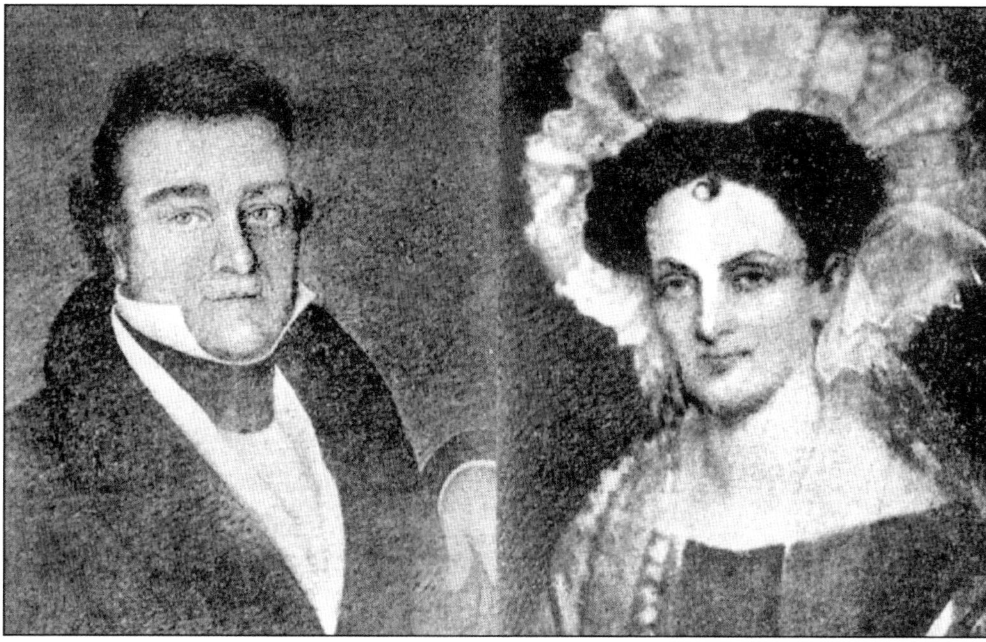

John Cain and his wife, Beersheba (Sullivan) Cain, were prominent early citizens of the new town of McMinnville. John was for many years the principal merchant of the town and was an extensive dealer in land speculation in Warren County. Beersheba was legendary for her great beauty and is credited with having discovered the now-famous iron water spring on the mountain for which the early summer resort was named. The Cains built this imposing two-story, brick house sometime between 1820 and 1825. At the time, it was known as the "handsomest private residence" in McMinnville, with expansive gardens that Beersheba oversaw. After her husband died, she converted their grand home into the McMinnville Inn in 1834, which, in the 1840s, became known as the Warren House.

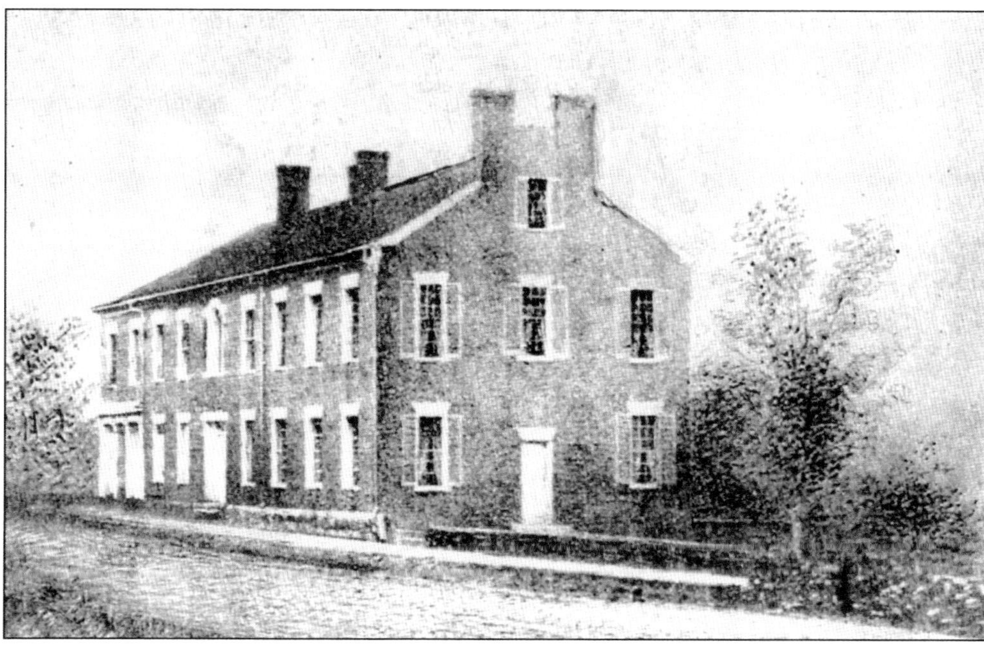

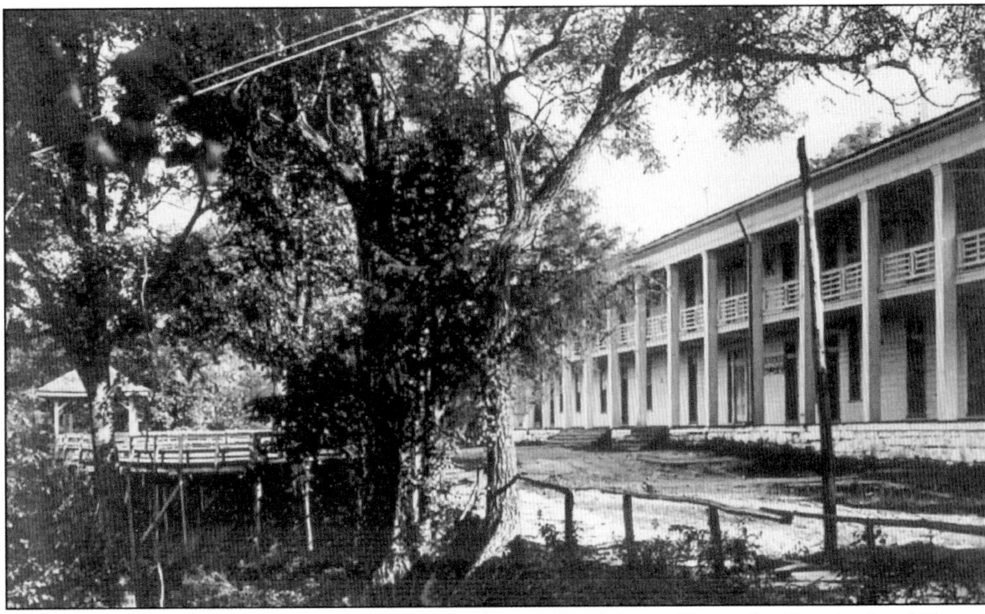

Beersheba Springs, located about 25 miles southeast of McMinnville on the Cumberland Plateau atop Beersheba Mountain, was established in 1839. When it was opened as a summer resort, the area was officially still a part of Warren County. Beersheba (Sullivan) Cain discovered a famous mineral spring there in 1833, after which a tavern and cabins were built. By 1860, it had become a popular summer resort, which continues today.

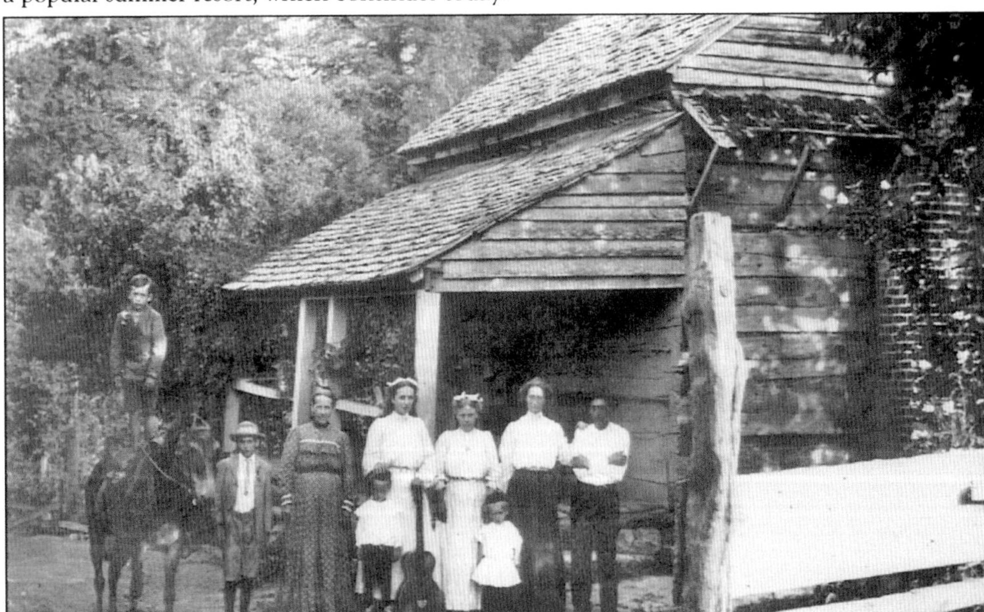

This early 1900s photograph depicts the Samuel Stoner and Nancy Jane Patrick Stoner family who, for many years, lived in an early log cabin built sometime around 1836 by pioneer Jacob Wanamaker. Pictured from left to right are son Louis (standing on horse), son Elza, mother Nancy Jane Stoner, daughter Allie, daughter Lucinda, Hassie Carter Stoner (wife of son Frank Stoner), with their children Marcus and Vernon.

This very rare, early-1800s photograph of some important buildings in downtown McMinnville was probably a stereoscopic view, showing the office of attorney Benjamin J. Hill marked on the photograph with an X, at left. The building marked with an X, at right, is the house in which Samuel Hervey Laughlin boarded. Laughlin was to become one of the town's greatest lawyers and influential politicians.

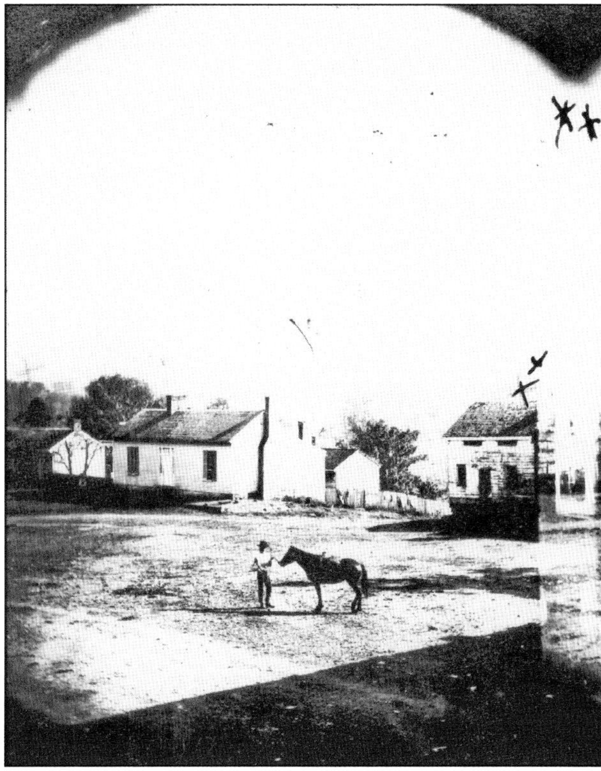

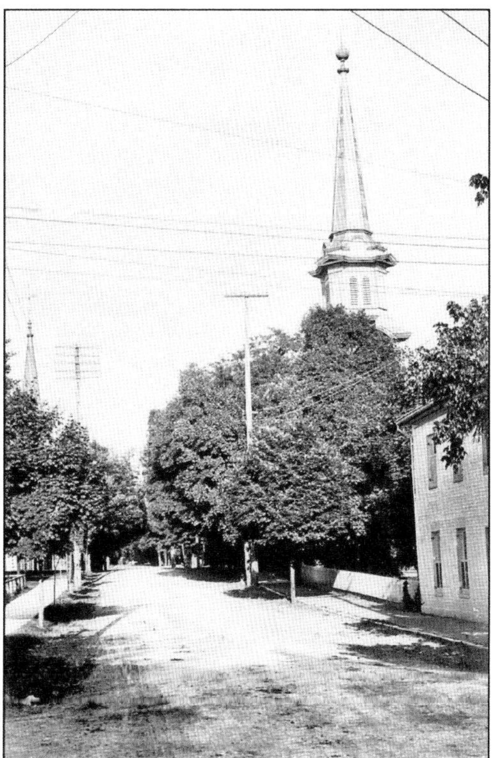

This 1800s photograph of West Main Street looking east shows the spire of Methodist Episcopal Church, far left, and a telegraph pole and lines adjacent to it. At right is the steeple of First Presbyterian Church, which was completed in 1878. A portion of the Annie Paine house can be seen at right, foreground.

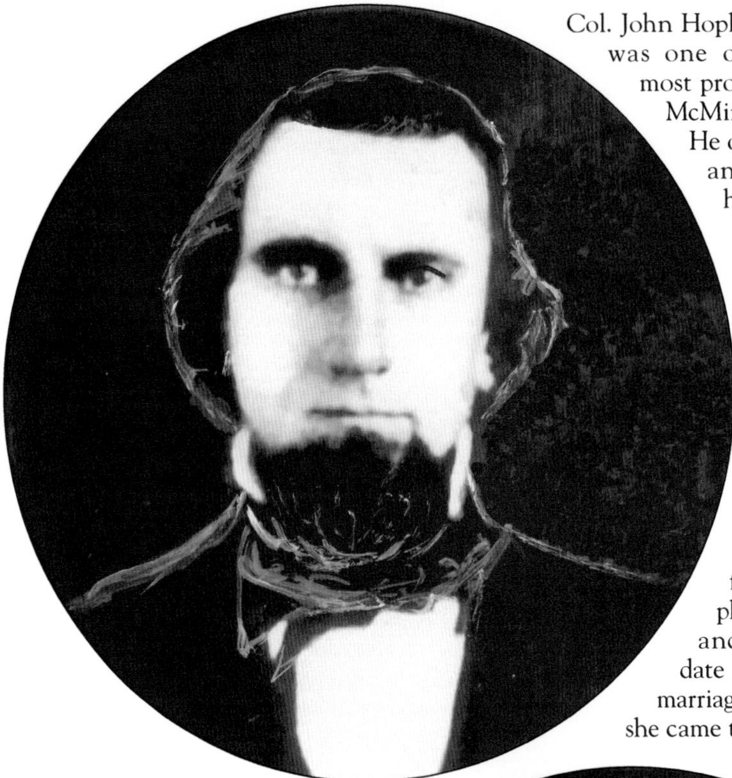

Col. John Hopkins French (1817–1892) was one of the wealthiest and most prosperous businessmen in McMinnville in the late 1800s. He owned vast land holdings and was a breeder of fine horses, often venturing to New Orleans to sell his stock. In 1853, during one such business trip to the city, he had a chance meeting with a young poetess, Lucy Virginia Smith, whose poetry he had read. At the time, French was actually carrying one of her poems on his person, which he had clipped from a newspaper. These photographs of Col. French and Lucy Virginia Smith date back to the time of their marriage in 1853, after which time she came to live in McMinnville.

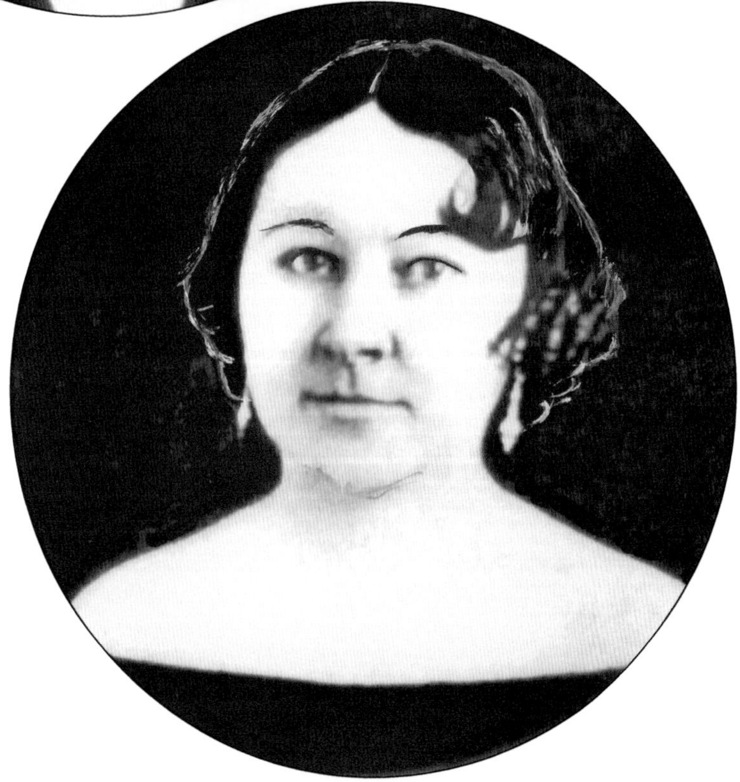

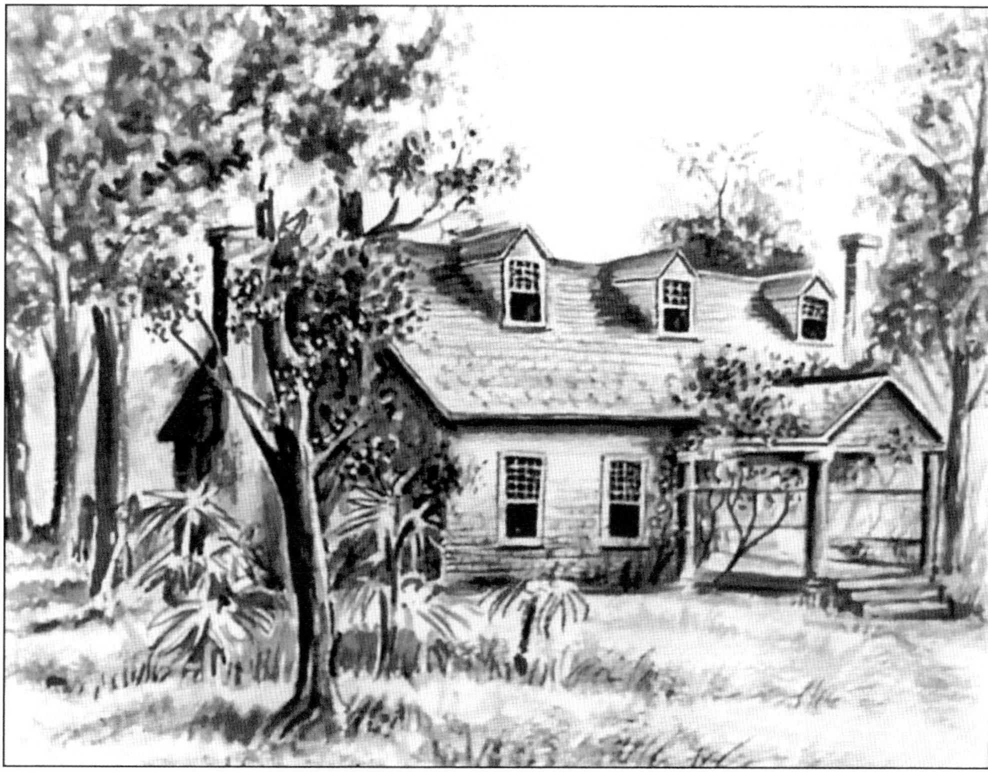

When Col. John Hopkins French married poetess and author Lucy Virginia Smith in 1853, it was Forest Home, the French homestead in Warren County, which became their legendary residence. The house was situated back on a 640-acre tract of land a short distance west of McMinnville along the Nashville Highway. This drawing of Forest Home was created by Monty Wanamaker in 2004, from the home's image in a 1900 magazine article.

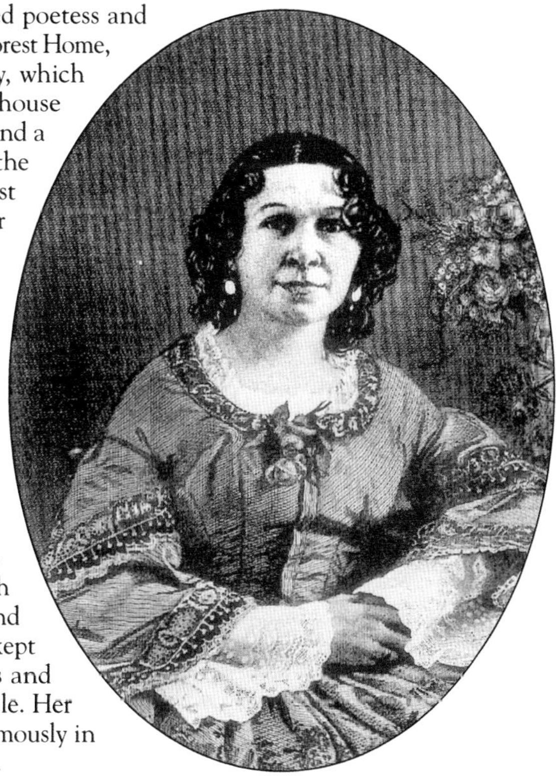

Lucy Virginia French (1825–1881), McMinnville's prominent Victorian author, was educated in Pennsylvania and her native Virginia. Already a published author, French subsequently published poetry, novels, and numerous newspaper articles. In 1862, she kept a detailed diary of the Civil War battles and conflicts of life in and around McMinnville. Her final book of poems was published posthumously in 1883 by her sister, Lide Smith Meriwether.

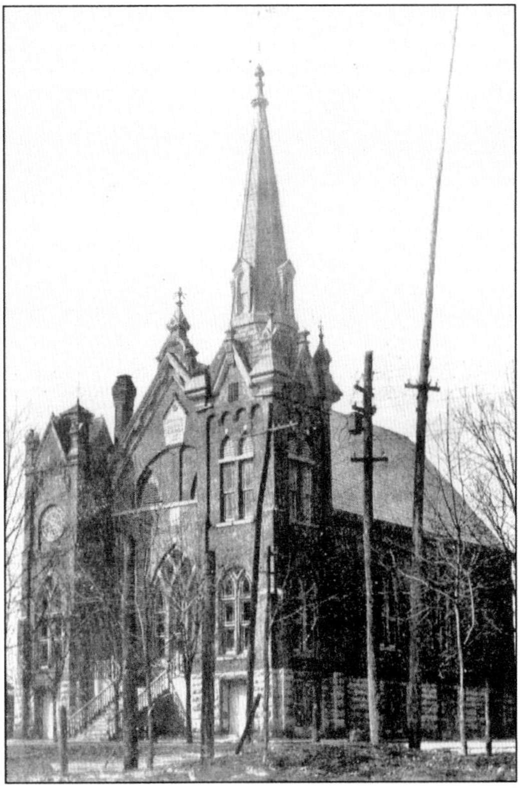

This photograph of the First United Methodist Church building was made around the time of the structure's completion in 1889. Located on the corner of West Main and Chancery Streets in McMinnville, when finished it was considered the handsomest building in the town, and its condition has changed little down though the years. The cornerstone was laid on August 25, 1886, with dedication ceremonies held in July 1889.

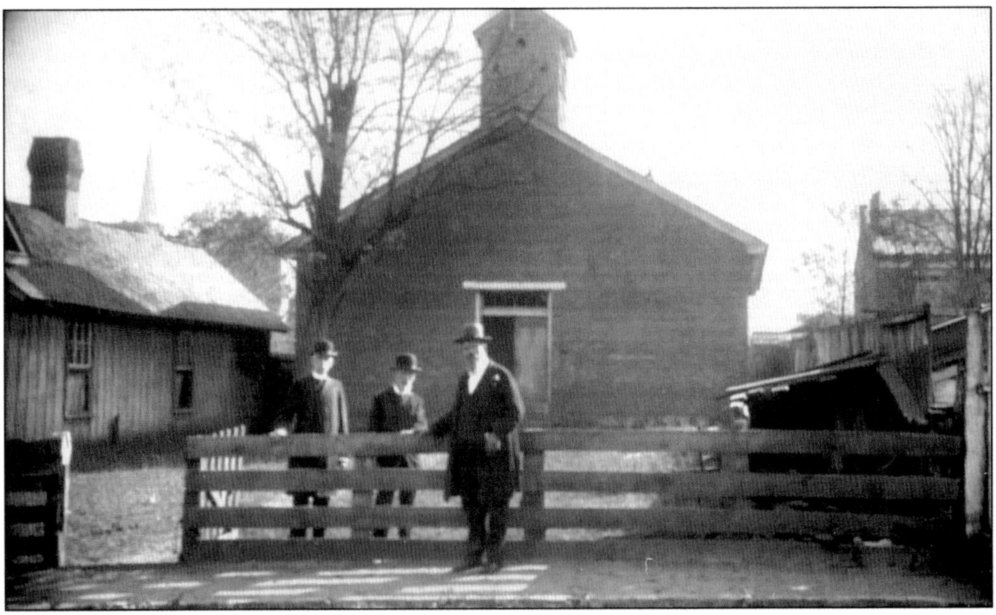

This little, brick Methodist Church building was erected in 1852 on the northwest corner of West Main and Chancery Streets in McMinnville, at the rear of the present Magness Memorial Library. Facing Chancery Street, the spire of the early Christian Church can be seen. The men pictured standing in front of the church are, from left to right, Rev. J. A. Orman, Rev. W. M. Green, and Rev. W. D. Cherry.

This pen-and-ink drawing by Chris Keathley depicts Houchin's Opera House, which was built in 1888 by William Houchin (1843–1895), a wealthy black McMinnville businessman and property owner. He was proprietor of a successful livery stable business and was at the time the wealthiest man in the town. The first permanent home of the town government was located on the second floor.

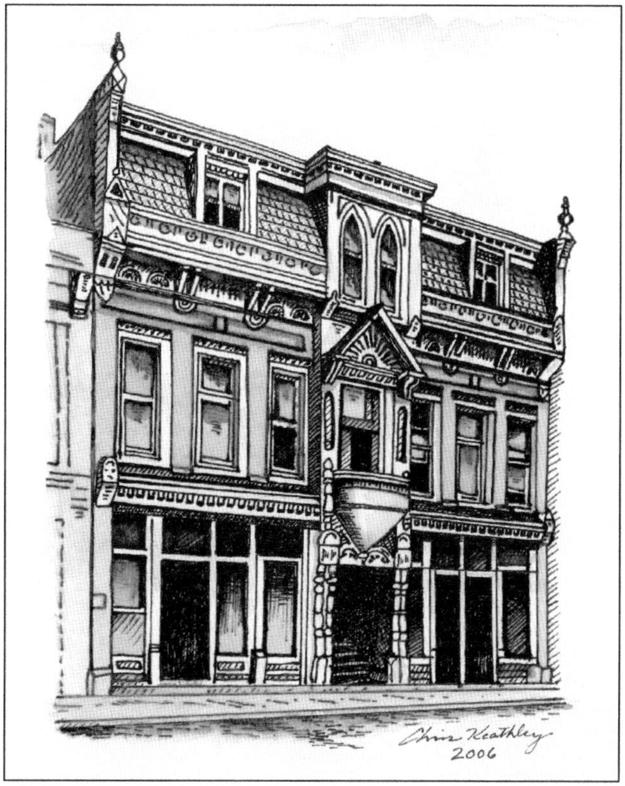

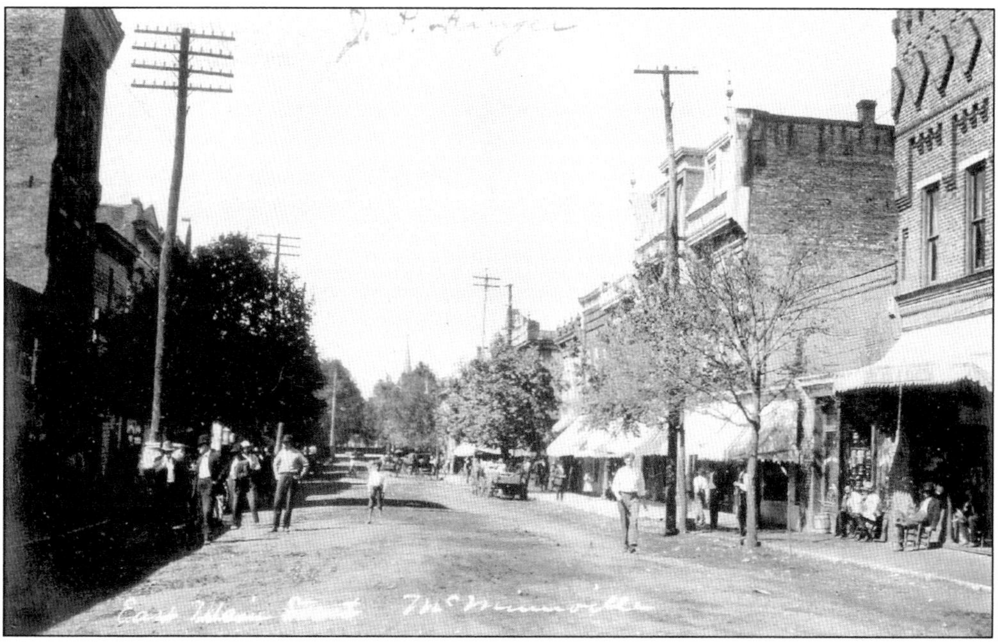

This real-photo postcard view of McMinnville's East Main Street, looking west, in horse and buggy days, shows, among other landmarks, Houchin's Opera House, partially blocked by the tree, at right, in the foreground. The photograph was made after the town had acquired telegraph and telephone service in the late 1800s, when the streets were still unpaved.

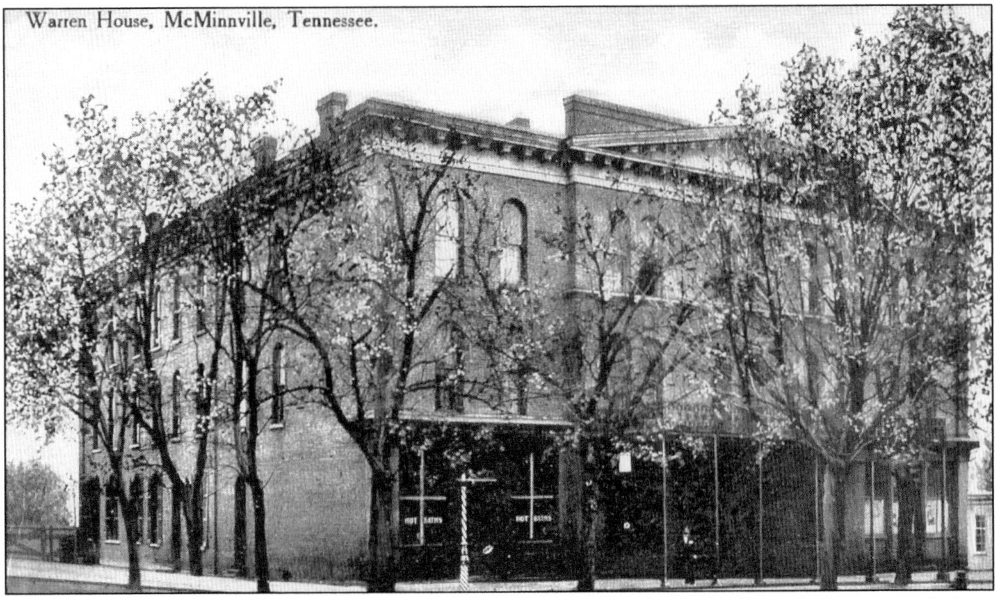

After the death of her husband, John Cain, around 1840, Beersheba (Sullivan) Cain turned their mansion into a hotel, which was first named the McMinnville Inn. In the following years, the establishment would be run by a number of individuals and would become known as the Warren House under the management of Dr. Sions Read. The original, three-story brick structure was destroyed by fire in 1870 and was immediately rebuilt to be successfully run as the Warren House until it was leased in 1913 by Oceana Sedberry, who, along with daughters Connie and Erby, began operating it as the Sedberry Hotel.

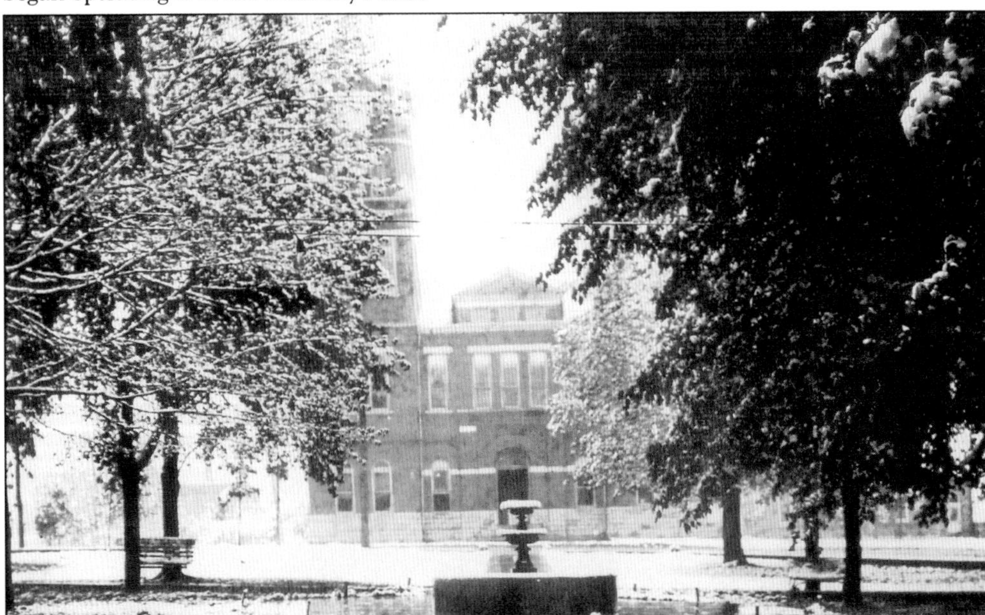

This early-1900s, real-photo postcard shows the serene McMinnville City Park covered in a blanket of snow with the leaves still clinging to the trees. The front of the fourth (and current) Warren County Courthouse, which was built in 1897, is visible in the distance with the fountain and surrounding pool seen in the foreground.

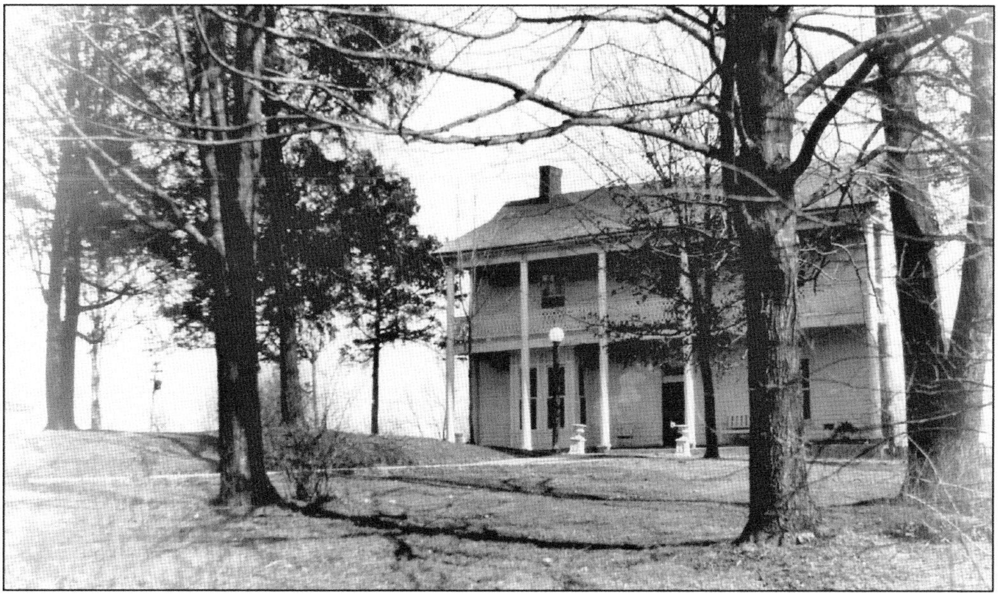

This imposing, two-story, Colonial-style house is located on North Spring Street, directly across from the First Baptist Church in McMinnville. The house was possibly built sometime before 1856 by George Jefferies Stubblefield. It was purchased in 1876 by prominent citizen Jesse Walling whose family lived in the house for several decades. In 1940, it became the residence of the Frank Winton family for more than 40 years. In recent years, the house has undergone a total renovation.

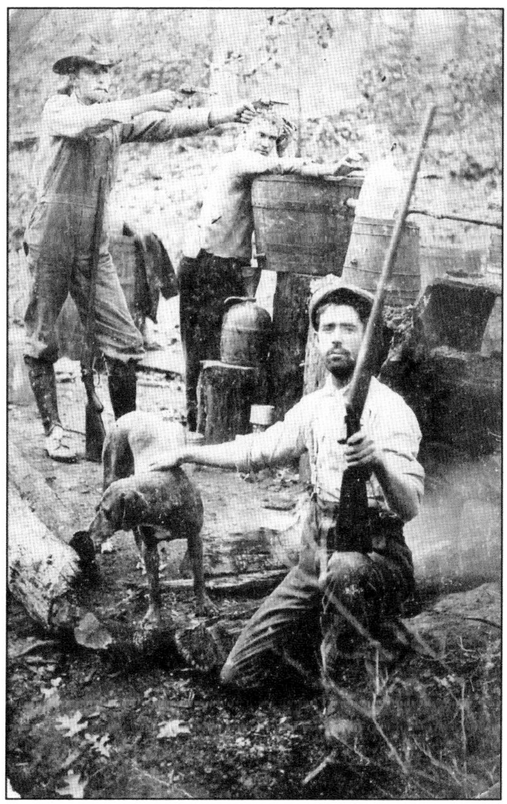

This image depicts three unidentified men guarding their moonshine still in the remote mountains of Warren County, possibly before the state of Tennessee voted out whiskey in 1909. By the late 1800s, apple brandy was a major Warren County industry; however, by the 1890s, little profit was being realized, and Warren County had been brought to near anarchy by overtaxation. After Prohibition, illegal spirits continued to be made.

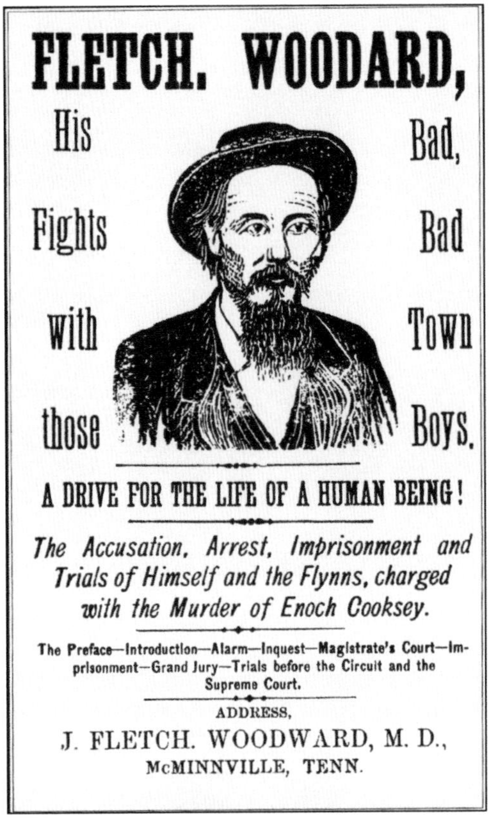

J. Fletcher Woodward, McMinnville's first known photographer, received patents for two photography-related inventions in 1871. He was also a medical doctor and, later in his life, was an author, publisher, engraver, and printer. He ran a commercial printing studio at his home and is known to have written at least 14 books. In 1878, Woodward published a little book detailing circumstances surrounding the murder of city marshal Enoch Cooksey on November 15, 1873. The killing was blamed on Woodward, who was arrested, jailed, tried by jury and found guilty of first-degree murder and sentenced to hang. The verdict was eventually overturned, and he was acquitted. Woodward created woodblock prints to illustrate his book, with the front cover shown at left, and the back cover image below, depicting the death of Cooksey.

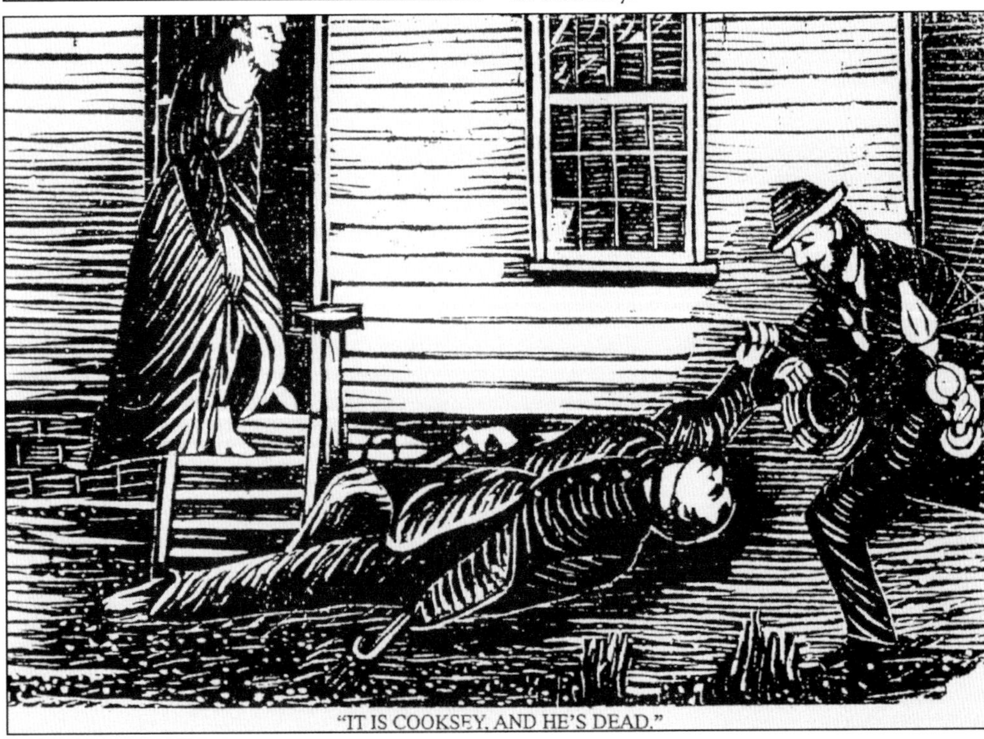

"IT IS COOKSEY, AND HE'S DEAD."

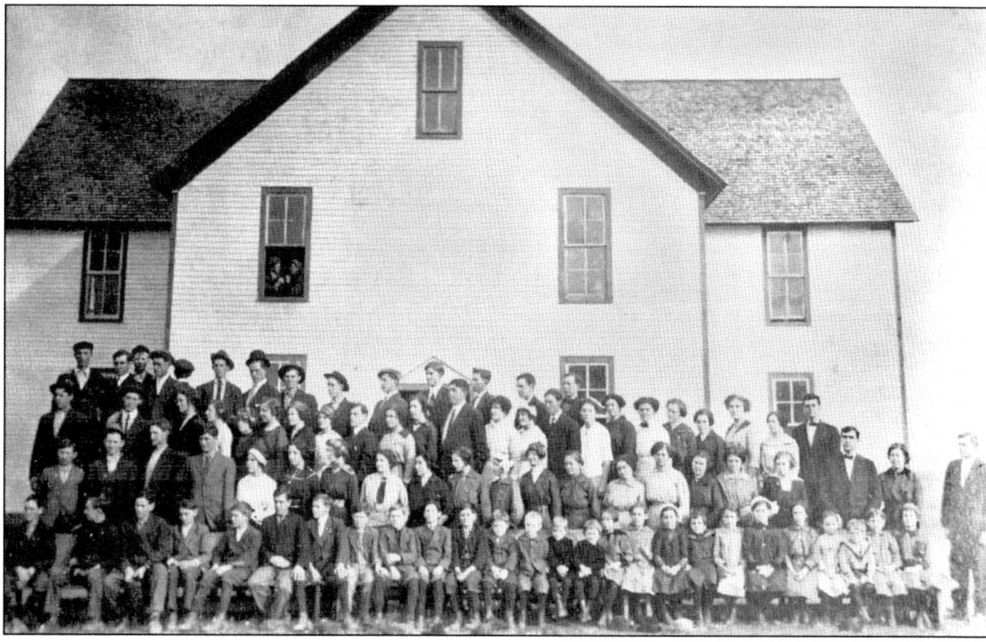

Trousdale, later known as Jacksboro, is located on the old Shelbyville Road about seven miles west of McMinnville. The exact dates of the Trousdale Academy are not known, only that sometime after the Civil War, it was in operation in the community. The school included several dormitories and large academy buildings, and it operated last under the direction of L. E. Summers. This photograph shows a group of unidentified students.

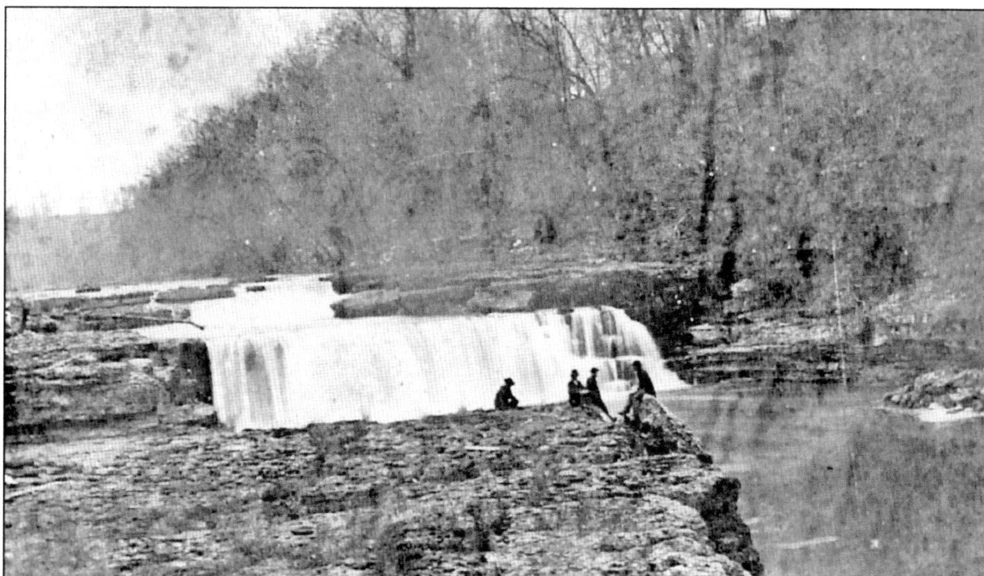

In the late 1800s, J. Fletch Woodward would have traveled on horseback the 30-mile trip with his cumbersome camera equipment to take this rare stereoscopic photograph of the Caney Fork Falls at Rock Island, northeast of the town of McMinnville. Revered as a special natural area to visit for special outings and sightseeing, Woodward's photograph captured picnickers on the rocks in front of the waterfall.

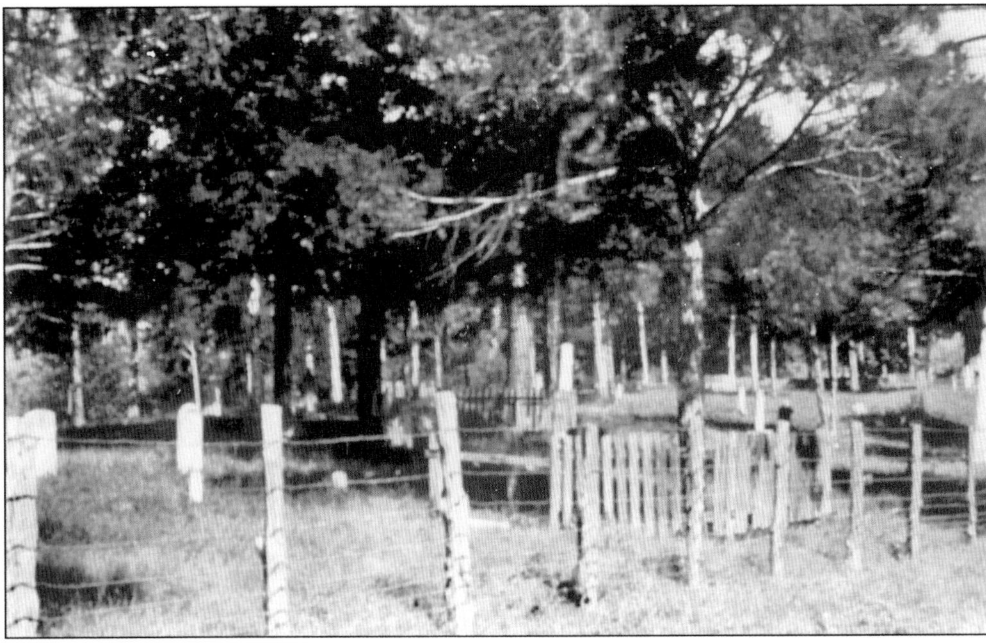

Improvement on McMinnville's old cemetery began in 1905 when the Memorial Circle was organized for the upkeep of the first town cemetery where many of McMinnville's earliest citizens were buried. The organization reset gravestones, repaired old fences, and enclosed the cemetery with a new wire fence and iron gate. Known as the Old Graveyard, the cemetery is now referred to as the Old City Cemetery.

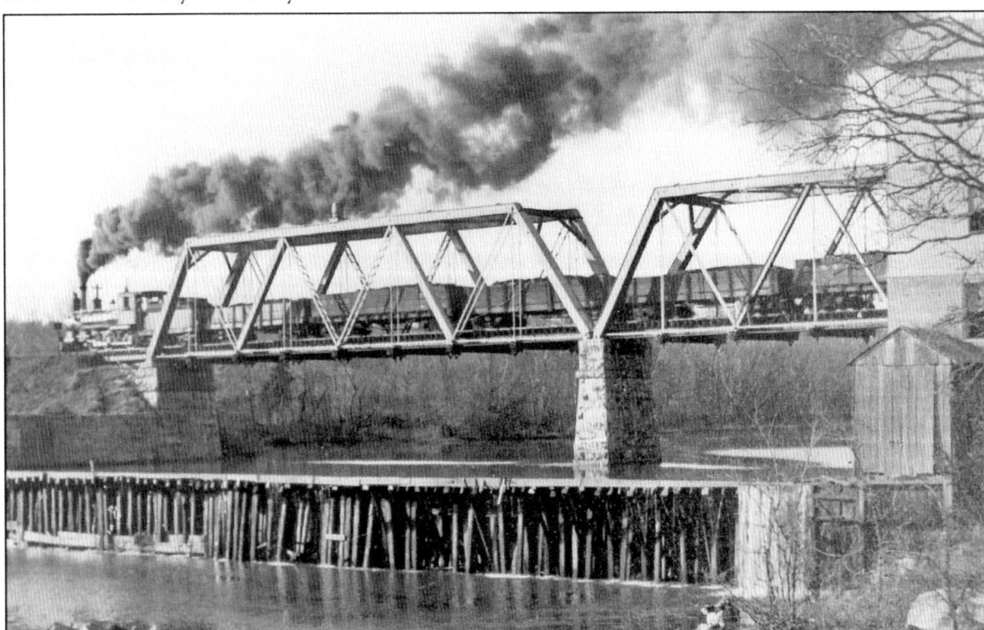

Asa Faulkner built many of the first county-owned bridges. Today's dam and railroad bridge, erected across the Barren Fork River on the stage road leading from McMinnville to Huntsville, Alabama, was the first recorded. The wooden dam, pictured in this photograph, was set afire and burned by Federal troops during the Civil War and was later replaced with a dam made of concrete.

Eliza Jane Lyon Mitchell was one of the most beloved and highly respected early citizens of Warren County. She had no children of her own, but cared for and educated some 15 children. Born in 1801, she was one of a family of 11 children born to James and Phila Lyon. Affectionately called "Grandma Mitchell," she and her mother were largely responsible for the building of the first church in McMinnville. She died in 1896.

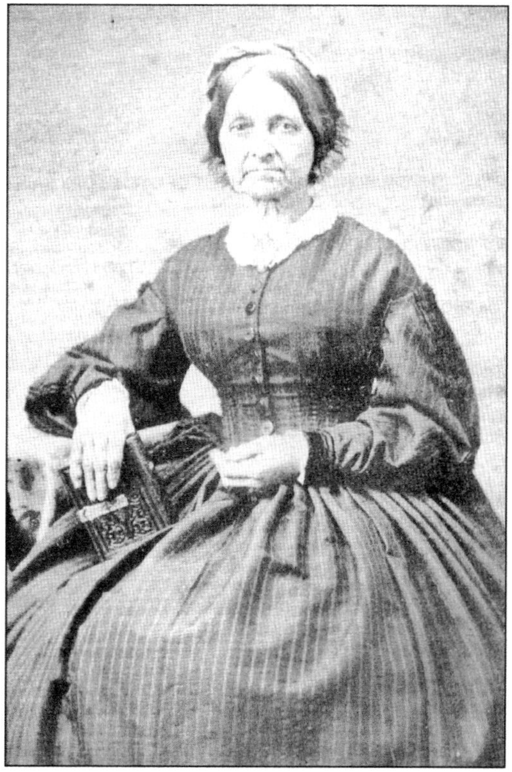

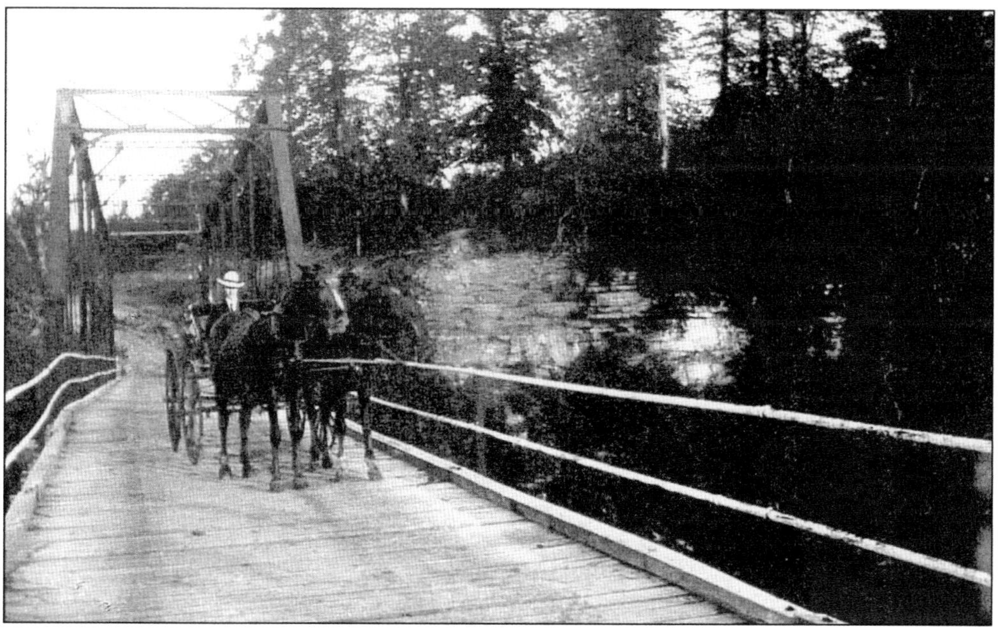

In the early 1900s, one of the many physicians practicing medicine in McMinnville was Dr. E. E. Northcutt (1881–1946), who is pictured in the above photograph by Southern School of Photography student Marion F. Kelly of Louisville, Georgia, who graduated from the school in 1906. The doctor driving his horse and buggy was captured by Kelley's camera as he crossed one of the many wooden bridges near McMinnville.

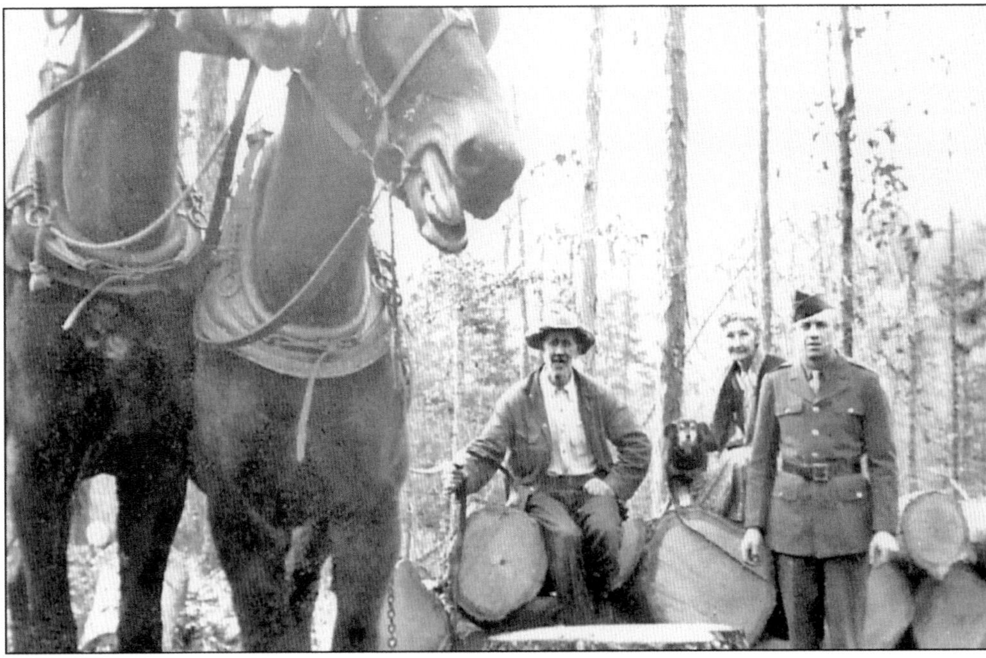

One of many pioneer families who settled in the Tan Yard Springs community was the Asmus family, who had roots in Germany. This November 25, 1944, photograph shows, from left to right, William Byrd, wife Mattie (Asmus) Byrd, with their son-in-law, Gentry Paul Gibbs, (in his military uniform). The dog's name was Sporty.

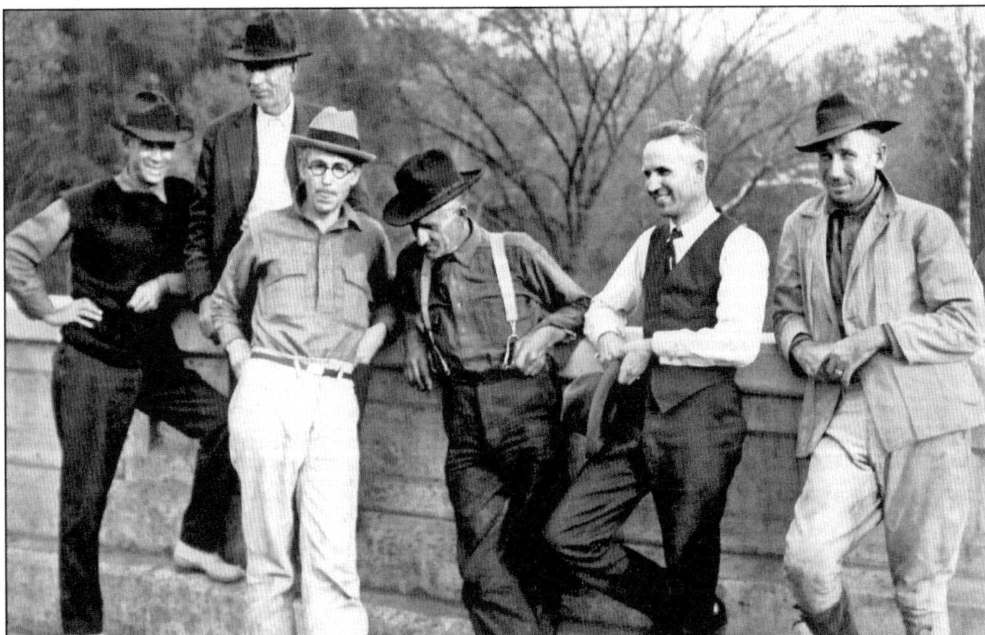

This photograph captured six men leisurely standing on a bridge somewhere in Warren County in the 1920s. Pictured from left to right are unidentified, W. V. D. Miller (sheriff of Warren County from 1898 to 1902), E. Q. "Tip" Miller (son of W. V. D. Miller), Dave Dunlap, Eugene C. Dunlap, and Raleigh Miller (son of W. V. D. Miller).

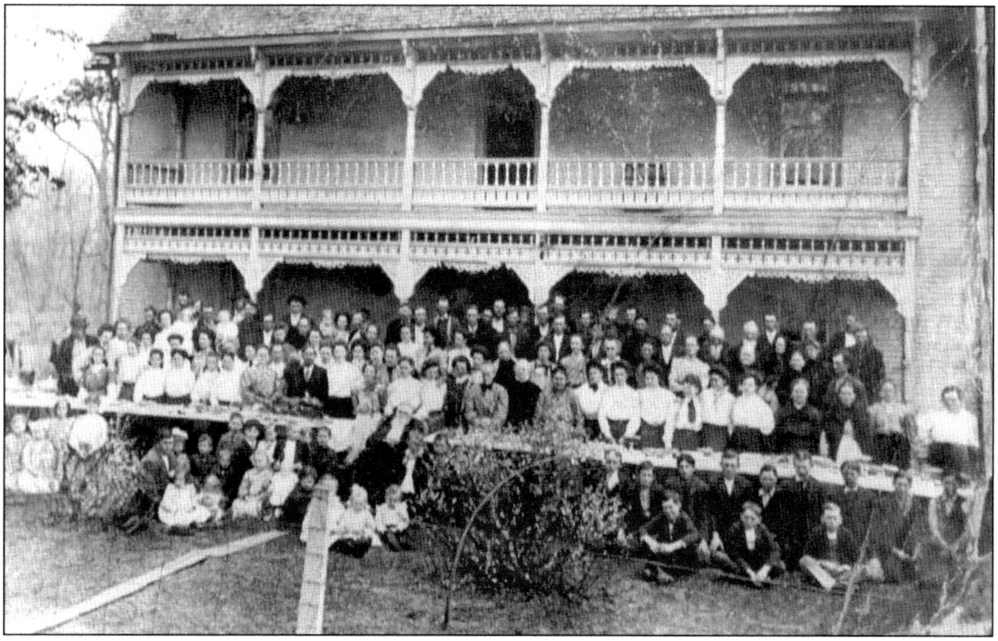

This photograph taken in 1909 at the home of Richard Russell shows family, friends and neighbors at a birthday dinner given in his honor. Grandpa Richard Russell and Grandma Russell are seen standing behind the table, left of center, behind the cooked whole hog, the main feature of the birthday feast. Such meals were often served at large family get-togethers.

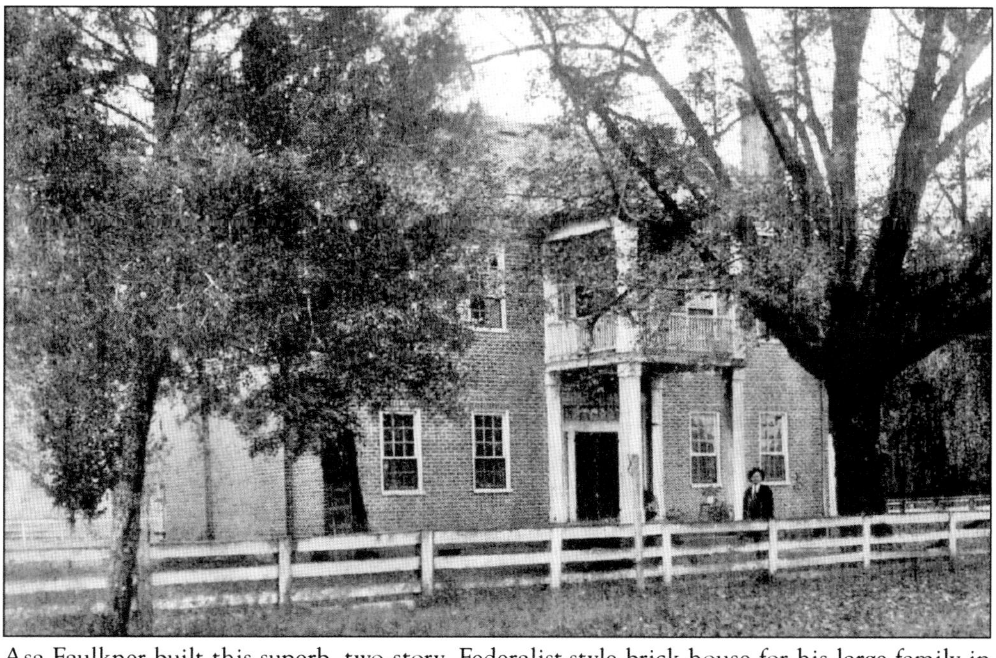

Asa Faulkner built this superb, two-story, Federalist-style brick house for his large family in the Faulkner Springs Community. The house, built of bricks made by slaves on the premises, overlooked Charles Creek and was originally the center of a compound of buildings. With 18-inch-thick walls, the house, completed in 1850, was named Falconhurst. The man standing in the yard is not identified.

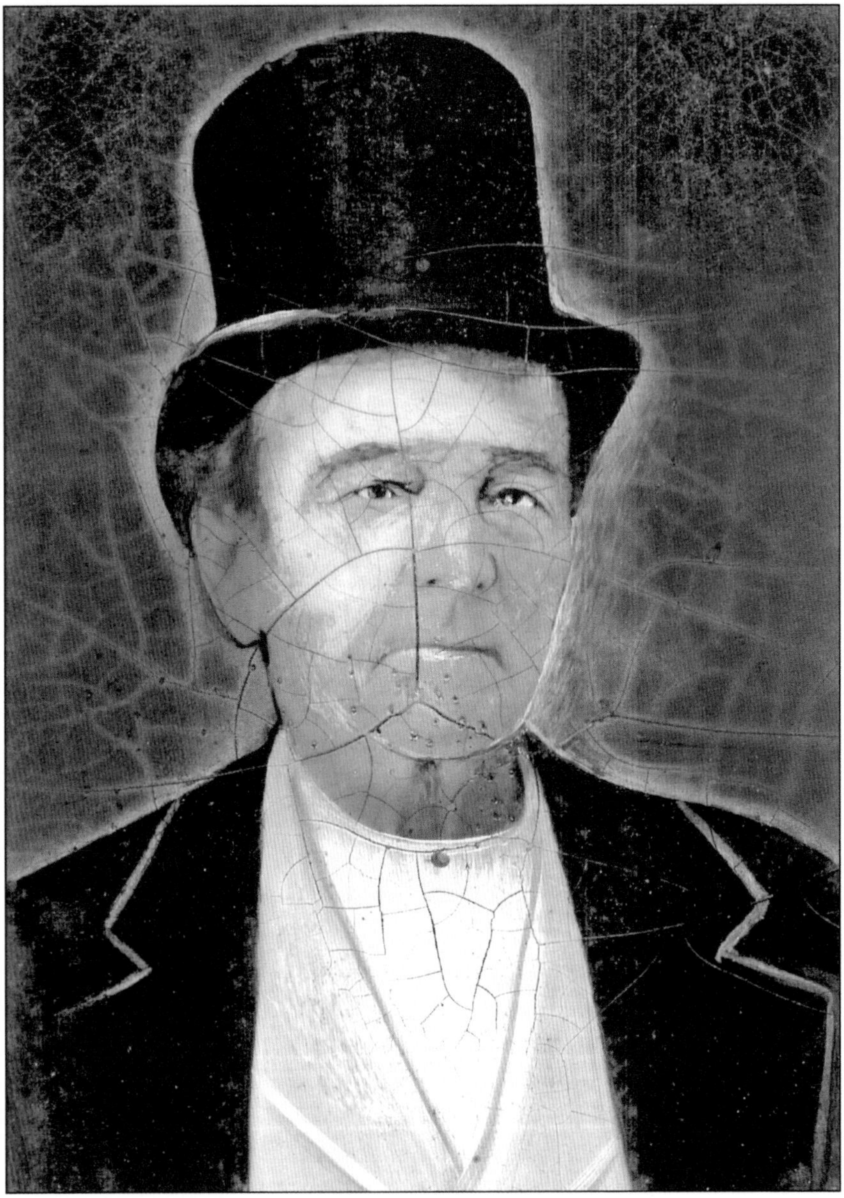

Born in 1802 in Edgefield District, South Carolina, Asa Faulkner was brought in 1808 by his parents, Dr. Archibald and Rebecca (Burkhalter) Faulkner, to the pioneer settlement that was Warren County. Dr. Faulkner soon erected a small woolen mill and cotton gin, which were the first recorded in the newly formed county. From this very early age, Asa's education was gained from his exposure to, and involvement in, the milling industry. After several years as a machinist apprentice in a cotton factory run by Henry Beidleman, Asa opened his own financially successful carding factory and gristmill. This led to a number of large, successful industrial enterprises throughout his long life. He became one of the wealthiest and most influential men in the county. Recognized as the patriarch of Warren County manufacturing, the visionary industrialist played a significant role in Warren County's—and McMinnville's—economic development and political processes during the 19th century. Married three times, he was the father of 18 children, with a large number of his sons involved in local industry as well. Asa died in 1886.

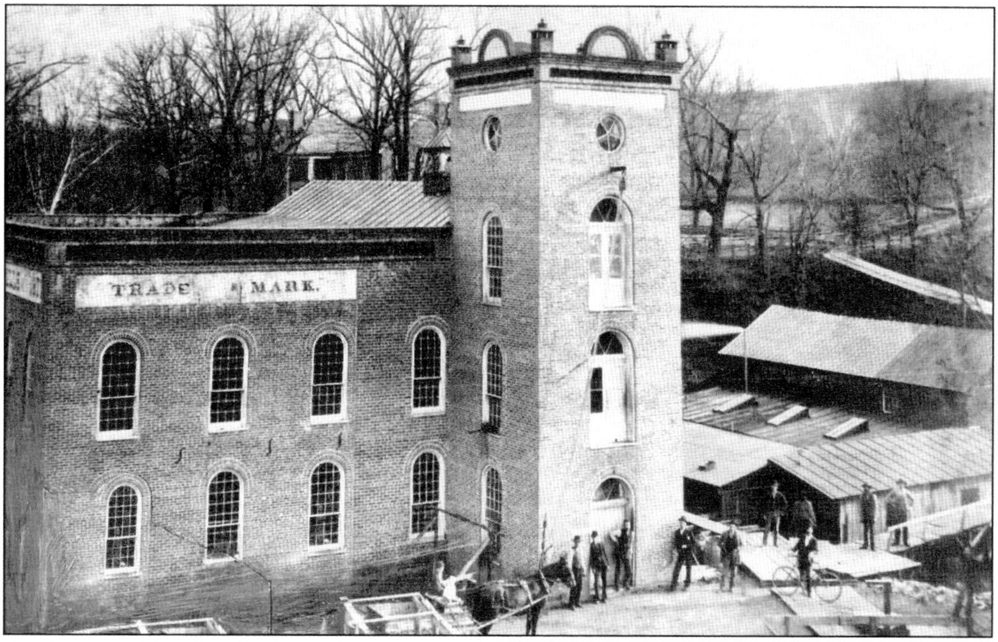

At the age of 16, Asa Faulkner became a machinist's apprentice in a small cotton factory run by Henry Beidleman some two and a half miles north of McMinnville. In 1841, young Faulkner purchased the entire farm of over 400 acres, and the cotton mill, on Charles Creek. With two partners, he opened the $10,000 mill named the Central Factory, which manufactured cotton yarn. The above photograph shows Faulkner's Central Factory in operation during its heyday. In 1861, Faulkner built an even more elaborate and costly mill, named the Woodman Cotton Mill, on the opposite side of the town of McMinnville, on the south side of the Barren Fork River near the railroad, at a cost of $100,000, which was torched and burned to the ground by Federal forces during the Civil War.

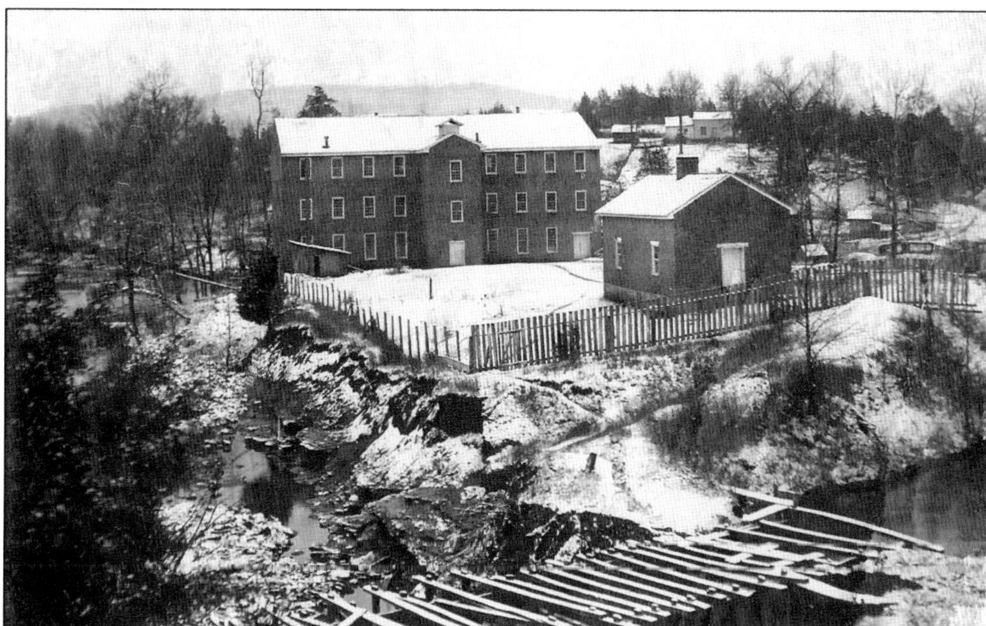

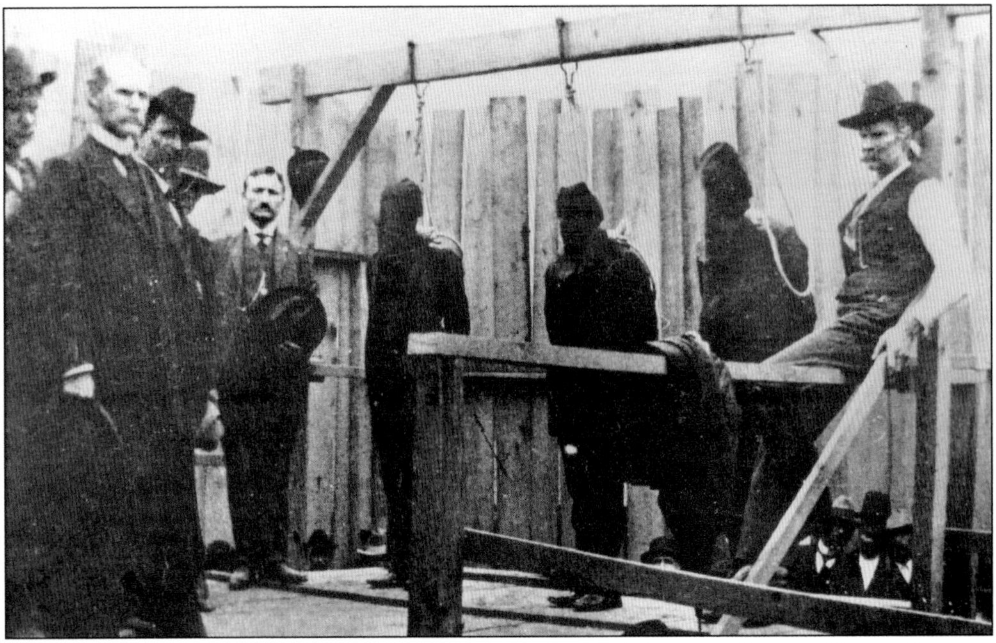

On April 25, 1900, three convicted murderers were hanged from a gallows in Deport Bottom, not far from the railroad depot. Hanged were John C. Watson, Bill Brown, and "Sonny" Crain (an African American). In the above photograph, Sheriff William "Bill" Van Doran Miller (in the big-brimmed hat) is seen with other unidentified officials minutes before the hanging. The condemned men are pictured hooded with nooses placed around their necks. The spectacle was carried out in the presence of a horde of curious onlookers who had made their way to the town from the far reaches of Warren and adjoining counties, the largest crowd ever to have assembled in the area to that date. From a series of six photographs, which were discovered in an old trunk, the bottom picture shows the convicted men hanging by their necks.

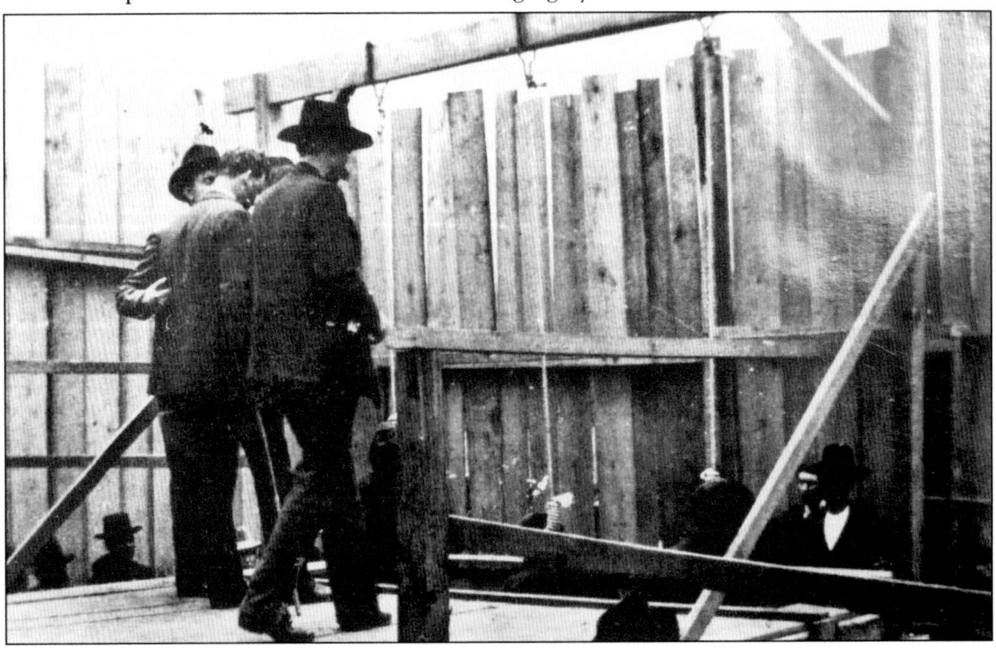

Dr. William Pitt Lawrence was a native of Massachusetts who came to McMinnville in 1815 and set up the practice of medicine. He had served as a surgeon in a division of Gen. Andrew Jackson's army during the War of 1812. His home in McMinnville was located on the northwest corner of Main Street and the public square. Dr. Lawrence moved to Nashville about 1830.

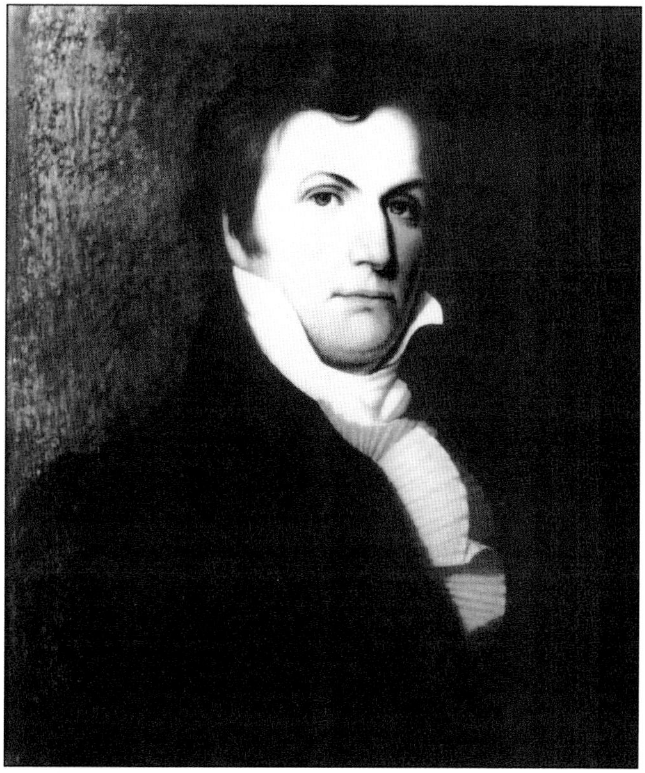

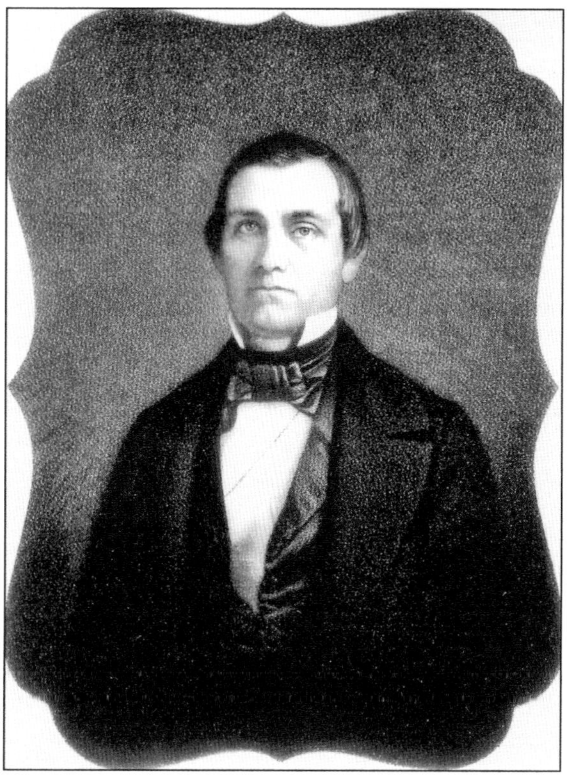

Sometime after 1820, pioneer attorney Andrew J. Marchbanks came to McMinnville to practice law. Around 1830, he built a small, brick building on the south side of West Main Street. Marchbanks served as circuit judge for 25 years. By the 1850s, he was a prosperous, highly respected citizen of Warren County, was considered one of its prominent leaders, and was one of the most esteemed lawyers and judges in Tennessee.

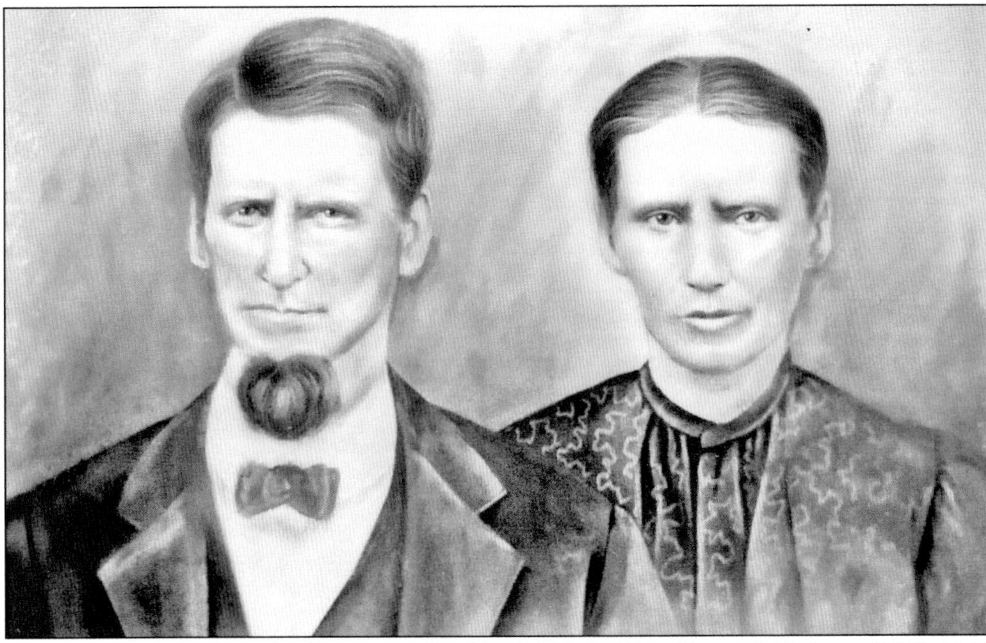

This portrait of Charles "Charlie" Pearson Bouldin (1856–1944) and Lucinda Beshears (1863–1947) was made around 1879, at the time of their marriage in Warren County. Both are buried in Warren County's Smyrna Cemetery. Nine children were born: William Elisha, Marion "Lum" Columbus, Octamaranda Margaret Lucinda, Jerima, Charles D. Bryan, Henry Atwood, Hallie Adella, Mary Leonora "Nora" Elizabeth, and Cora Melissa Bouldin.

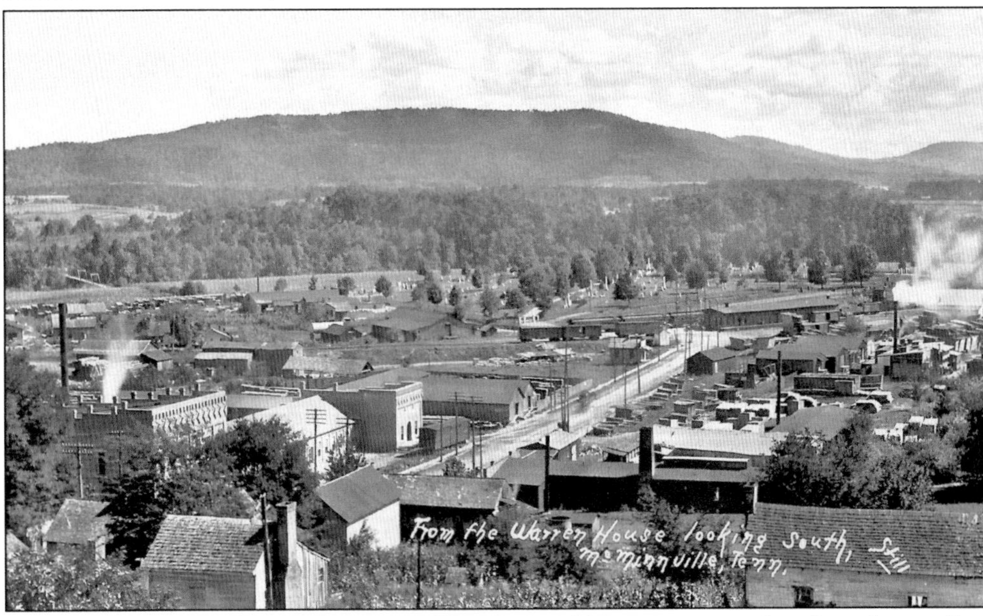

This late-1800s view of Depot Bottom and Ben Lomand Mountain was taken from the top floor of the Warren House. In the far distance can be seen the new cemetery, with the railway station visible in the distance, at far right. Smokestacks and buildings of Burroughs-Ross-Colville Lumber Company and McMinnville Manufacturing Company, prominent early industries in the town, can be seen on either side of Depot Street.

Pictured is the handsome McMinnville Mercantile Building, a large, three-story brick building on the corner of Main and Spring Streets, which was erected as the "Magness Block." The building housed the McMinnville Mercantile Company, as well as a number of businesses, including Tennessee Electric Power Company, Henegar Hardware Company, and the Southern Standard Printing Company on the second floor. In December 1925, the building was completely destroyed by fire. The photograph below was taken inside the McMinnville Mercantile Company Store, with unidentified individuals.

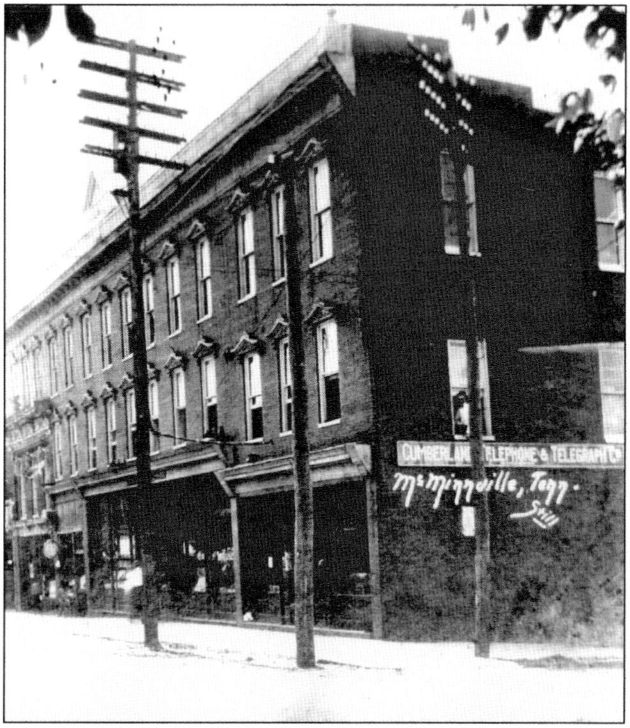

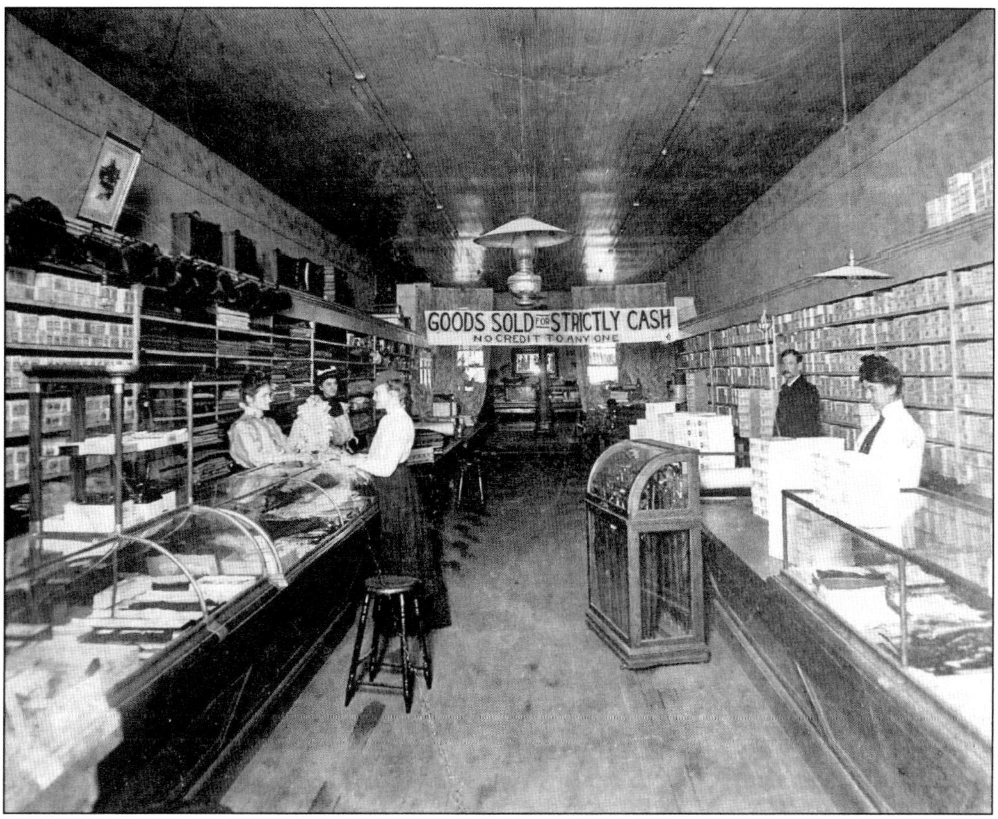

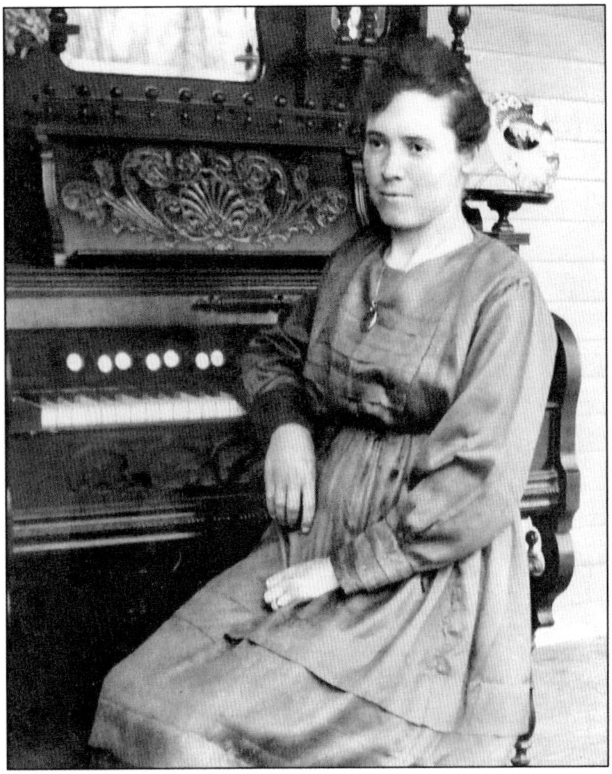

This portrait of Jackie Arnold—seated at the family's pump organ—was taken in 1915 when she was 16 years old. In 1919, she married J. R. Cantrell with whom she had two sons, Grady and Kenneth. She died in 1982 and is buried in Smartt Memorial Gardens in McMinnville.

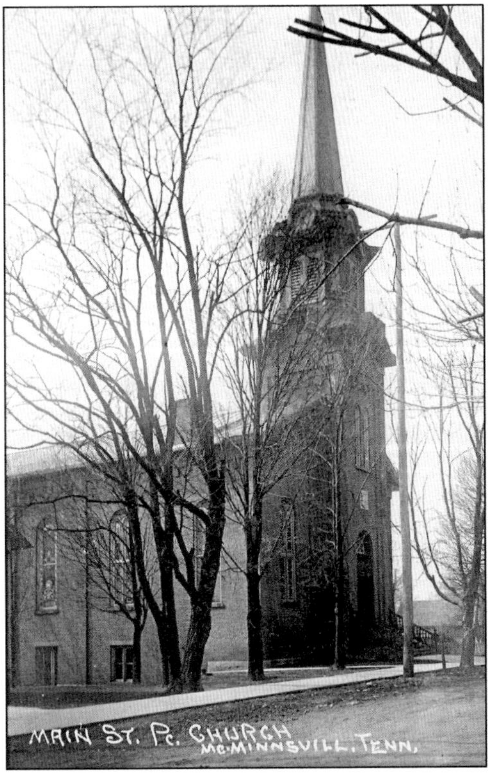

When fire destroyed McMinnville's first Presbyterian church building in 1866, the present First Presbyterian Church on West Main Street was built and completed in 1872, its sanctuary finished in 1878. Although its interior has been restructured, the church's original wooden pews and grand pipe organ (installed in 1890) are still in use today. Listed on the National Register of Historic Places, the church is pictured in this early-1900s photograph.

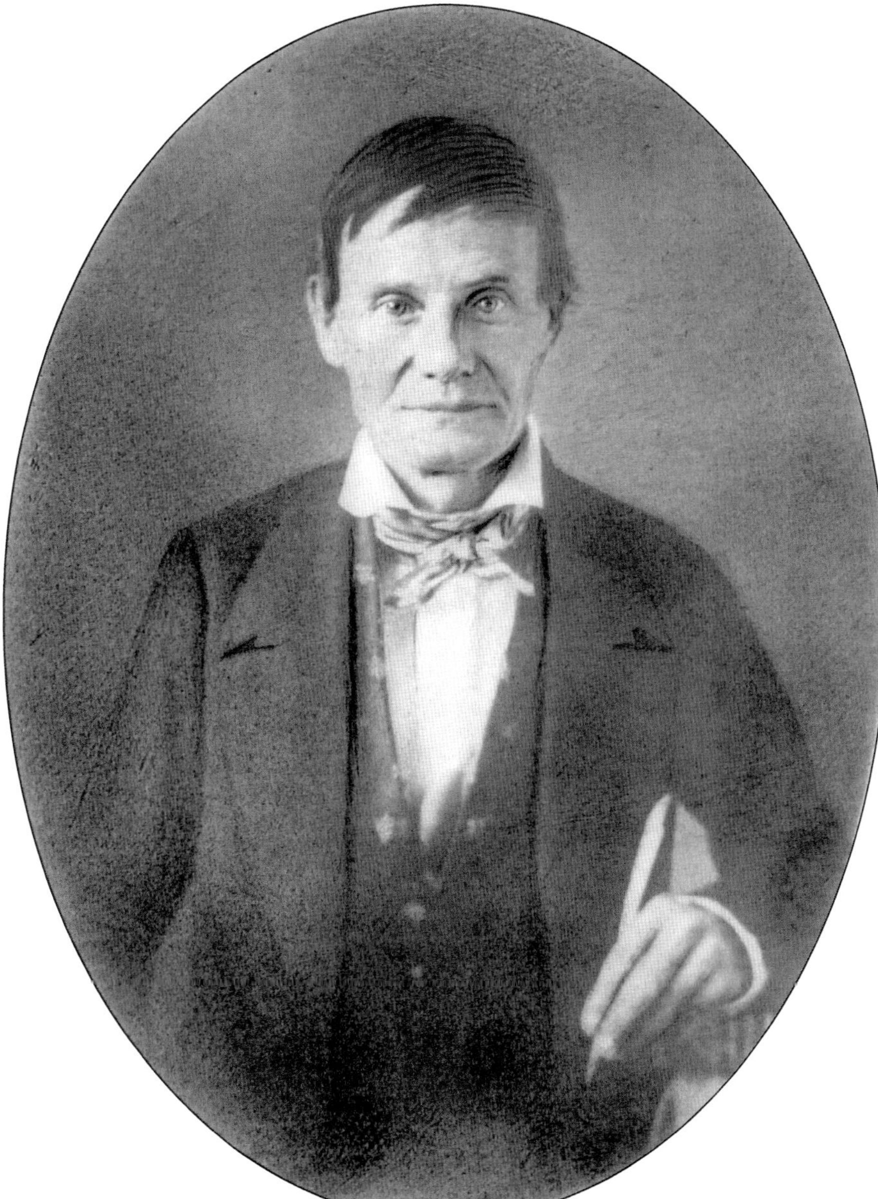

Samuel Hervey Laughlin, brilliant lawyer, farmer, politician, and newspaperman, came to McMinnville in 1811 at age 15 to work as clerk in a new store run by Andrew Buchanan, and spent most of his illustrious life as citizen of the town. Aspiring to become a lawyer, he read law under the tutelage of famed Virginia attorney James McCambell. After developing an interest in politics, he became acquainted with Felix Grundy and James K. Polk, serving in the Tennessee Legislature from 1836 to 1838. He served as delegate of the Democratic Convention in 1840, traveling with James K. Polk to the convention. As a delegate in 1844 to the Democratic Convention, he played a decisive role in Polk's nomination. In 1845, he left McMinnville to accompany by steamboat from Nashville the president-elect, James K. Polk, and his family, to Washington for the inauguration. The new president appointed him to the position of recorder of the General Land Office. For the remainder of his life, Laughlin stayed in the capitol, where he died on May 5, 1850.

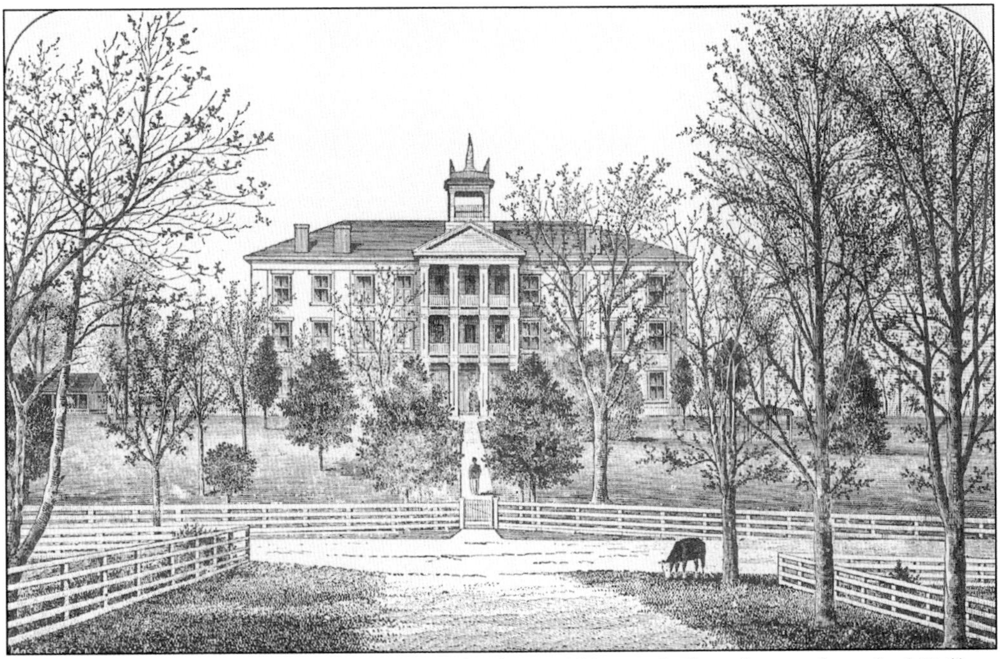

Cumberland Female College, pictured, was built in 1850 on a hill at the north end of College Street in McMinnville. Founded as Cumberland Female Seminary by the Middle Tennessee Synod of the Cumberland Presbyterian Church, it was chartered by the Circuit Court of Warren County and was in operation as an important institution of learning for 50 years, with the final sessions held during the 1899–1900 school year.

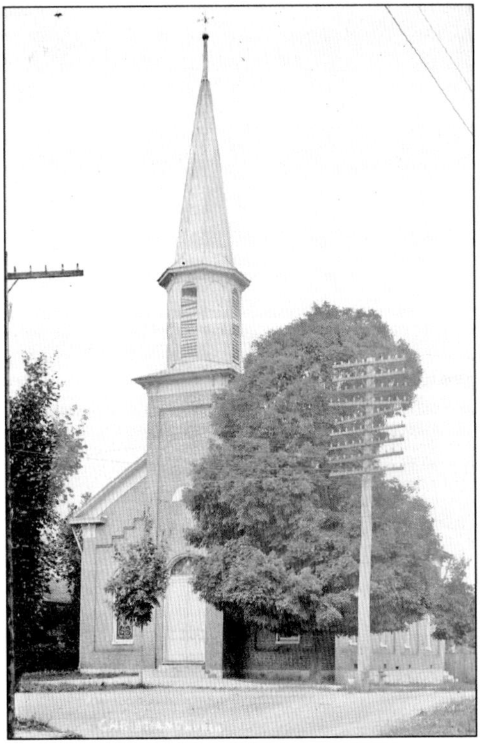

In 1877, H. L. Walling undertook the task of raising funds to erect a larger building for the McMinnville Christian Church congregation, which had outgrown their "little meeting house" erected in 1840. Completed in 1878, the new Christian church building, pictured, stood at the present site of Central Church of Christ on the corner of Morford and College Streets, and served the congregation until 1926.

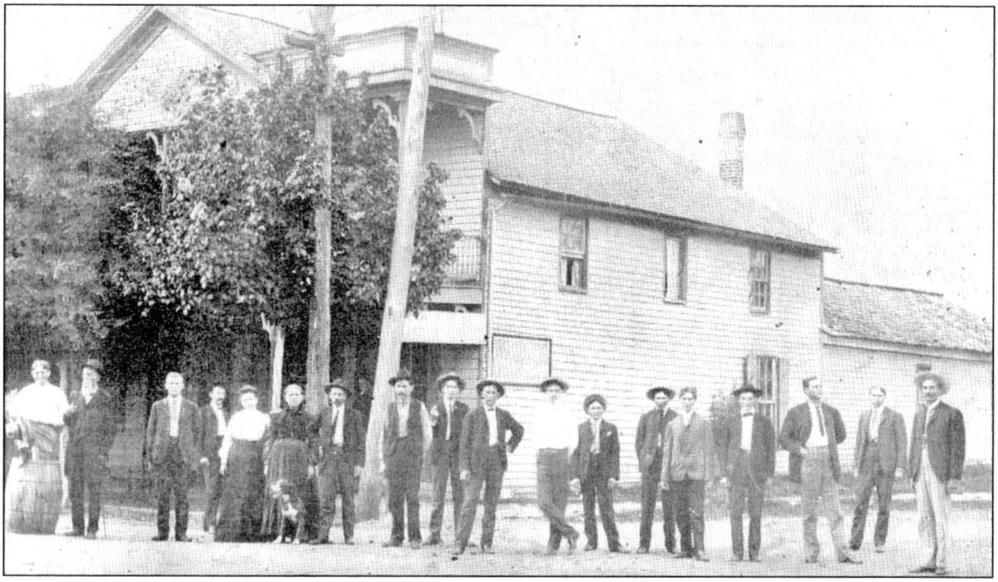

The Tate House, a boarding house, built before the Civil War, stood on East Main Street in McMinnville and was destroyed by fire in the mid-1920s. The Brown Hotel was erected on the site in 1926. The lady standing behind the dog is Mary Jane Tate. To her left and right stand Charles Mitchell (son-in-law) and Martha Mitchell (daughter). G. T. Schmitz, husband of Beta Lively, stands beside the man in a white shirt near the center of the picture.

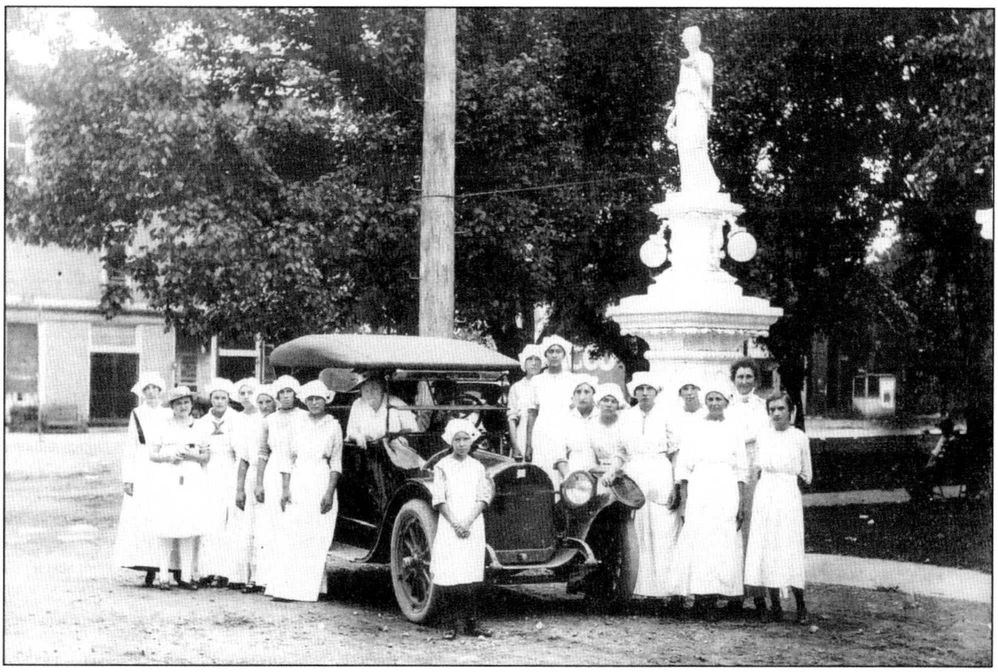

The Tomato Club later became the Warren County Agricultural Extension Service—the 4-H Club. In this photograph, members of the club, along with their driver and Bettie Smithson (the county's first extension agent), pictured second from right, prepare for an outing. The group has assembled in McMinnville's City Park near the backdrop of the newly installed Davis Memorial Fountain.

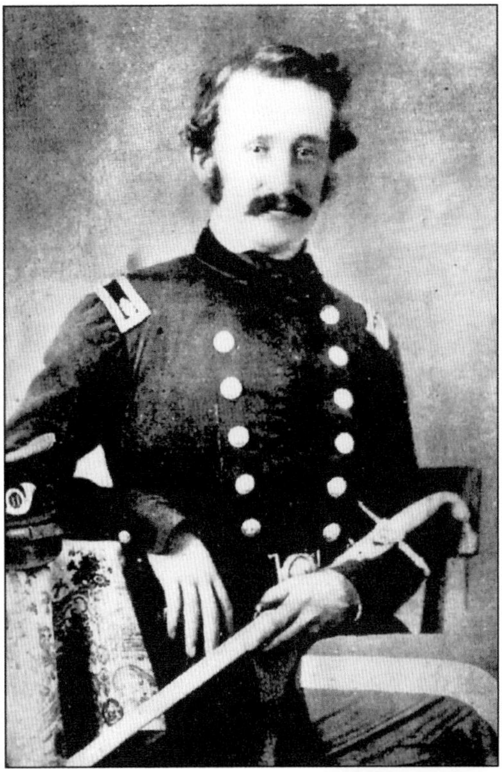

John Houston Savage, flamboyant lawyer, politician, and leader of the 16th Tennessee Regiment CSA during the Civil War, was born in Warren County in 1815. He never married, served brilliantly in three major wars, and served on three occasions in the Tennessee State Legislature. He also represented the state as senator. His autobiography was published in 1903, and he died in 1904.

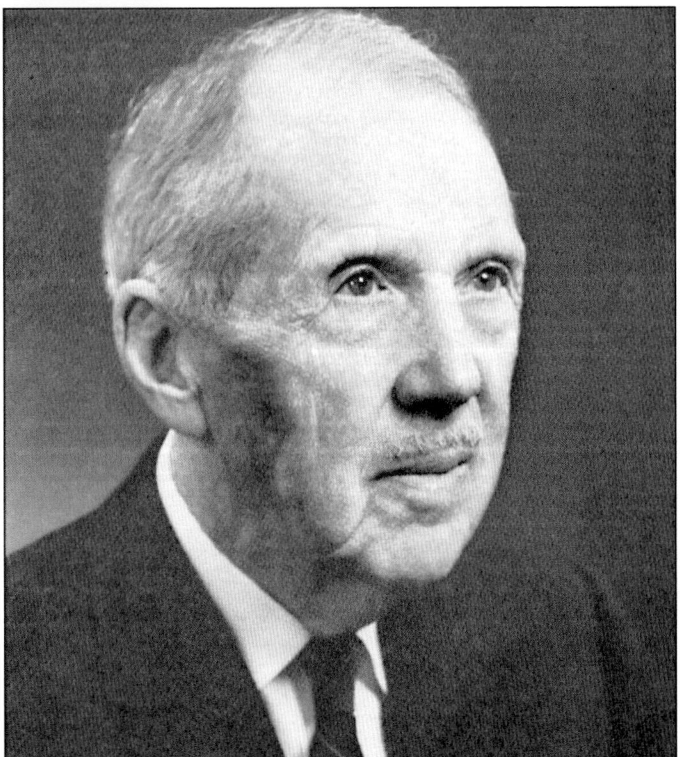

Samuel Colville Lind, born in McMinnville June 15, 1879, became undoubtedly Tennessee's most famous scientist and the only native Tennessean to be elected to the National Academy of Sciences in 1949. After studying at several American universities, he studied at the University of Leipzig in Germany and with Madame Curie in Paris. He later worked in Oak Ridge, Tennessee, as a member of the Manhattan Project. He died in 1965.

This is the wedding picture of James Monroe and Mary Steakley Cunningham made in 1890. Mary, born in White County in 1869, moved to Warren County and attended McMinnville public schools and later graduated from McMinnville's Cumberland Female College. She established a large, early library and later Magness Memorial Library where she served as caretaker and librarian before her death in 1941.

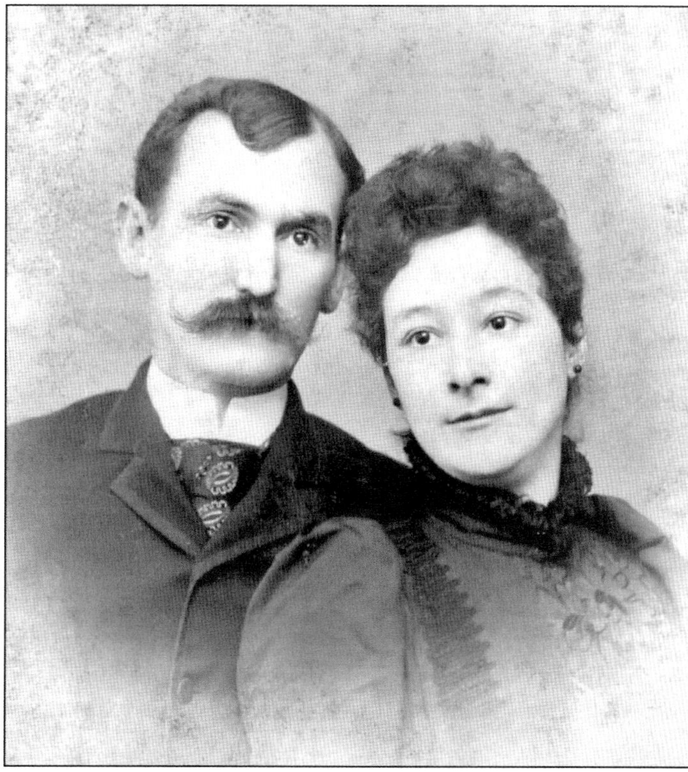

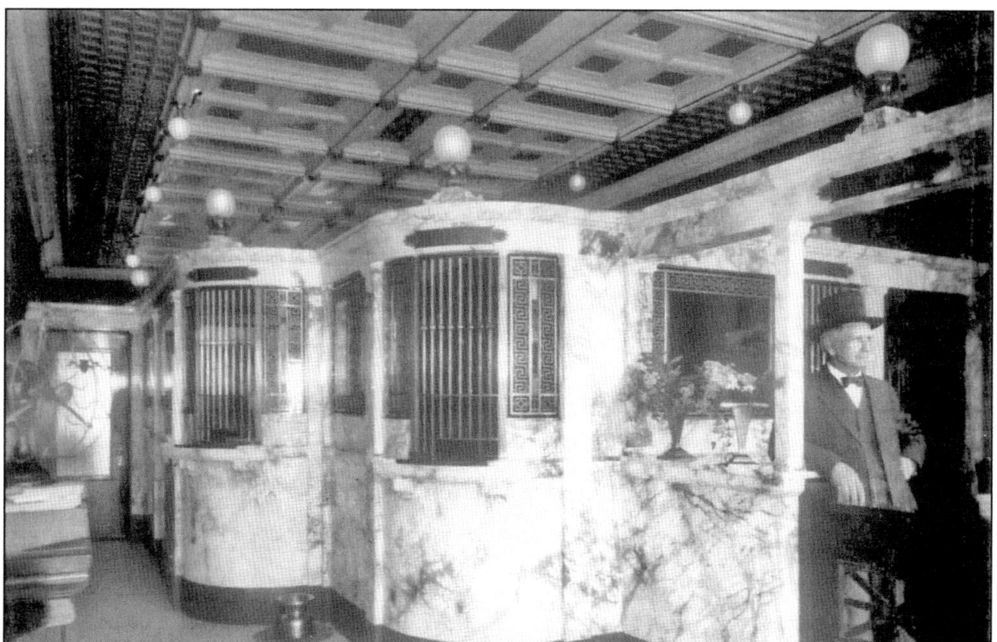

The City Bank and Trust Company was chartered April 5, 1912, and remained operational under that name for many years as one of McMinnville's strongest and most substantial banking institutions. This 1912 photograph captured Jesse Walling, the bank's original president, in the bank's lobby. Walling served as president until 1922.

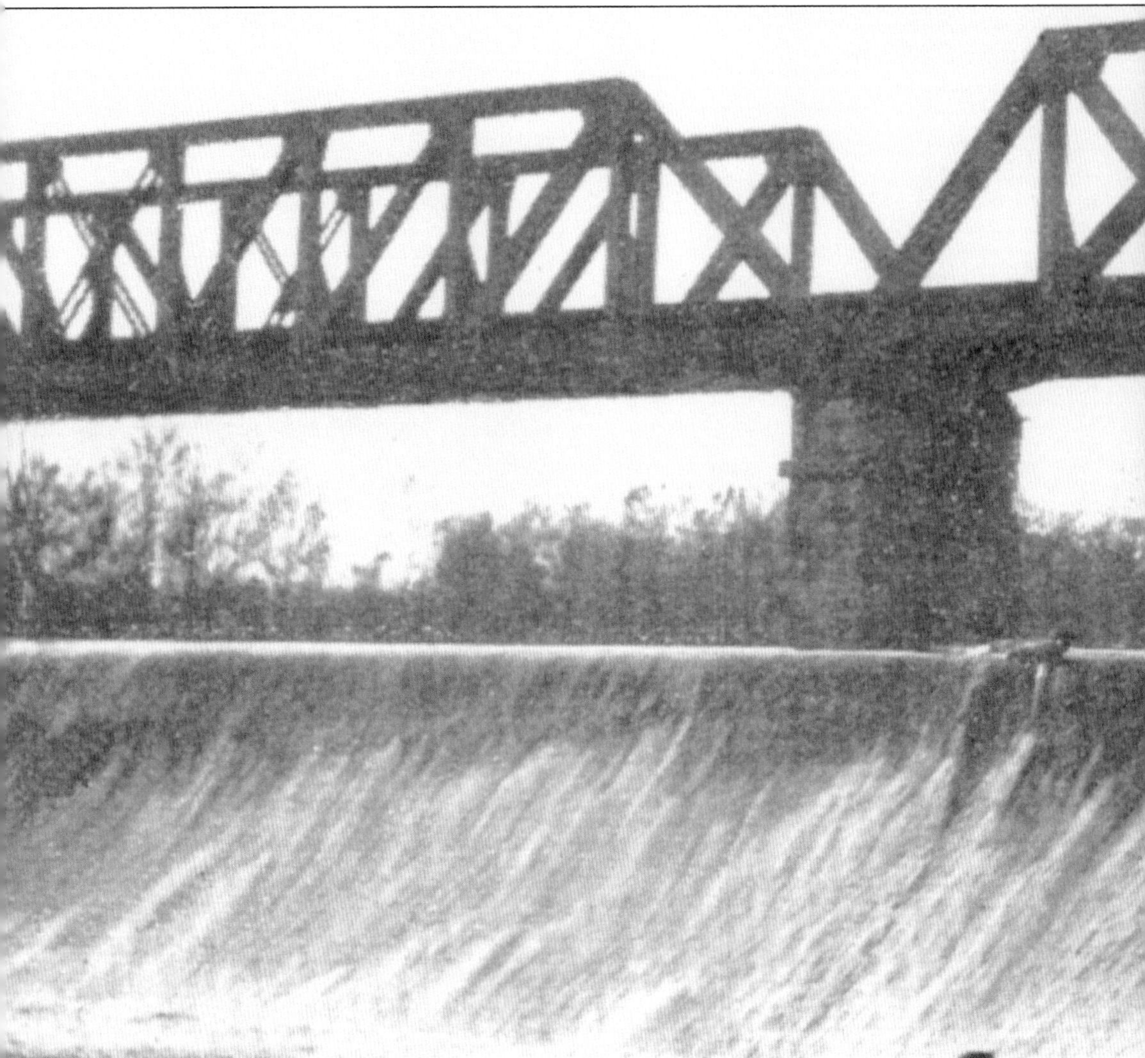

In this photograph, thought to have been taken by famous local photographer William Spencer Lively, a trio of individuals is pictured on the rocks beneath the old mill dam that spans the Barren Fork River, located a short distance southwest of McMinnville. For a number of years, steamboat rides were provided up the course of the river for recreational pleasure. Two early, large, water-powered mills were located on the banks of the river near the dam. During the 1902 flood,

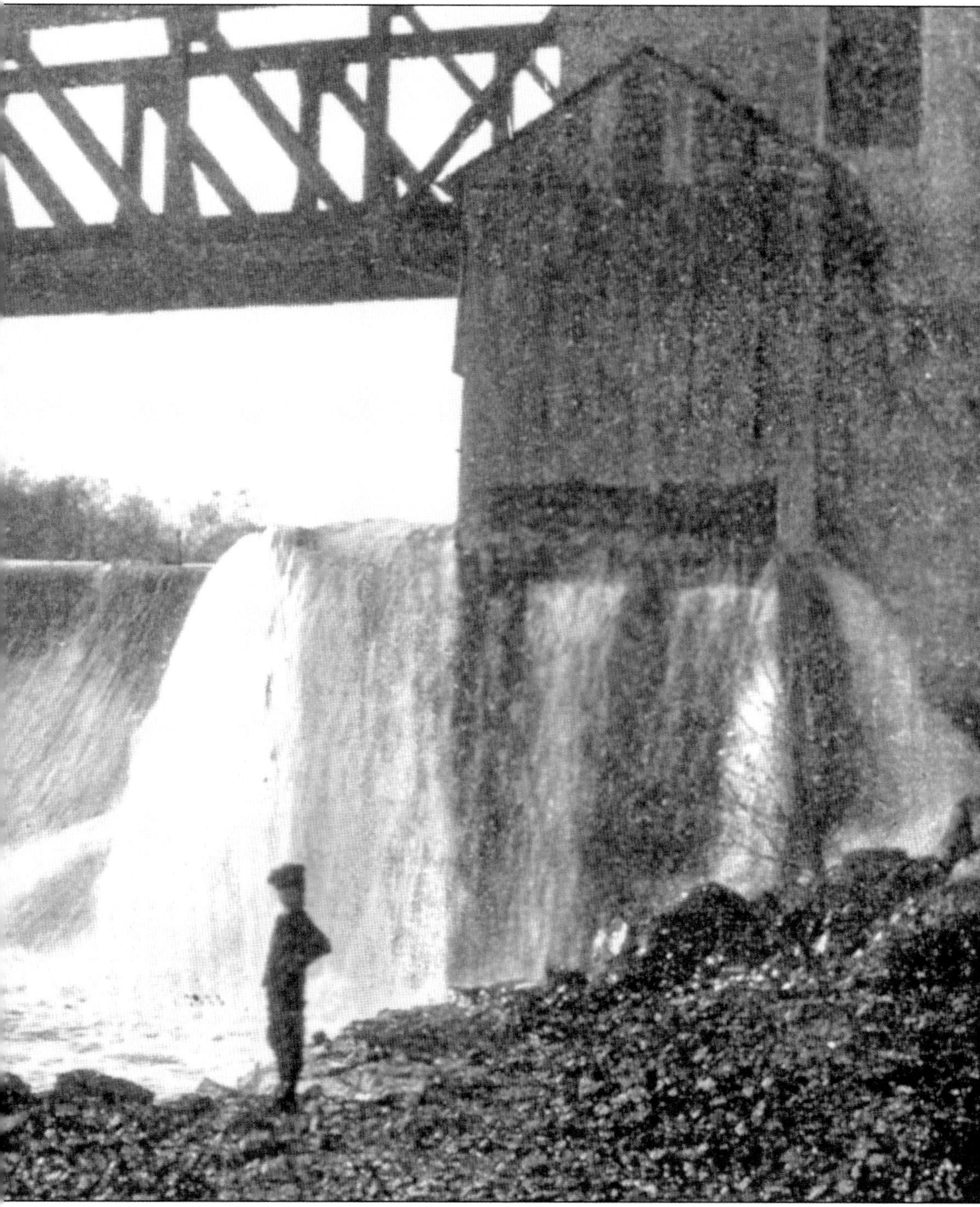

which a short time later the *Southern Standard* newspaper described as "the greatest calamity that has ever befallen Warren County," the Annis Cotton Mill suffered severe damage but survived after water reached the sills of the second-floor windows. The Falcon Flowering Mill was totally swept away by the flood. Only the foundation was left.

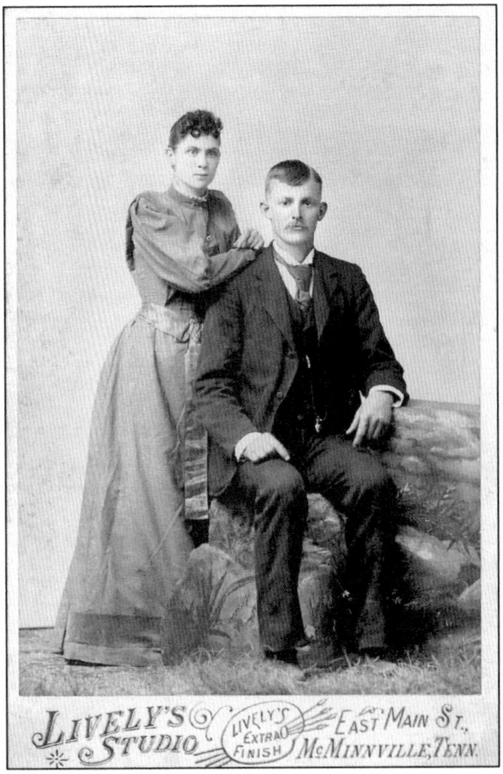

The early community of Steppsville, located some 10 miles southeast of McMinnville, got its name from the early pioneer, Frederick Stepp II. A wealthy landholder, Stepp was a land surveyor by trade. This photograph is the wedding picture of Alice Ware and Abner Lawson Stepp, son of Frederick Stepp III and Serenia Clark Stepp. They were married on October 13, 1892.

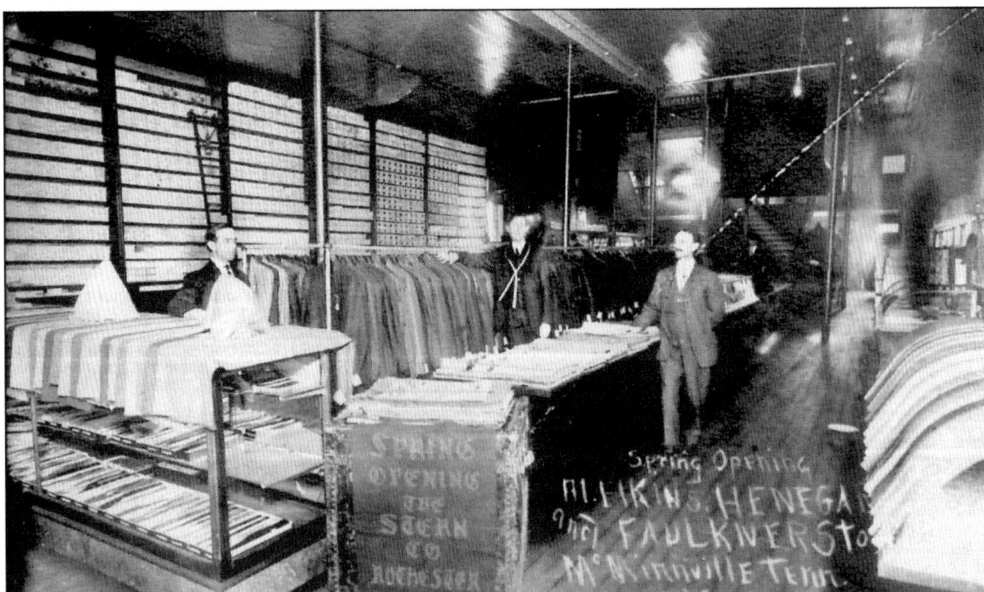

This 1912 photograph was made inside the Elkins, Henegar, and Faulkner Store in downtown McMinnville at the time of the spring opening. The store specialized in men's tailoring and was one of several tailoring and millinery shops operating in the early 1900s in downtown McMinnville. Pictured from left to right are Elvin Elkins, Joe Thomas Henegar, and R. Will Elkins, proprietors.

This rare, late-1800s photograph captures the early People's National Bank Building in downtown McMinnville. A Ferris wheel is in operation in front of the building. From left to right, Lila Walling, Susie Beaver, and Sallie Frazer are seen sitting on the curb at far right. At that time, carnivals and circuses often came to the town and set up equipment in various locations.

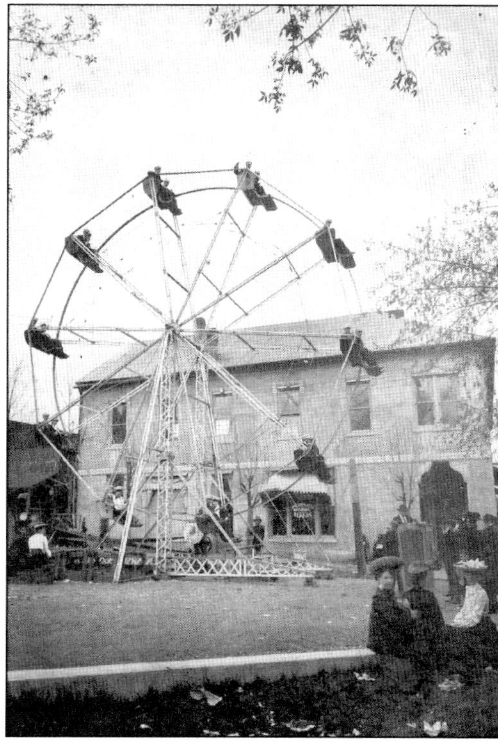

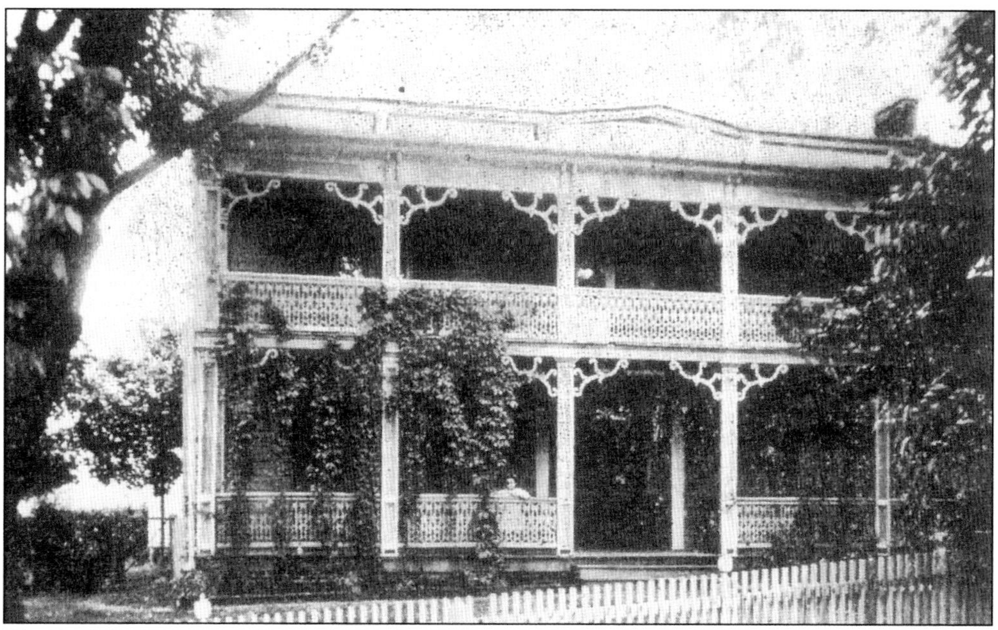

The Dr. J. B. Armstrong house, located on College Street, became a legend during the Civil War when Brig. Gen. John Hunt Morgan and his bride, Martha Ready, came to live in the house shortly after their wedding in Murfreesboro on December 14, 1862. Armstrong was Ready's cousin in whose house the newlyweds spent their honeymoon. The house served as his headquarters until shortly preceding his departure on his ill-fated Ohio Raid in the summer of 1863. In about 1920, Central Church of Christ demolished the house to make way for additional church space.

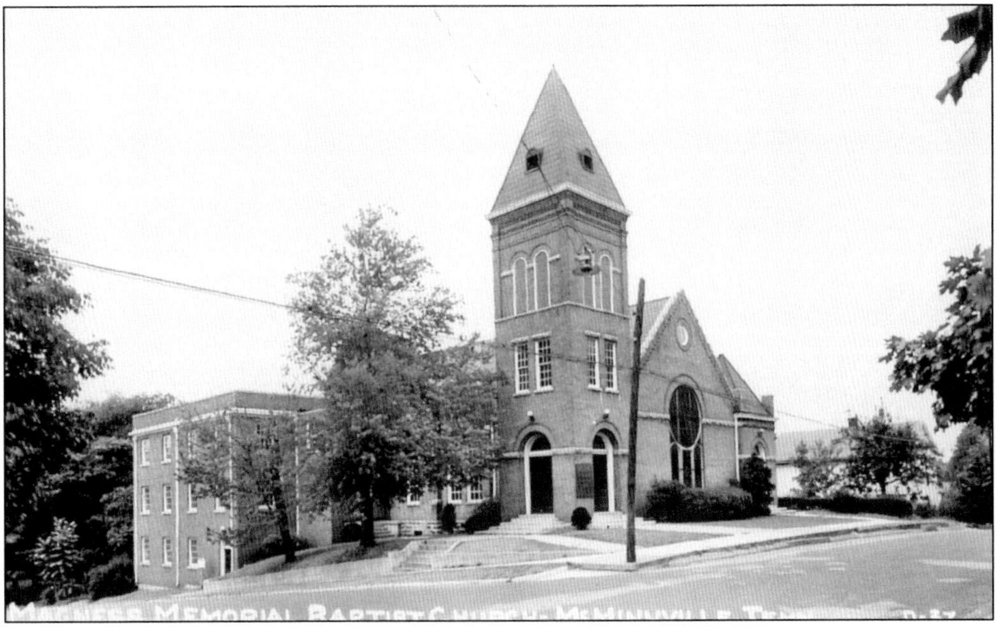

In 1930, the McMinnville Baptist Congregation purchased the old Southern Presbyterian Church building located on the corner of Spring and Donnell Streets, and they later changed its name from First Baptist to Magness Memorial Baptist, in honor of benefactor William H. Magness Sr. A large addition was constructed soon afterward, with subsequent renovations and enlargements in 1958 and 1959. On April 16, 1973, a fire destroyed much of the church.

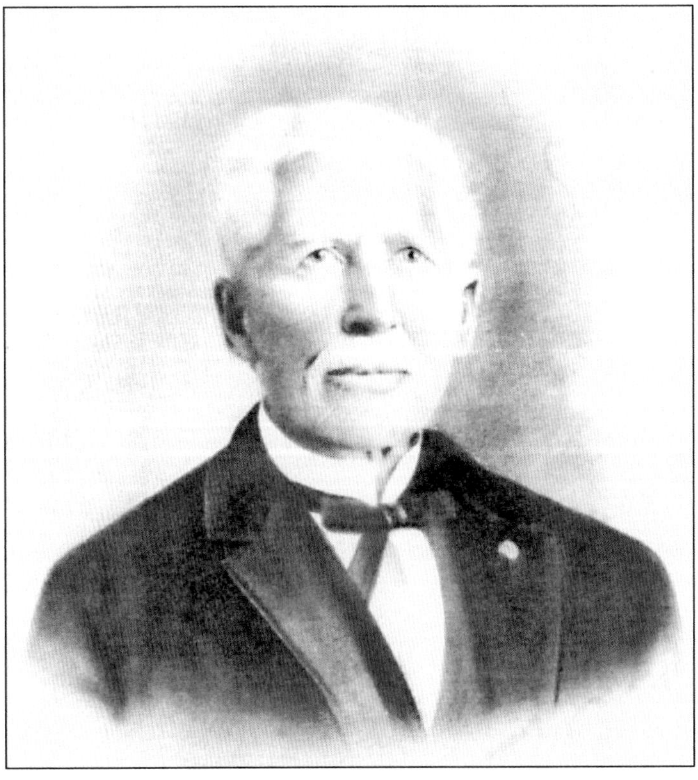

The grandfather of Capt. James J. Womack came to Warren County from Rutherford County, North Carolina in 1810. Captain Womack was born in 1834, was a farmer and lawyer, and is known in McMinnville historical circles for the diaries he kept during his days as a soldier in the Confederate army during the Civil War. He died in McMinnville July 18, 1922, and is buried in Riverside Cemetery.

Two

COMMUNITIES

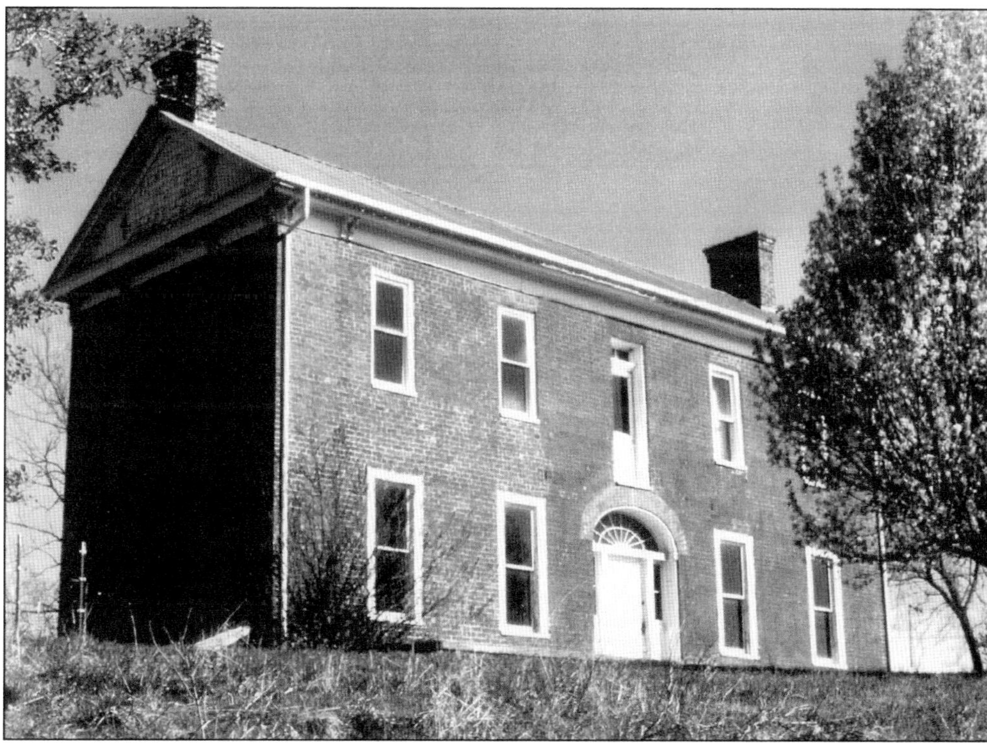

This large, two-story, Federalist-style brick house was built with the work of slave labor, probably in the 1820s, by William "Rock" Martin. Still standing at Mud Creek, and listed on the National Register of Historic Places, the legendary house was a resting place during the Civil War for Gen. Nathan Bedford Forrest and his soldiers prior to their famous Murfreesboro Raid.

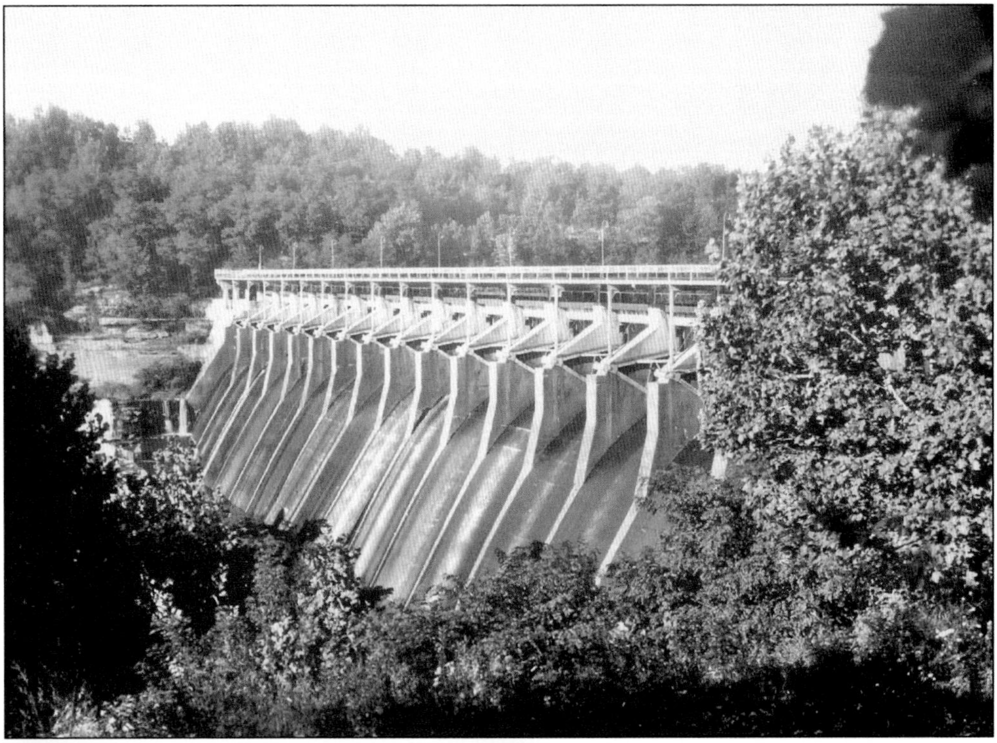

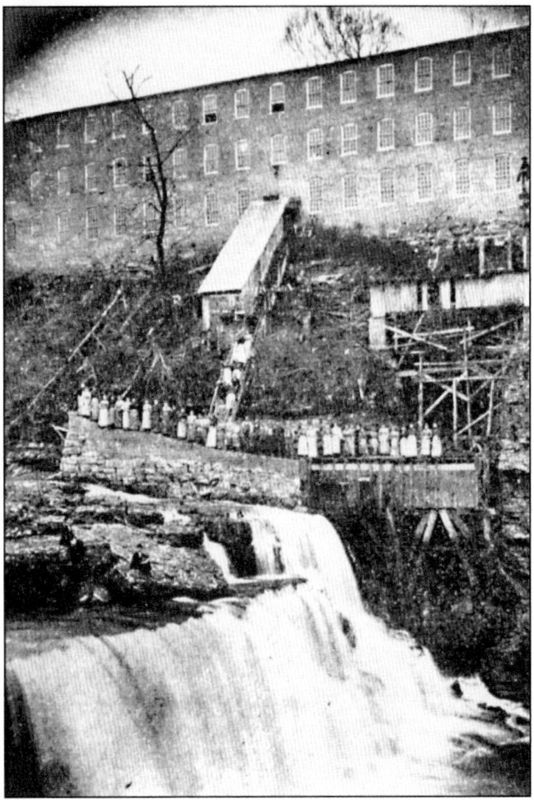

Rock Island was the first permanent settlement in what is now Warren County. The early Supreme Court sessions were held here, with Andrew Jackson in attendance. With the railroad completed in 1881, a hydroelectric plant and dam were completed by the Tennessee Electric Power Company in 1917, creating Great Falls reservoir with 125 miles of shoreline. This photograph of the dam was taken around the time of its completion.

By April 1883, the aged Asa Faulkner had built a long, Howe-Truss bridge across the Collins River near the falls on the Caney Fork River at Rock Island. By 1892, the Great Falls Cotton Mill project had been completed by his son, Clay Faulkner, and Jesse and H. L. Walling, who ran the grand mill successfully until the great flood of 1902.

Clay Faulkner, son of Asa Faulkner, was born in 1845 and also played a dramatic role in Warren County's early growth. He was a partner with his father in the Great Falls Manufacturing Company, and he ran his own woolen mills successfully. During the Civil War, he served secretly in the Unionist 5th Calvary U.S. Faulkner died in 1916.

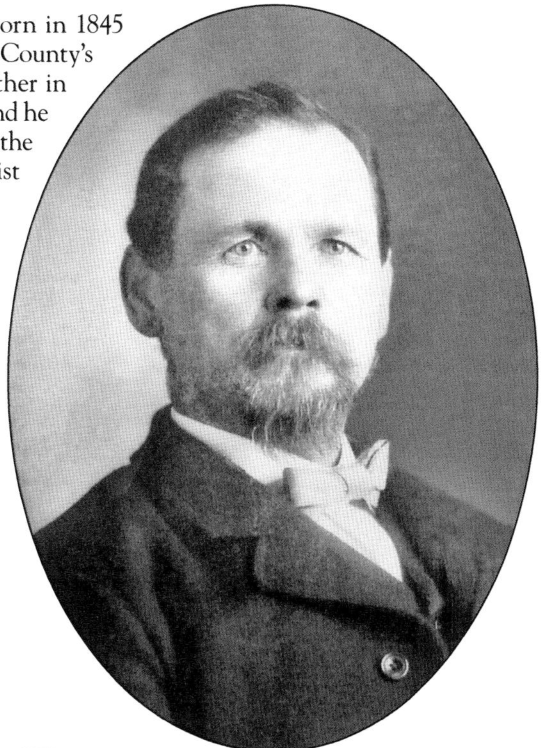

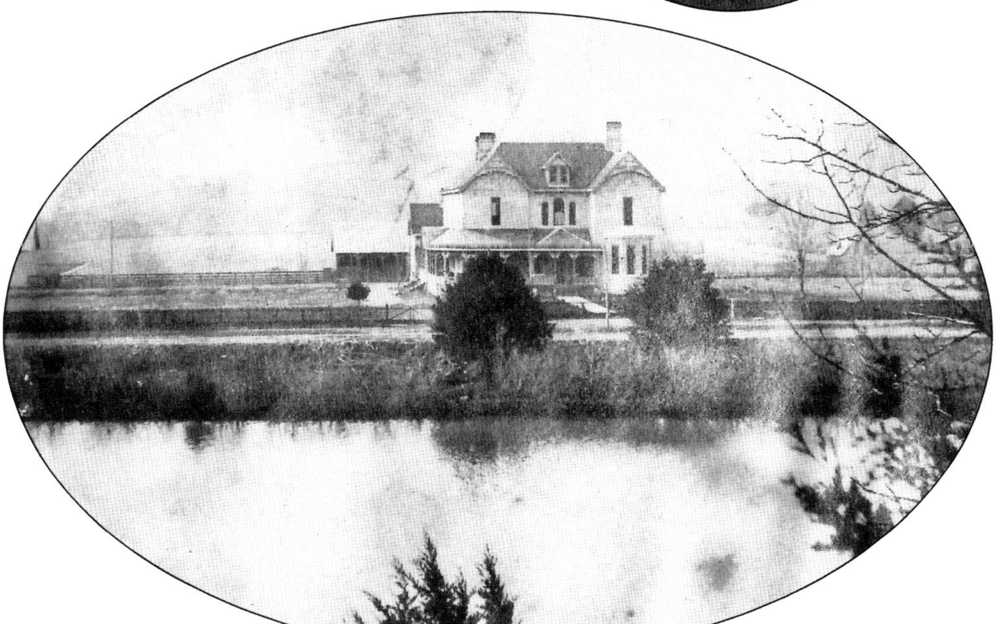

Clay Faulkner built this 10,000-square-foot, solid-brick mansion in 1896 to entice his wife, Mary, to move closer to his woolen mill along Charles Creek. He supervised every aspect of the gracious, Queen Anne residence where they reared their five children. This rare, late-1800s image of the mansion, seen from across the lake, may have been recorded by pioneer photographer J. Fletch Woodward.

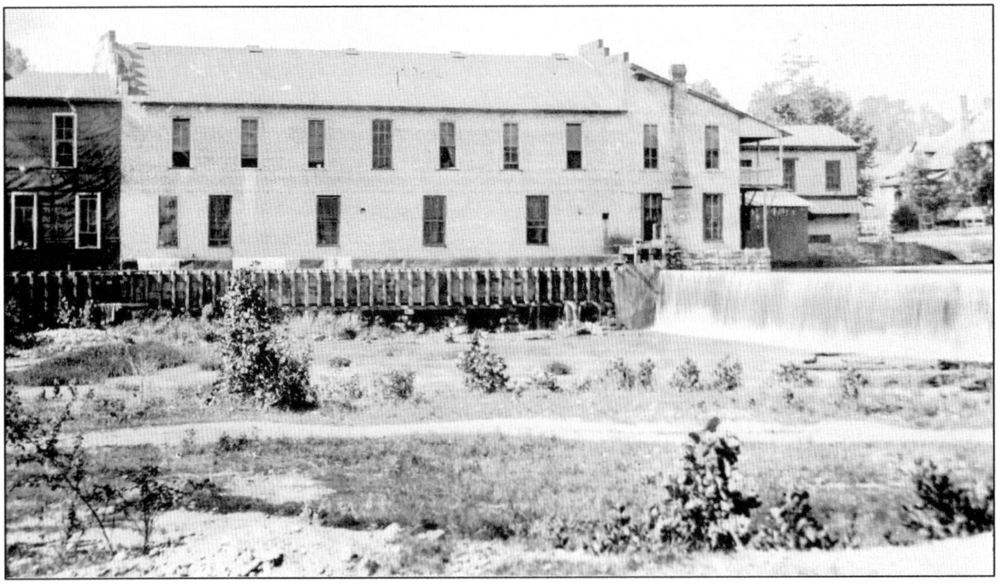

In 1872, Clay Faulkner erected this cotton mill, named the Mountain City Woolen Mills, in which he successfully manufactured jeans, pants, and overalls until 1905 on the banks of Charles Creek, in the Faulkner Springs Community. Here the enterprising merchant perfected his "gorilla pants" market in clever advertising, which ensured great success to his mill.

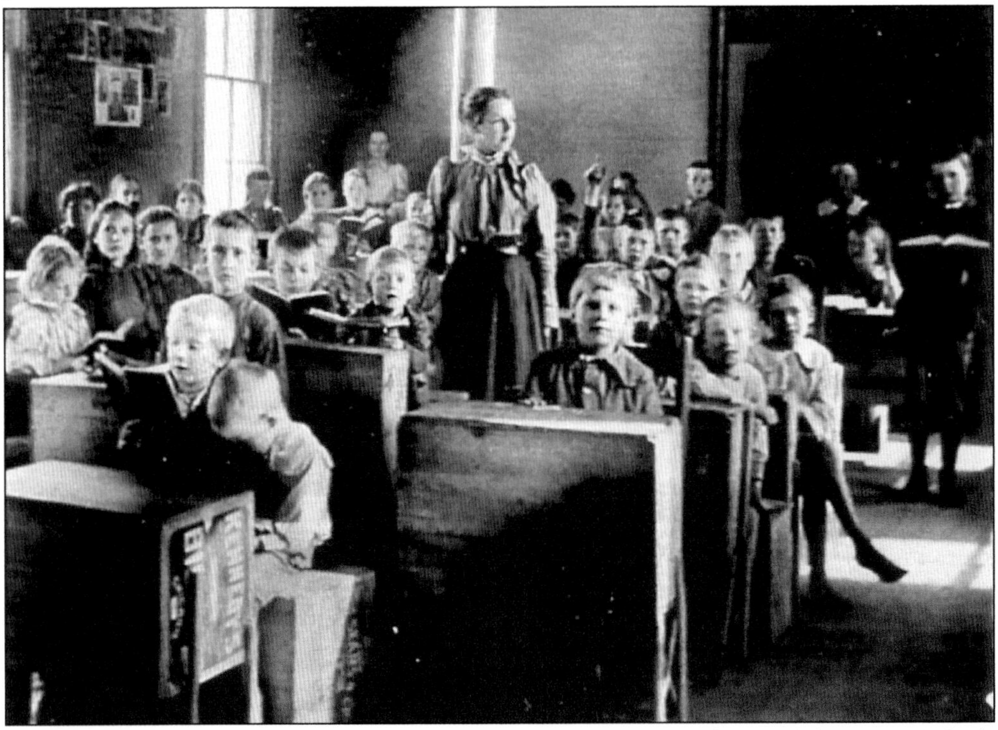

Clay Faulkner's vision encompassed social and religious as well as financial dictums. He built a church and erected a small school in which he employed a teacher for his own mill workers' children and orphaned children. This photograph depicts the interior of his school, with students and teacher, sometime in the late 1800s.

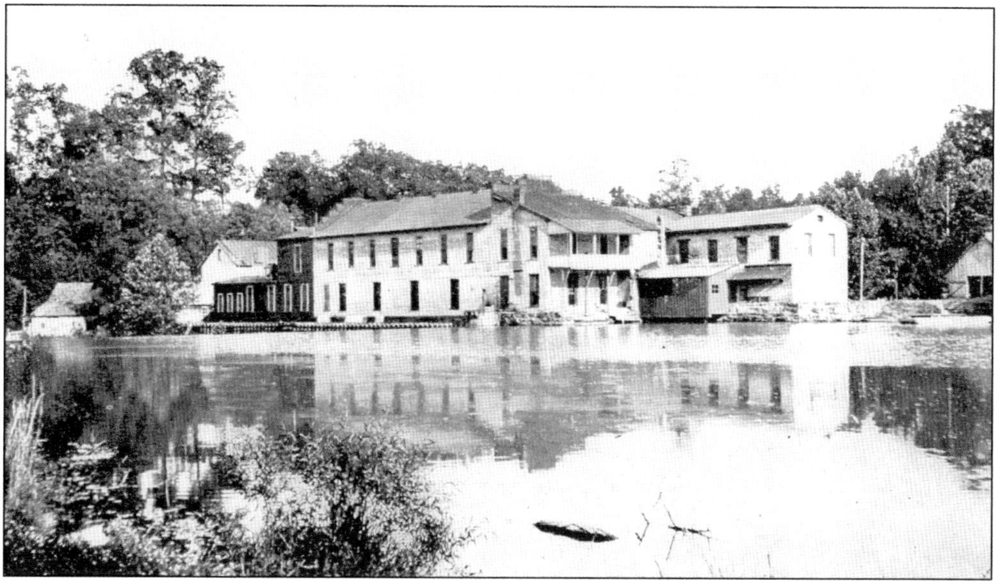

After the great flood of 1902 enacted great damage to his water-powered Mountain City Woolen Mill, established in 1873, Clay Faulkner converted the structure into a resort hotel, which he named Faulkner Springs Hotel. With the exploitation of medicinal spring water on the property, the hotel flourished and enjoyed great success up until the advent of World War I. This is a postcard view of the hotel.

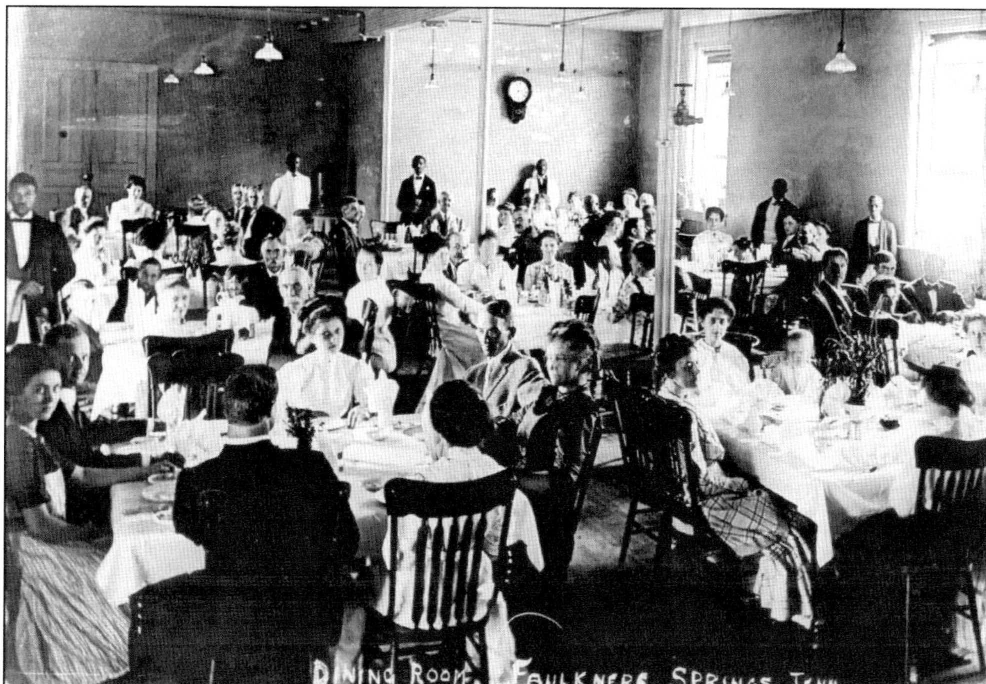

The Faulkner Springs Hotel registry shows that its confluence of guests came from far and wide and included many prominent Nashville visitors, many of whom were repeat visitors to the hotel. The hotel's dining room, pictured in its heyday, was a popular eating place for McMinnville and Warren County residents as well.

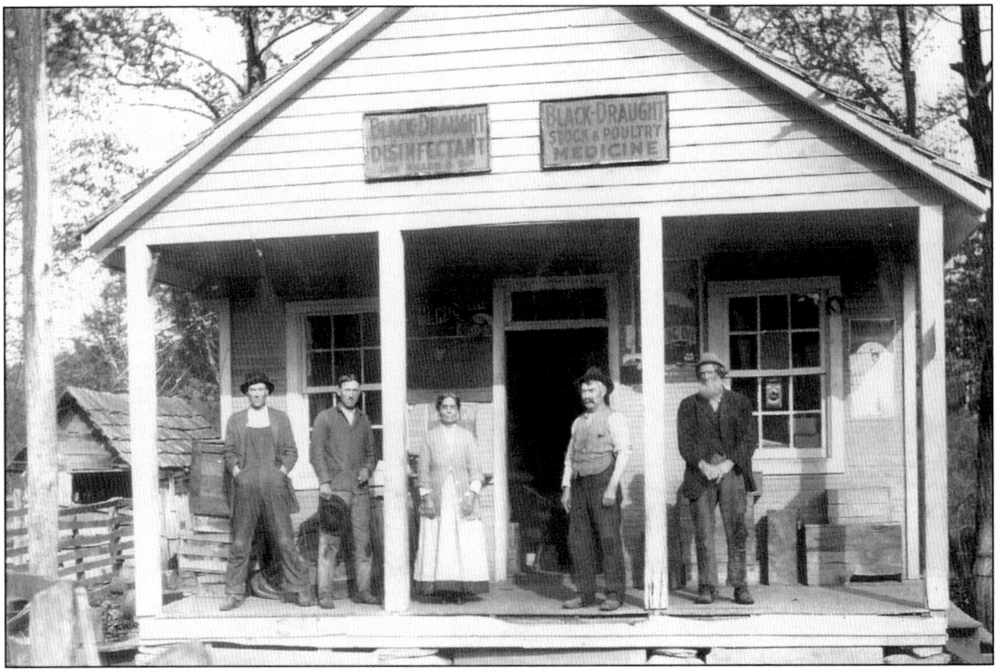

The Elijah L. Moffitt Store, called Roleta General Merchandise Store and Post Office, was operational from about 1880 through the 1920s in the Hill's Creek Community of Irving College. Pictured in an early 1900s photograph are, from left to right, Bill Moffitt, Lester B. Moffitt, Laura Moffitt, Elijah L. Moffitt, and unidentified.

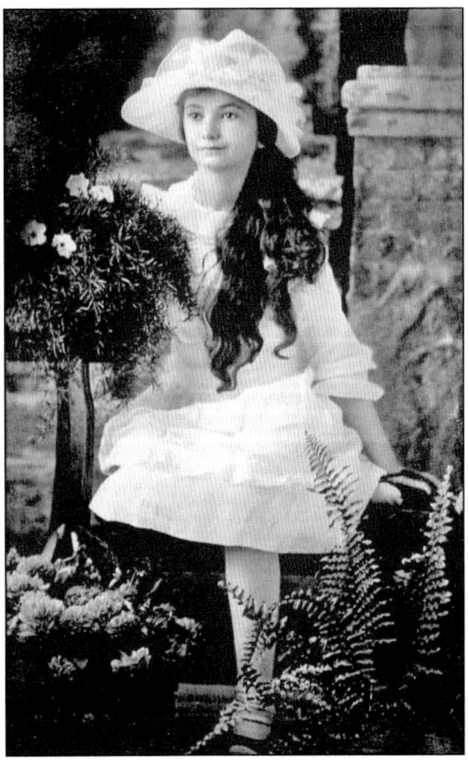
Elizabeth Hume Rowan was born April 7, 1909, in McMinnville, the daughter of Stokley Donalson and Jennie Emmaline Higginbotham Rowan of Warren County. Elizabeth worked as a switchboard operator at the YMCA in Nashville before moving back to McMinnville. She was married in November 1967 to Buford Woodlee (born 1893) of Warren County. Elizabeth died May 25, 1995, and is buried in Liberty Cemetery, alongside her mother, grandmother, and great-grandmother.

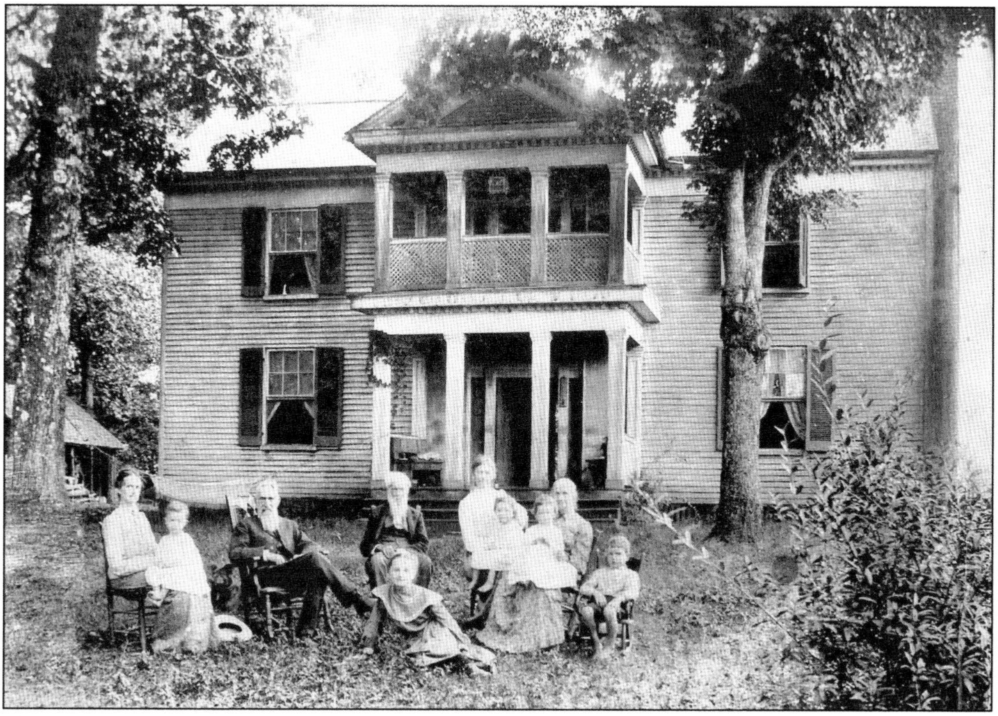

The Mabrys were a prominent pioneer family in the Viola Community. Pictured in this 1903 photograph are, from left to right, Martha Mabry and son Charles Brown, Buck Cunningham, Thomas E. Mabry, Mary Mabry and Nell Smith, Grandma Mabry (holding Edith Mabry), Ed Taliaferro, and sitting on the grass in front is Julia Brown, (sister of young Charles). The Mabry House, located in the Wesley Chapel area, burned in the 1990s.

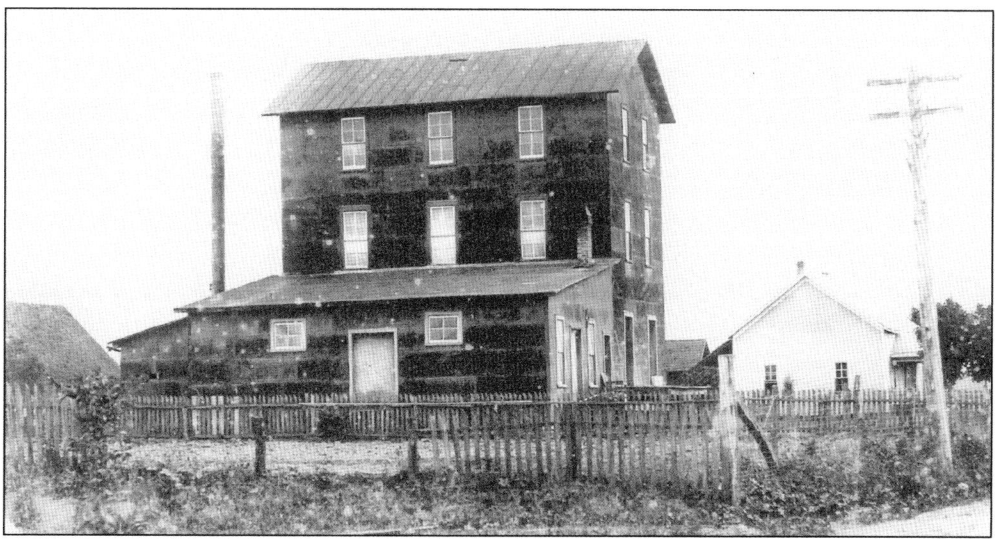

The community of Viola was one of great prosperity and industry early in the county's history. The Viola Mill was known far and wide for its famous "Viola's Best" flour and other grain products. Built around 1906, it was owned by Robert Stove and Robert H. Bonner, who later sold the enterprise to Tom Smith. The popular mill was in operation until 1973.

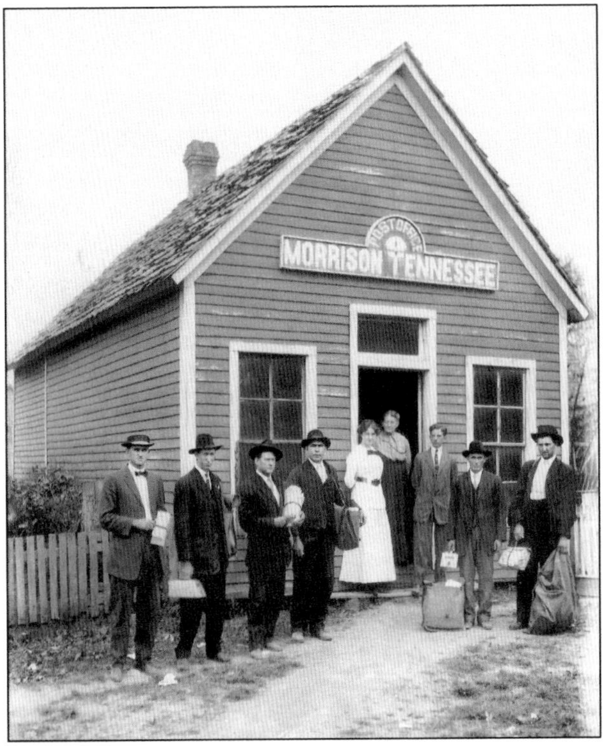

Morrison is one of four municipalities within Warren County. Samuel Morrison came to the area about 1838 and staked off his claim on what is now property in the center of the town. The first Morrison post office was established officially on March 17, 1857. John Crisp, extreme right, is the only person who can be identified in this 1900 photograph of the post office.

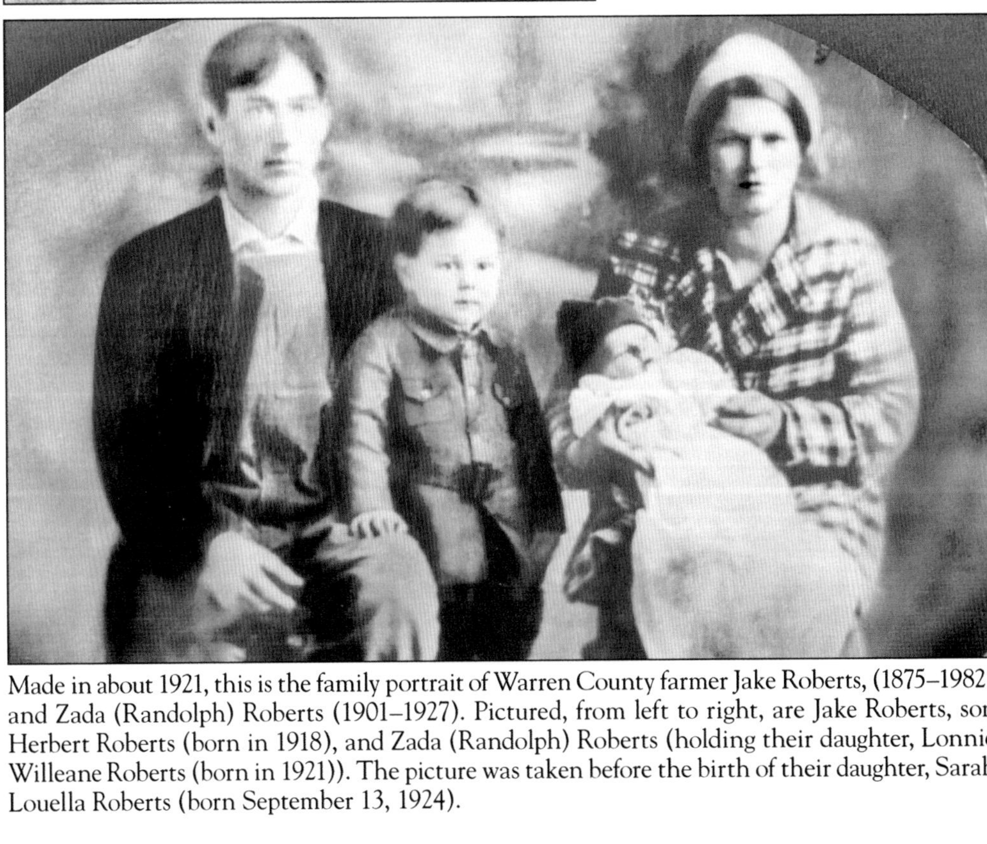

Made in about 1921, this is the family portrait of Warren County farmer Jake Roberts, (1875–1982) and Zada (Randolph) Roberts (1901–1927). Pictured, from left to right, are Jake Roberts, son Herbert Roberts (born in 1918), and Zada (Randolph) Roberts (holding their daughter, Lonnie Willeane Roberts (born in 1921)). The picture was taken before the birth of their daughter, Sarah Louella Roberts (born September 13, 1924).

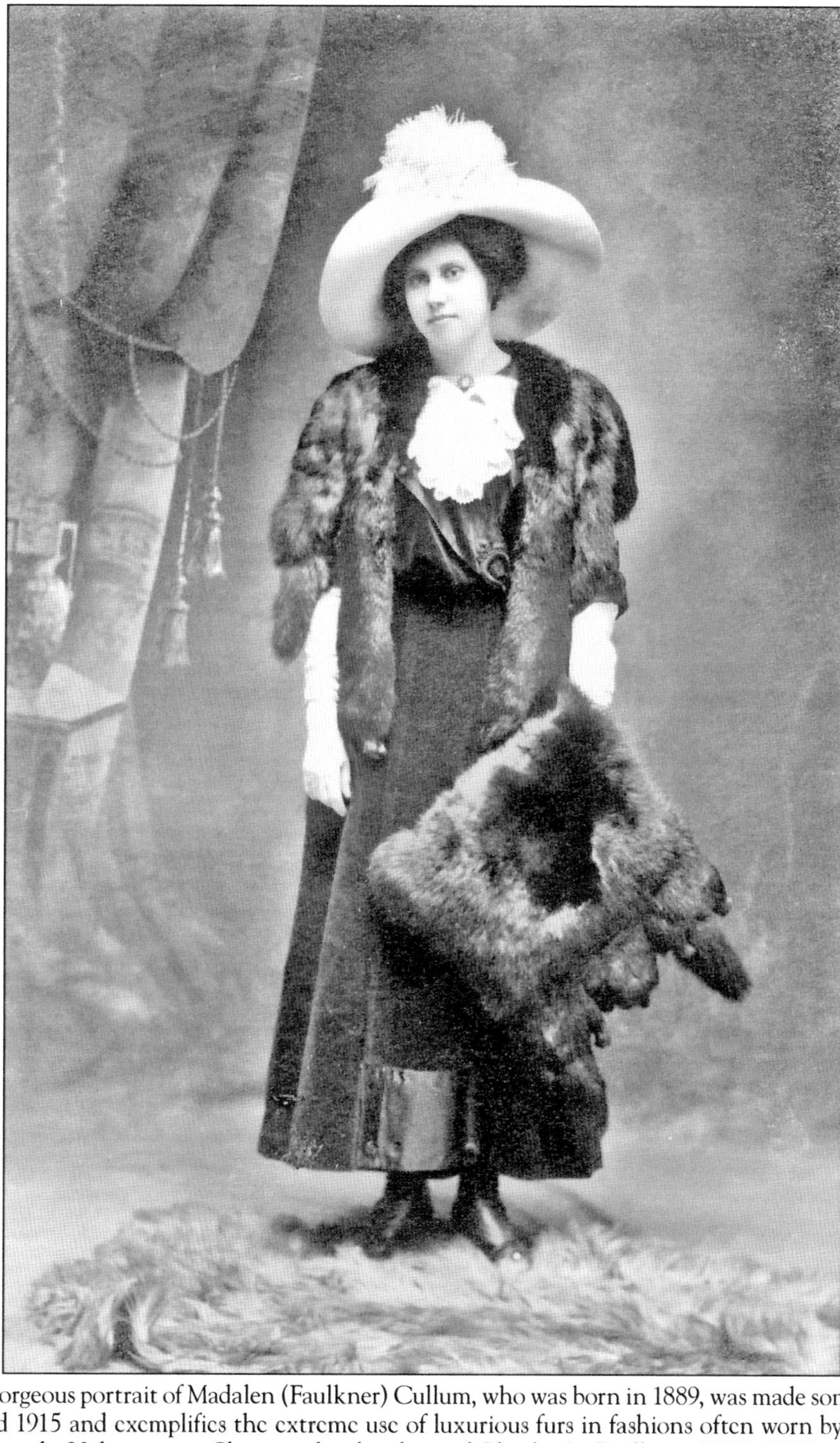

This gorgeous portrait of Madalen (Faulkner) Cullum, who was born in 1889, was made sometime around 1915 and exemplifies the extreme use of luxurious furs in fashions often worn by ladies in the early 20th century. She was the daughter of Charles L. Faulkner (1859–1937) and Ida G. Faulkner (1859–1913). Madalen died at an early age in 1918 and is buried in McMinnville's Riverside Cemetery.

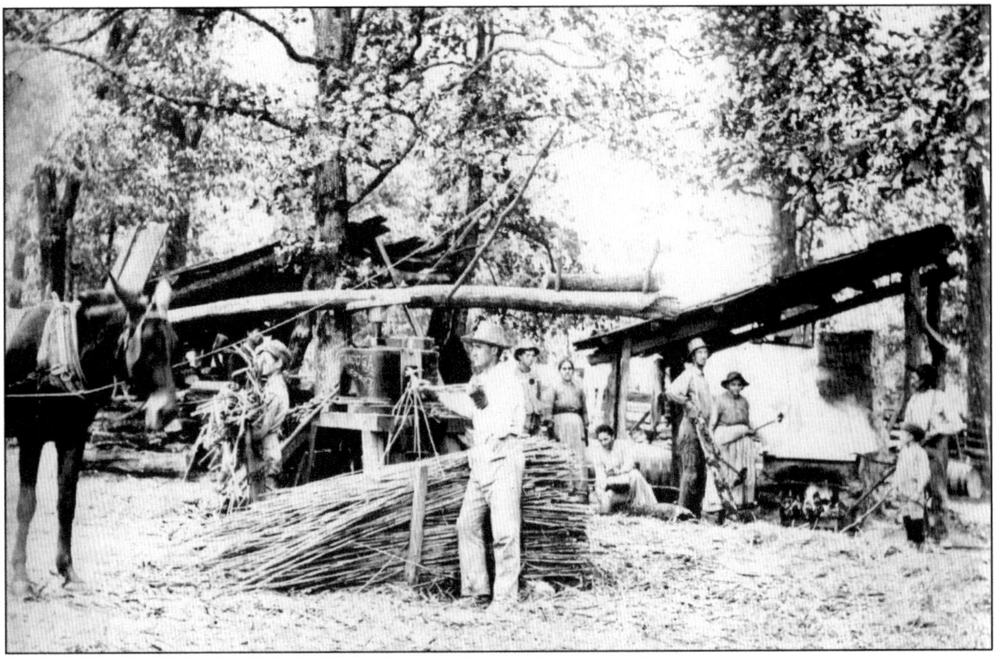

This photograph taken in the early 1900s shows a sorghum mill, near the Oak Grove Baptist Church near McMinnville, in full operation. Those in attendance include Walter and Louise Davenport, Jessie Davenport (feeding the cane), Alton Davenport, Tennie Robertson (pouring syrup), Bryon Bess (firing), Ernest Robertson (carrying stalks), and Jessie Robertson (small child).

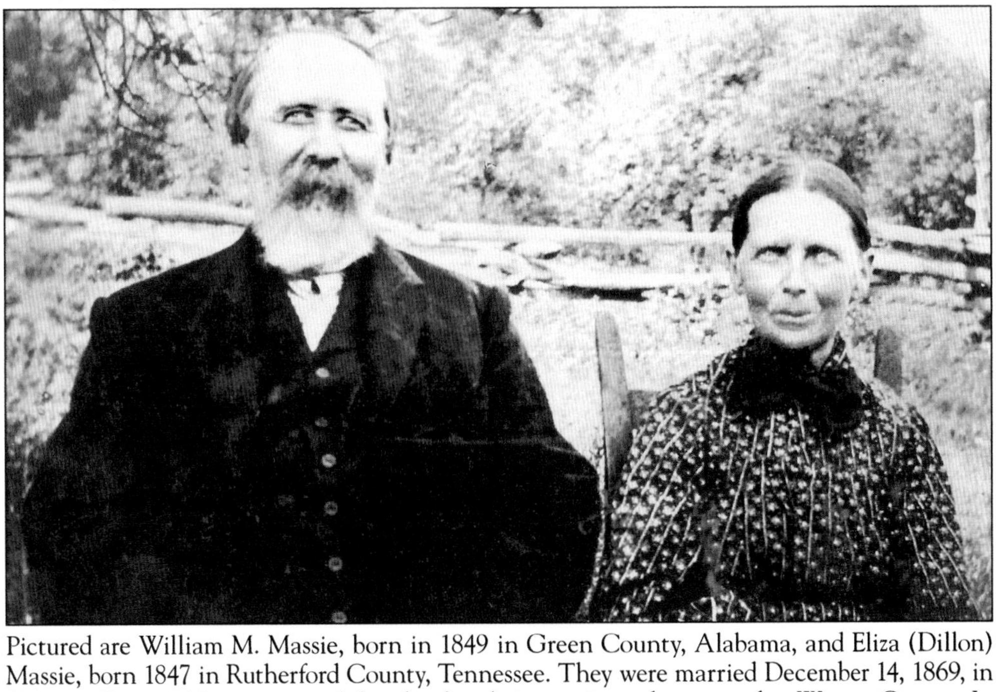

Pictured are William M. Massie, born in 1849 in Green County, Alabama, and Eliza (Dillon) Massie, born 1847 in Rutherford County, Tennessee. They were married December 14, 1869, in Cannon County, Tennessee, and shortly after their marriage, they moved to Warren County. In 1889, they purchased a large farm along the Collins River in the McCollum Bend area, where they lived in a log house and raised seven children.

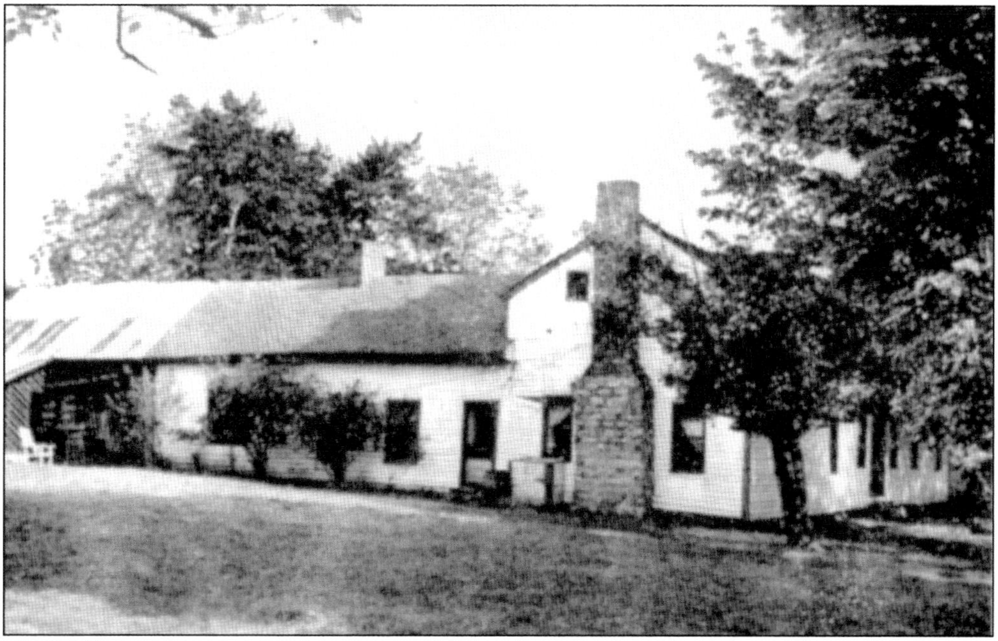

The William C. Smartt family was one of the early pioneer families who settled in the territory of Warren County. Born in 1785, he came from North Carolina in about 1806 and settled along Hickory Creek. He served as the county's first sheriff. The George Madison Smartt (son of William) home, shown here in a late-1940s photograph, was built in 1810 and was enlarged in 1840 and again in 1865.

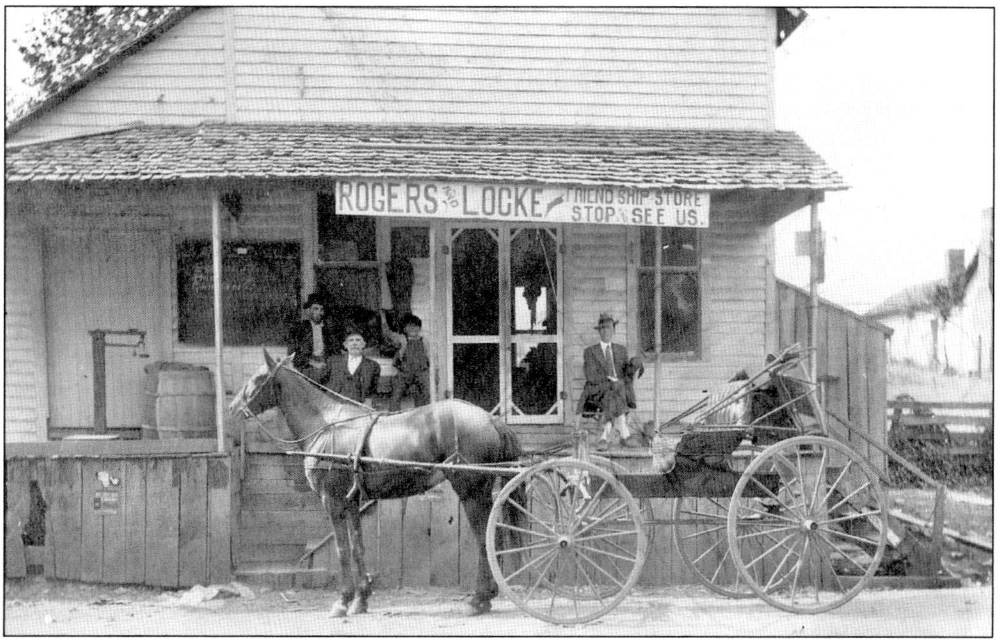

The Rogers and Locke Friendship Store was in operation in the early 1900s in the West Riverside Community. Run by Jeff Rogers and Will Locke for a number of years, the store was the forerunner of Locke's 5 and 10 Store on Main Street in downtown McMinnville. This photograph shows three unidentified individuals at left with Will Locke sitting in the chair beside the front door.

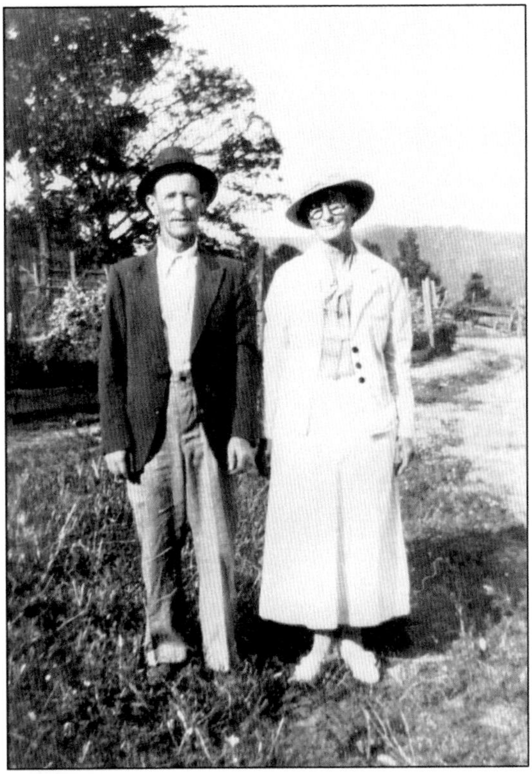

This photograph of Jimmie J. Wanamaker (1875–1937) and wife Nancy Ann Wanamaker (1879–1950) was taken sometime around 1925. Married July 6, 1899, they lived at the Warren/Grundy County line near Wanamaker's Branch at the Collins River, some 12 miles south of McMinnville. They had 11 children: Mary, Martha, Jacob, Nancy, James ("Jimmy"), Naomi, Ruthie, Lassie, Haywood, Deliah, and Charity.

The first band organized in the rural areas of Warren County was organized in 1910 by Hackett Barnes in the Dibrell community. Members of the band pictured from left to right were (first row, seated) Walter Bragg, Hall Tenpenny, and Director Barnes; (second row, seated) Thomas Chastain, John Roy Bragg, Perry West, Jim Green, Bob Clark and I. G. Gribble; (third row, standing) Clyde Potter, G. W. Hinkley, and Dr. G. G. Fisher.

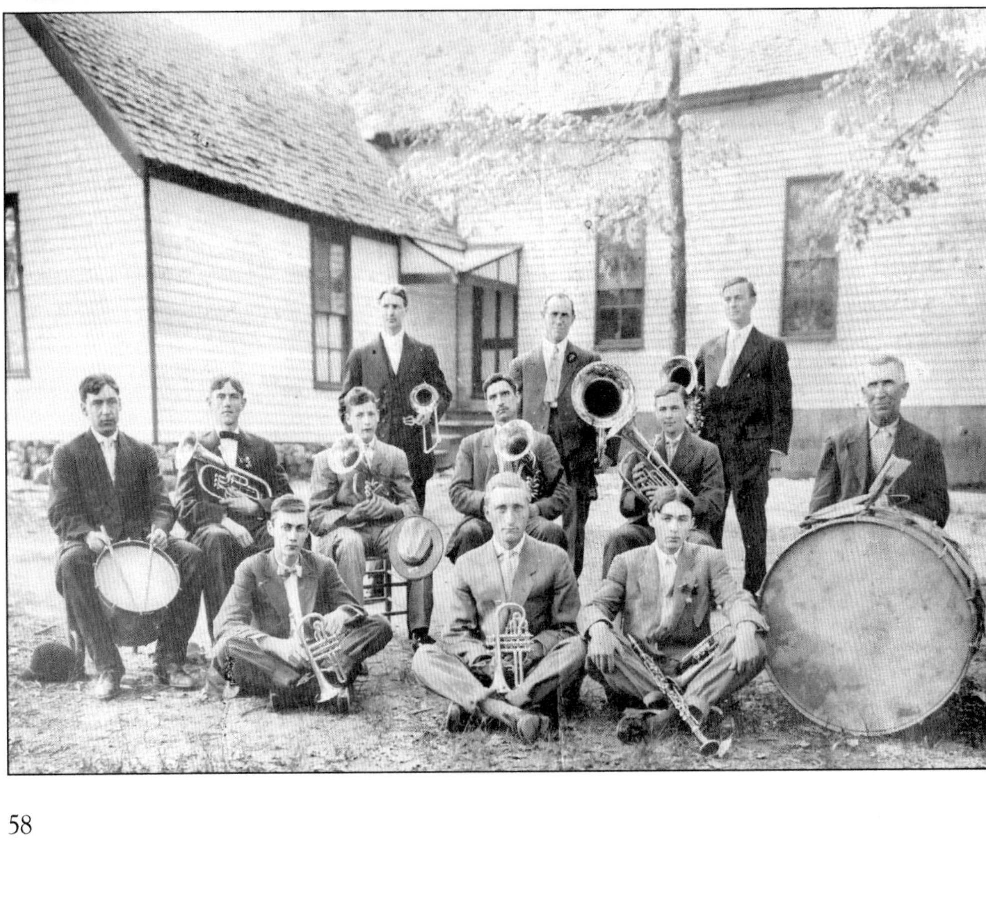

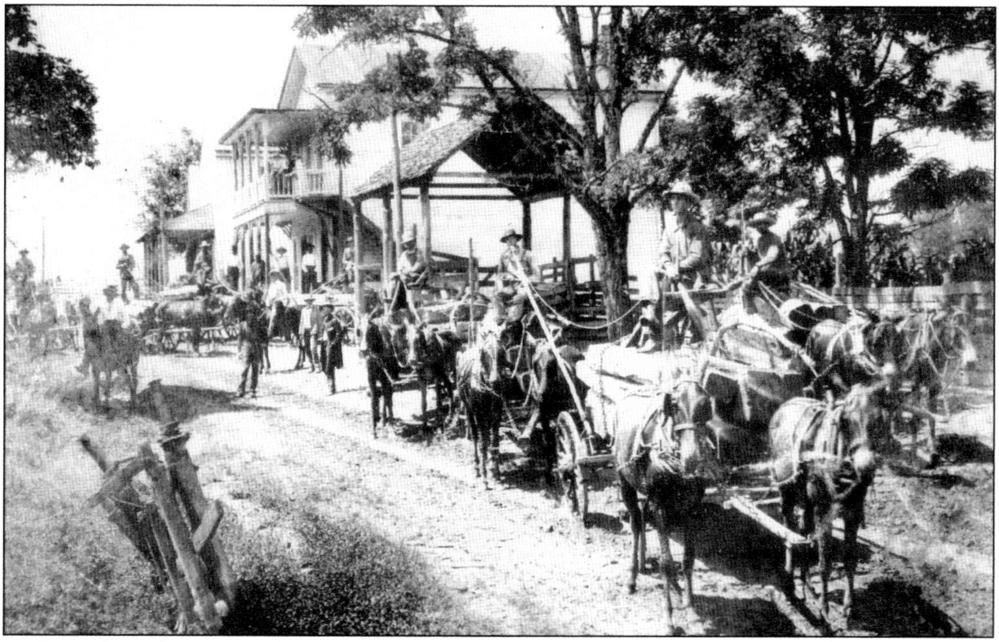

In the early 20th century, the community now known as Irving College was known as Morrison's Crossroads, so named after Samuel Morrison who first settled there and later had the community of Morrison named for him. In the early days, there was a mercantile store, a mill, blacksmith shop and a cattle scale facility. This photograph was taken at a time when one traveled on horseback or in a wagon pulled by mules or horses.

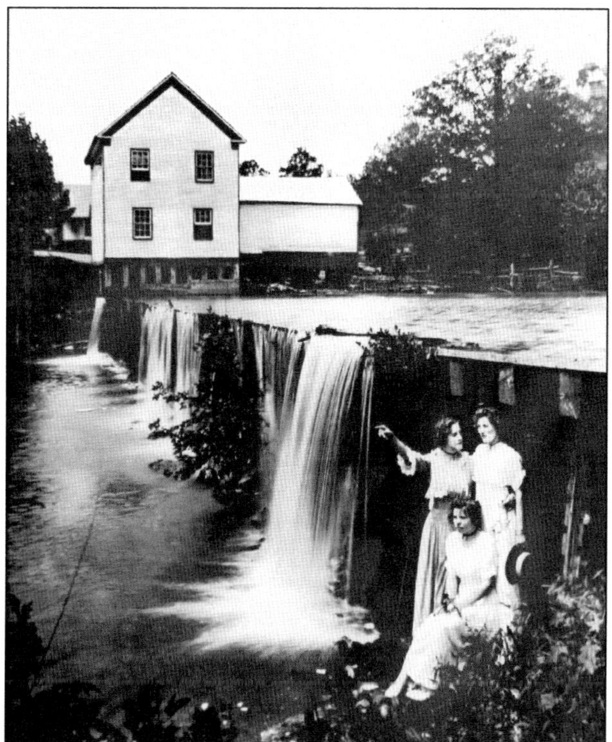

The old Clearmont Mill, located in the Ivy Bluff community, operated from the early 1800s, and was one of many water-powered gristmills operating in the early days of Warren County. The center of community life, it was owned and operated in later years by Doyle Barnes up until 1947. Some years later, it was struck by lightning and burned to the ground.

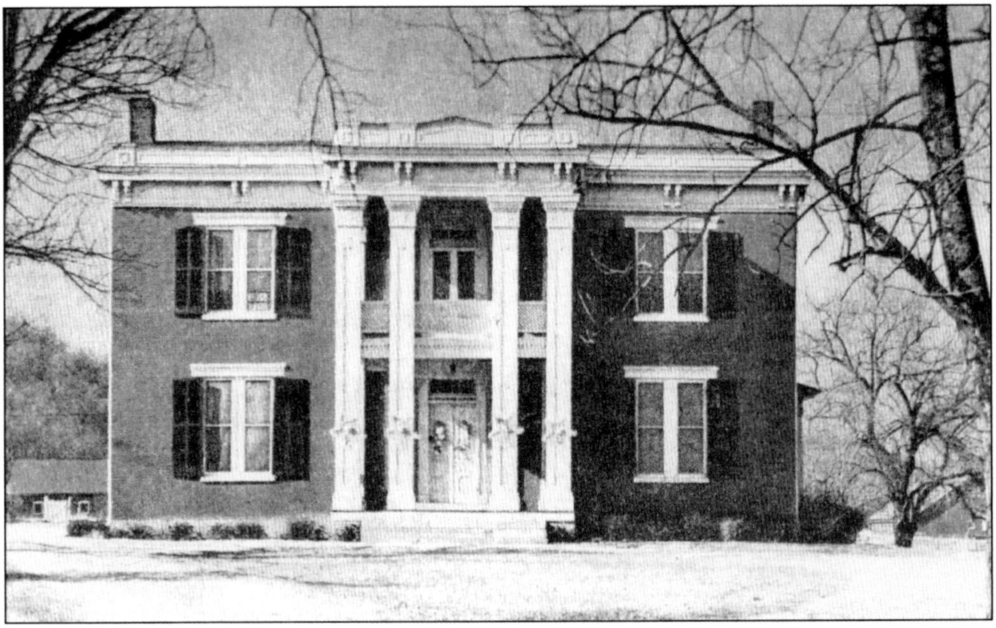

This brick mansion, which was gradually torn down in the 1990s, was built prior to the Civil War, probably by Capt. Thomas Benedict Rust (1831–1910), whose family occupied the residence during its formative years. Built with the help of slave labor, it was located in the Plainview Community, a few miles southeast of McMinnville. Rust was married to Adaline Faulkner (1834–1918), and the couple had nine children.

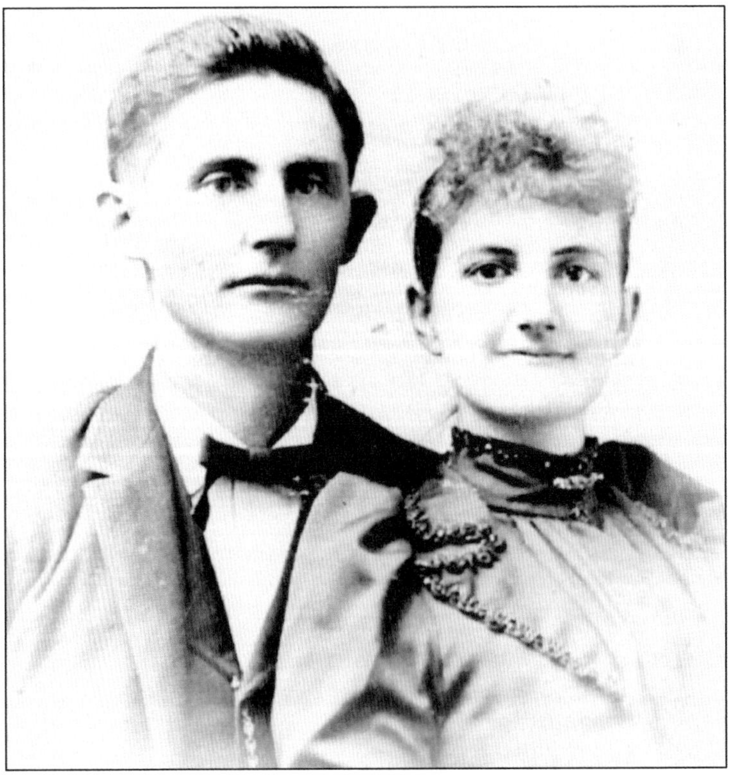

Charles Mabry Brown may possibly be the oldest living citizen of Warren County. He was born in 1902 in Ladonia, Texas, to Andrew George Brown (1865–1908) and Martha (Mabry) Brown (1870–1951) of Warren County. This is the wedding portrait of Charles and Jessie Mae (Stubblefield) Brown (1898–1986) who were married in 1927. George Mabry Brown still lives in the original dogtrot, log house in the Wesley Chapel Community, where he has lived since 1921.

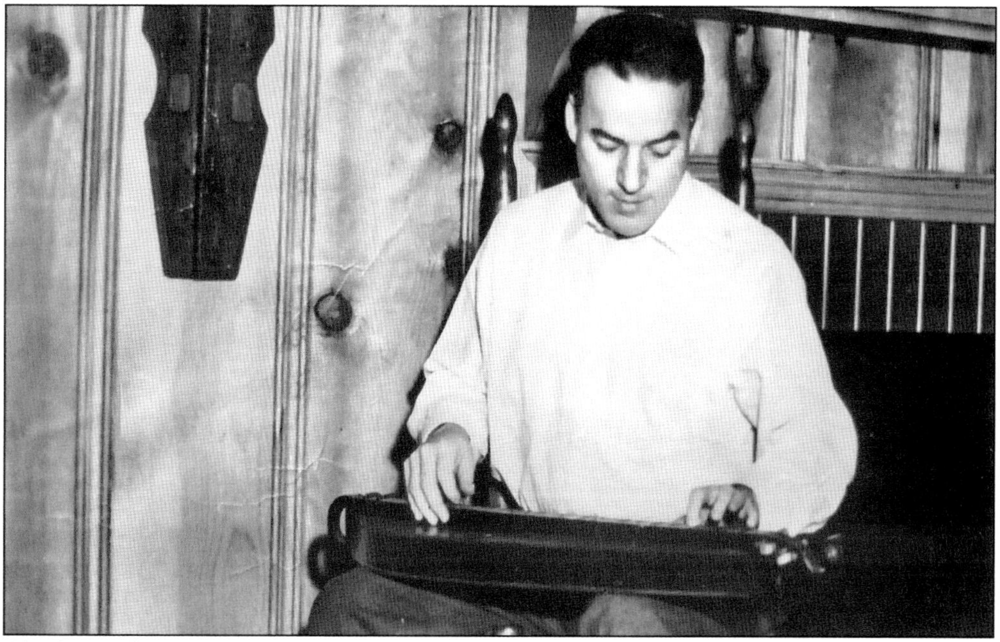

Charles Faulkner Bryan was born in 1911 and grew up in Falconhurst, the Asa Faulkner house. He gained wide acclaim as a musician and composer, and gained worldwide recognition for his pioneering work in preserving southern folk music. His most famous work, *The Bell Witch Cantata*, premiered in Carnegie Hall in 1947, under the direction of Robert Shaw. Bryan died unexpectedly in 1955 from heart complications.

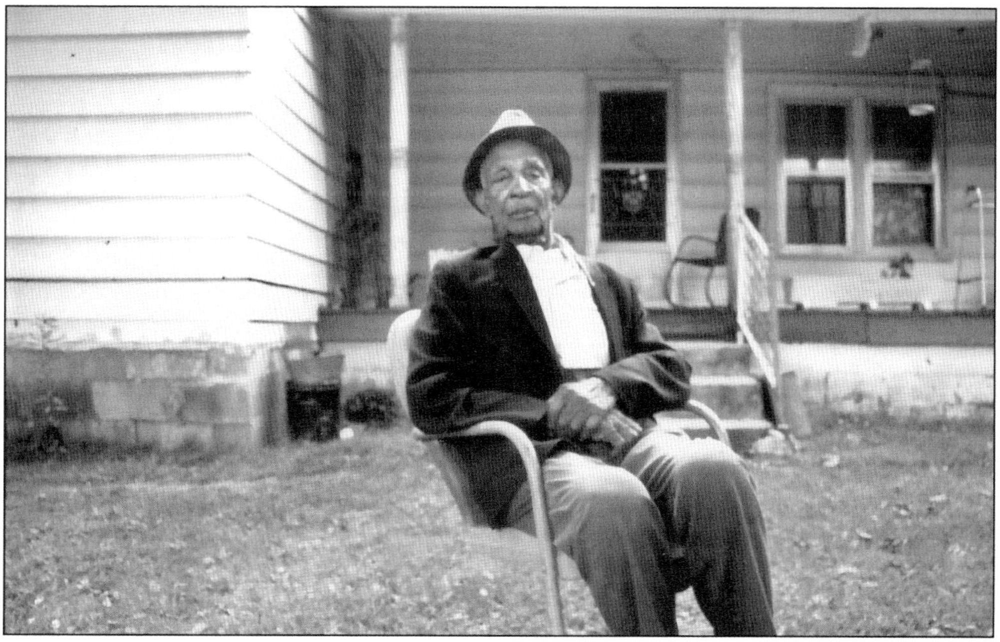

In this photograph, probably taken in the 1960s, Roy Webb is pictured sitting in front of his house in the Bolden Green community of Faulkner Springs. Born in 1889, he was one of 10 children born to Richard and Suzy Webb. As a youth, he worked for Clay Faulkner, and later as his carriage driver. Webb's grandmother was one of Asa Faulkner's numerous slaves. Webb died in 1989.

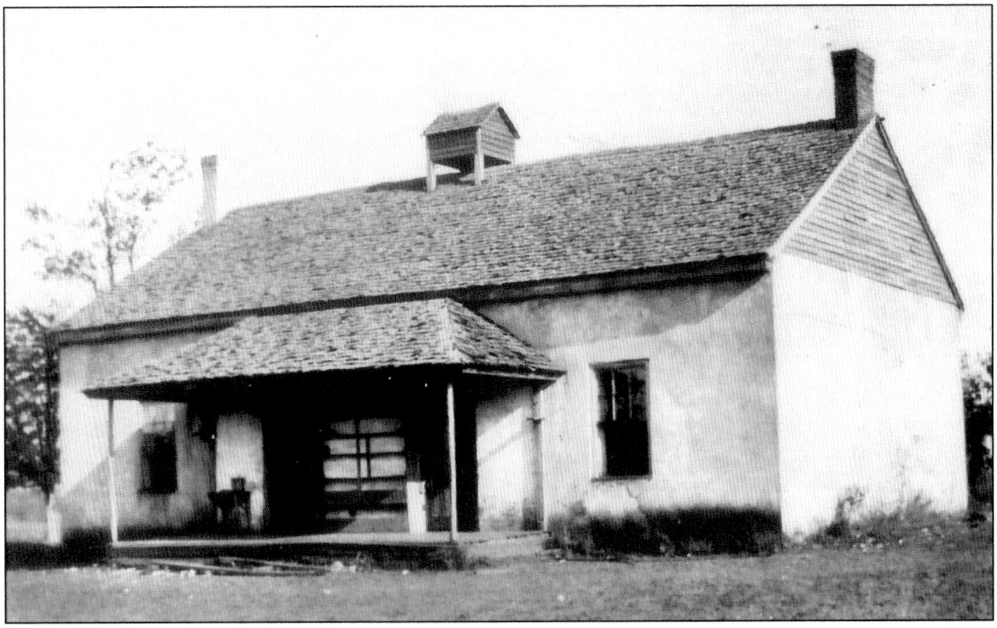

In 1835, a small neighborhood school was built in what is now known as the Irving College community. In 1845, called Irving Academy, the enlarged school became very successful as one of the leading male schools in the south. The building pictured was called East Congress Hall, one of a complex of early buildings for the famous school. This building was still standing at the site in the 1920s.

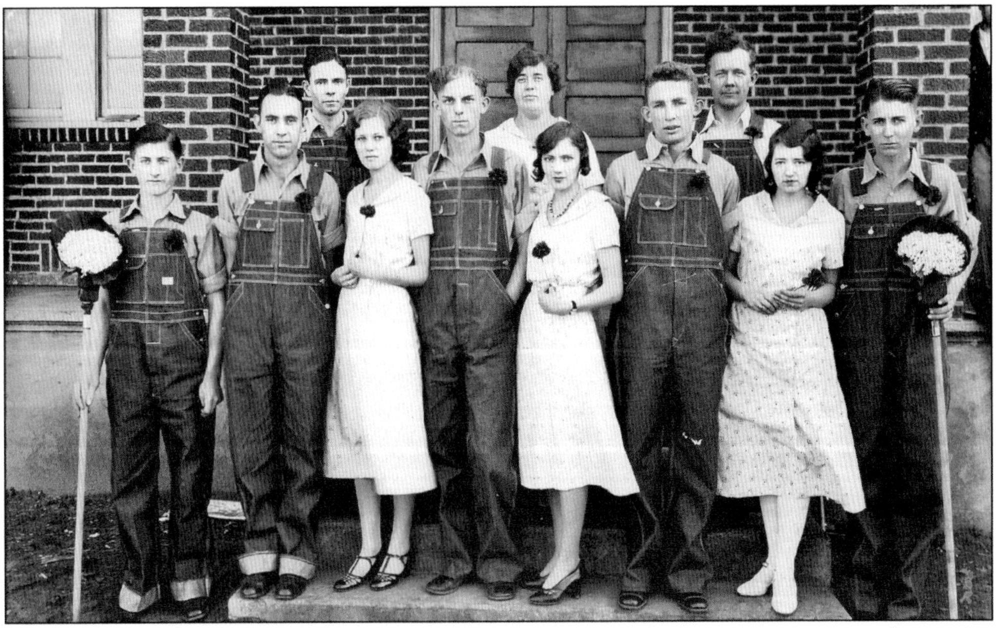

The Irving College School has continued to operate since its early inception, except during the Civil War. Pictured in this rare photograph of the 1932 Irving College Class are, from left to right, (first row) Baxter Safley, Doyle Masey, Wilma Hobbs, Brown Doak, Pauoline Ware, Harold Sain, Clara Northcutt, and Lowell Turner; (second row) Haskell Newman, Adina Golden, and Reece Rogers, principal.

This is a rare daguerreotype of Benjamin Jefferson Hill who was the son of pioneer Henry J. A. Hill, who came from North Carolina and settled in the area of wilderness southeast of McMinnville in 1801, since known as Hill's Creek. In 1858, Benjamin Jefferson Hill operated the famous Warren House Hotel, and before the Civil War, he was engaged in the mercantile business in McMinnville. The highest-ranking officer from Warren County who served in the Civil War, he was commander of the 35th Regiment, Tennessee Volunteers. He served as mayor of McMinnville in 1872. His last days were spent practicing law in McMinnville. Perhaps the first water-powered mill to be built in Warren County, Hill's Mill, pictured below, was built in 1808 by pioneer J. A. Hill. It remained in the family and operated by means of a turbine wheel for some 130 years.

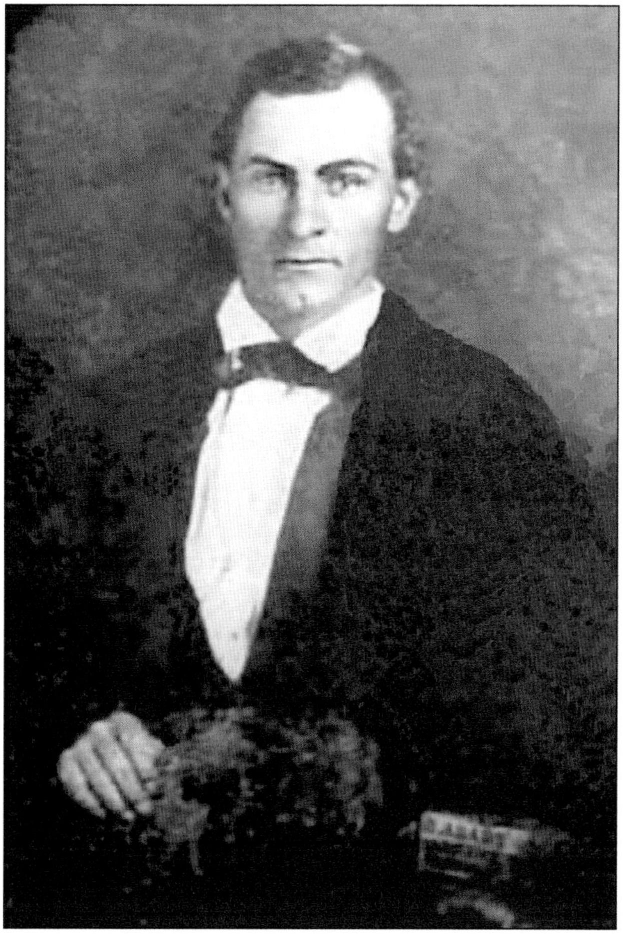

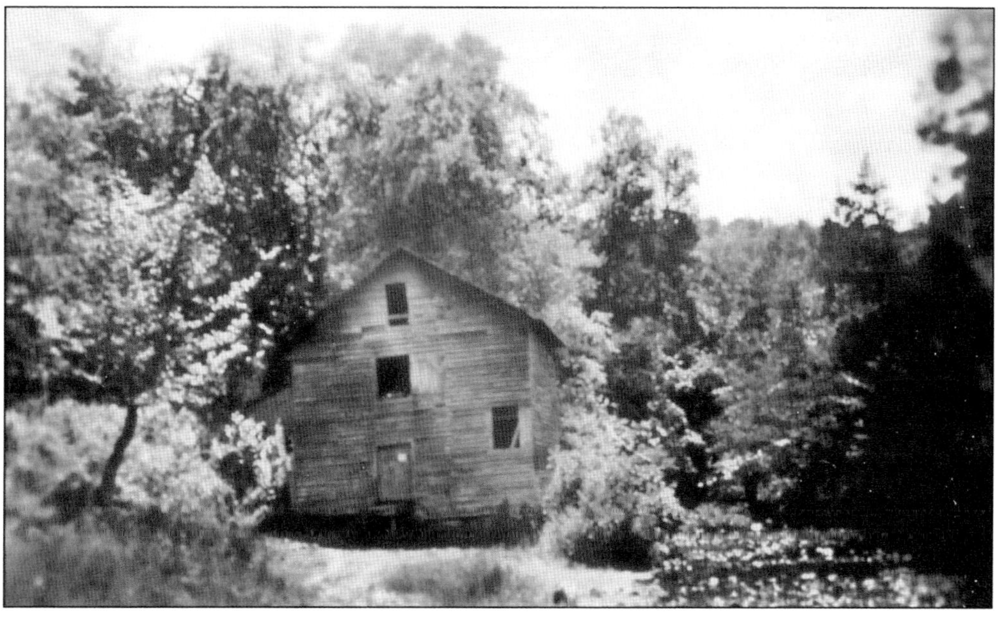

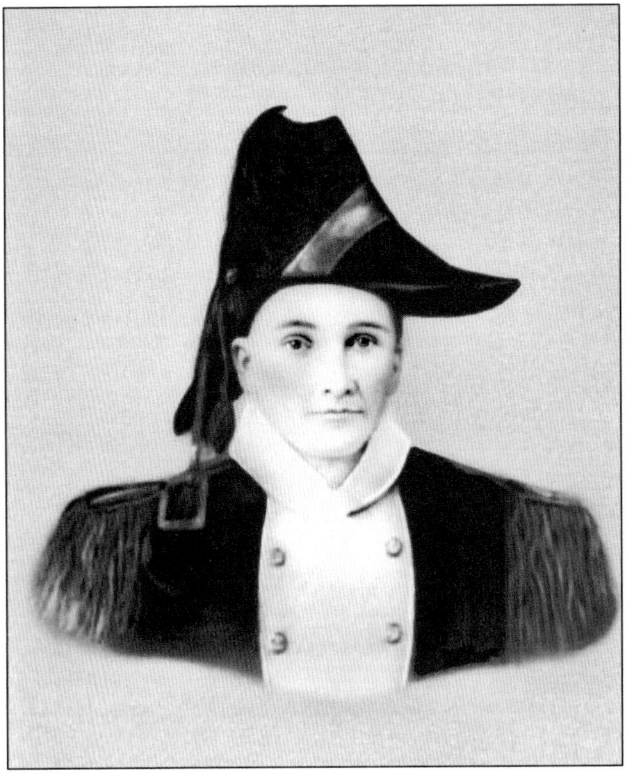

Adrian Northcutt (1799–1869) was born in Virginia and came to Warren County with his parents and settled in the Northcutt's Cove community, later named for his family. He married Sarah Cope in 1819, and they had 16 children. He served as captain in the war with Mexico and was later commissioned general in the Tennessee militia. In this image, Northcutt is dressed in his general's uniform.

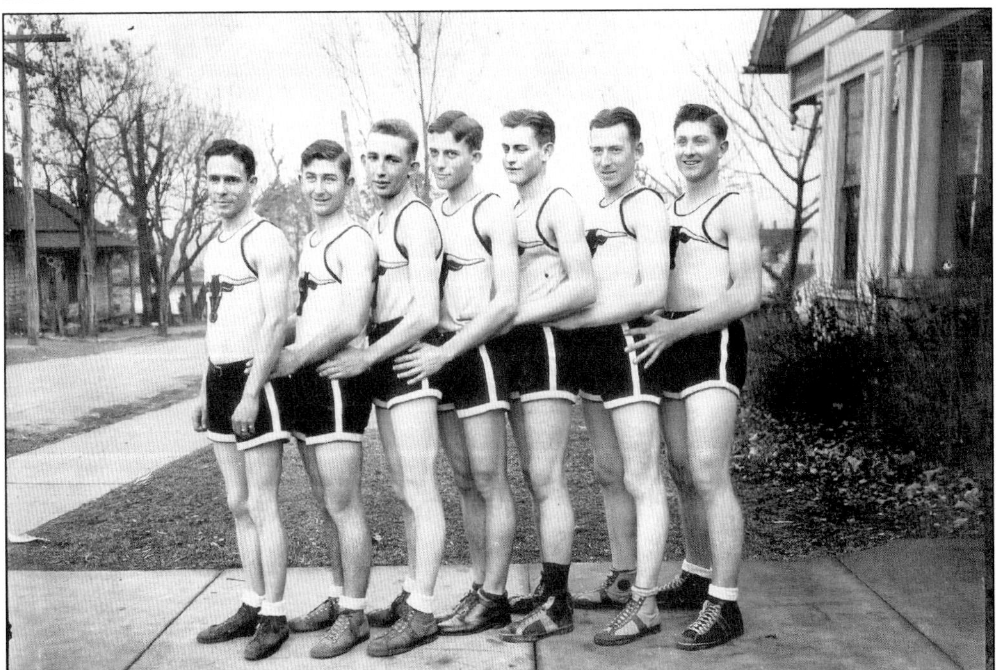

This rare, 1932 photograph pictures members of the Longhorn Independent Basketball team of the Irving College School. From left to right, are Haskell Newman, Lonnie Safley, Harold Sain, Charles Lewis, Overton Hillis, Noah Woodlee, and Marcus Safley.

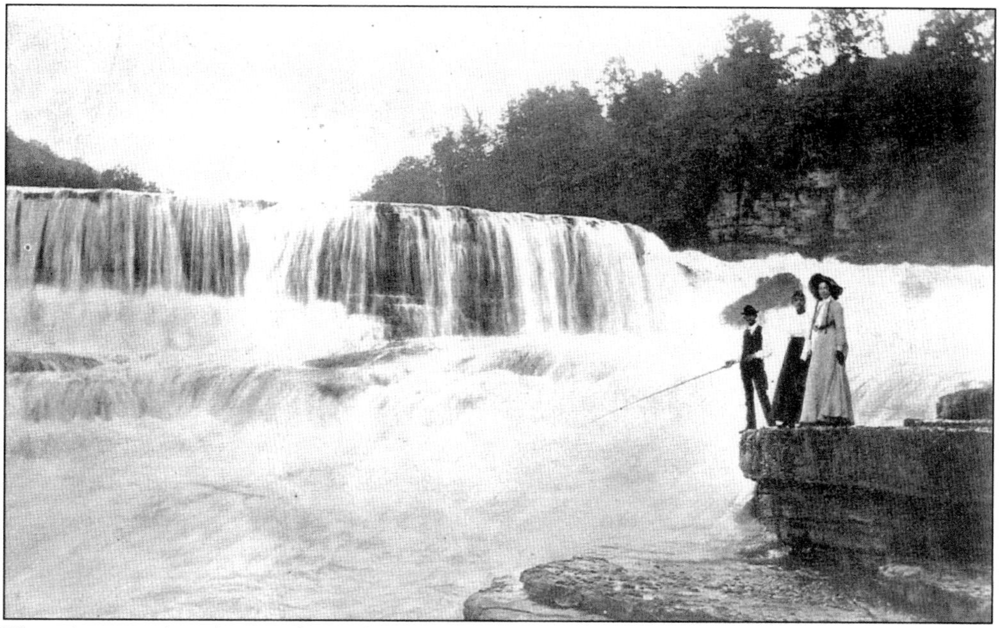

This photograph, taken in the early 1900s at Rock Island and thought to have been taken by local photographer William Spencer Lively, depicts family members standing on an outcrop above the spectacular Caney Fork Falls in the background. Seen standing on the rock are Mrs. Lively (Lela Jones Lively); daughter Nancy Pearl (wearing the hat); and Nancy's husband, Joseph Austin (with the fishing pole).

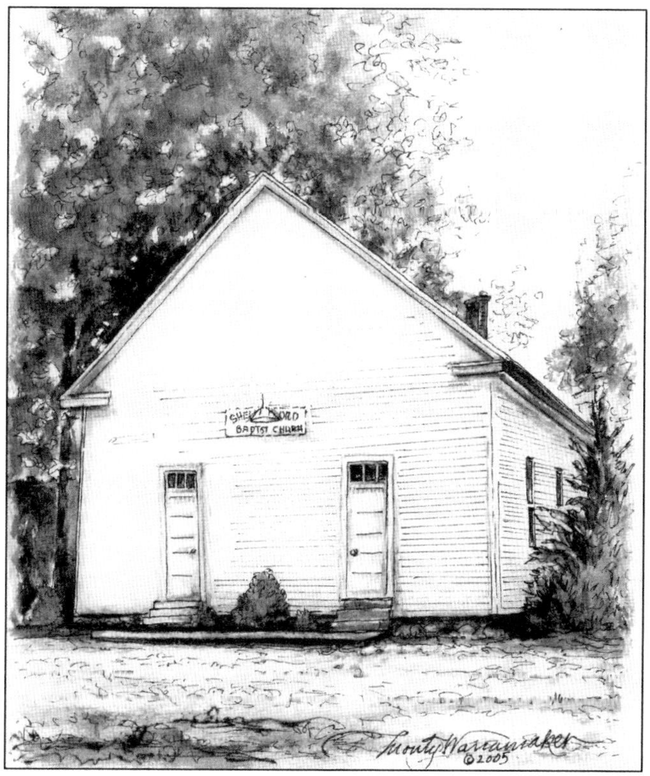

One of the earliest settlements in Warren County, Shellsford, got its name from Christian Shell, who owned and operated an early mill there along the Collins River. The church was established in 1810 in a log cabin, which was replaced in about 1857 with a frame building. After 1855, the name was changed and was later known as Shellsford Church, pictured in a drawing by Monty Wanamaker.

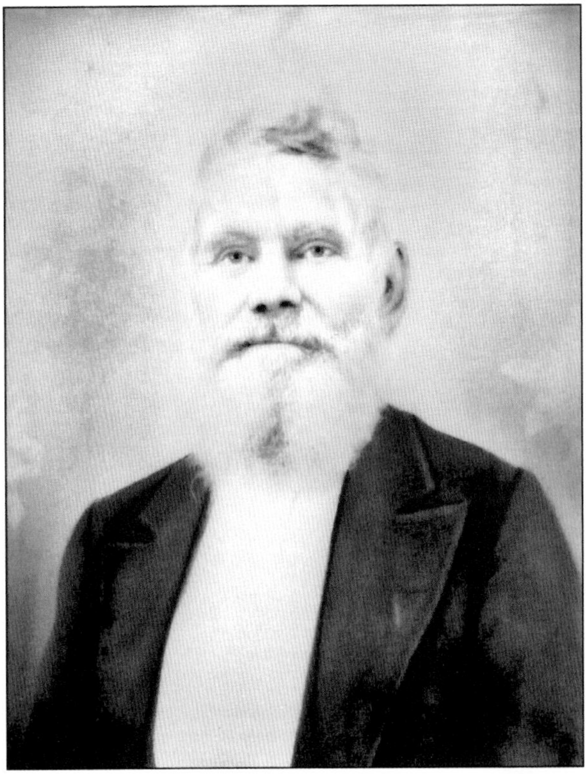

John R. Madewell, born in 1818 in White County, came to Warren County prior to 1844 where he settled in the Steppsville community, and worked as farmer and laborer. He married Sarah Phillips in 1838 and later in 1867 Melvina Dica Thaney Meadows. They had five children: William M. (born 1839), Thaney (born *c.* 1842), James A. M. (born 1844), Allison Woodville (born 1849), and Jesse (born 1852). John Madwell died in 1911.

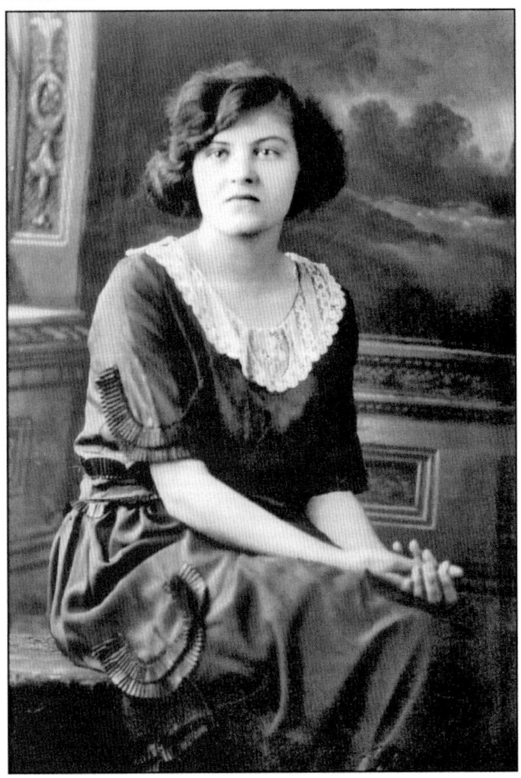

Carrie Lee McGregor (1903–1970) was the daughter of Horace McGregor and Gilley (Kesey) McGregor. This portrait of her was probably made around the time of her marriage in June 1923 to Osmond Cain Woodlee. They lived in a large, pre–Civil War, dogtrot log house, probably built by Jacob Woodlee, in the Hill's Creek area near Irving College. They had four children: Rebecca, E. K., Lierd, and O. C. Woodlee.

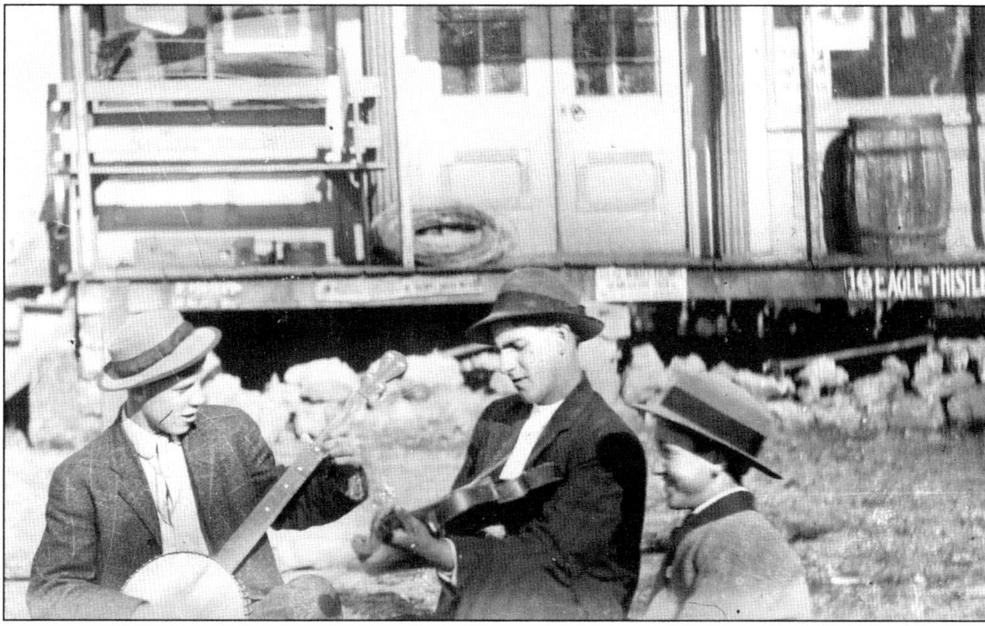

The Daylight Post Office was established in the late 1800s in a general store owned by merchant Oliver Towles, who served as its first postmaster. In 1963, after Arsey Womack, the last postmaster, retired, the post office was closed. Newspapers from across the United States published a photograph depicting the post office established in a lean-to shed, which had been built around a tree growing out of its roof.

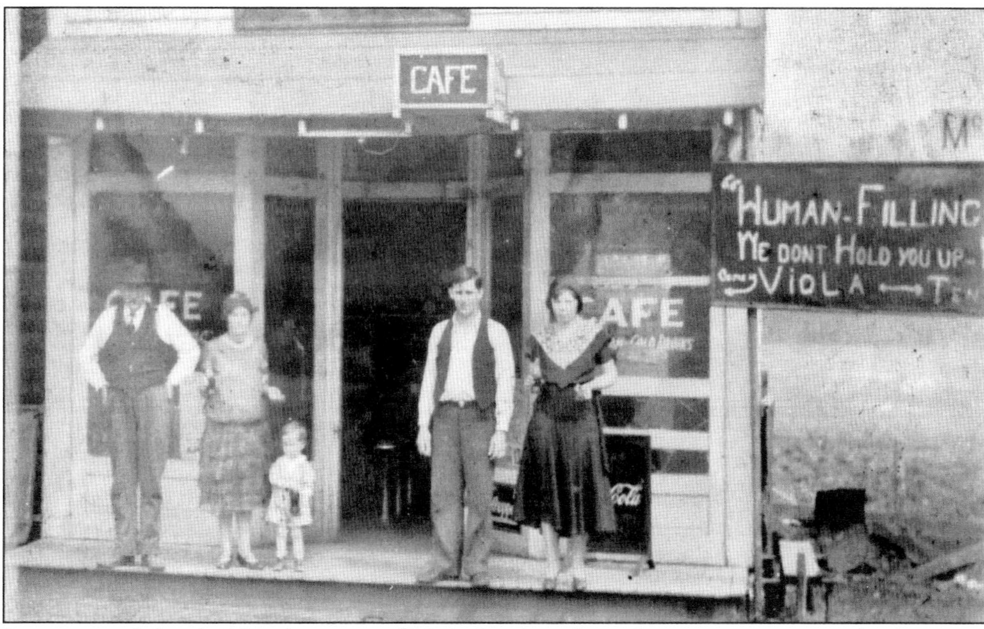

Incorporated April 1901, the town of Viola has long been known as a center of culture and refinement, with its early progressive schools and numerous churches. The town has had numerous practicing physicians as well as a bank, hardware stores, groceries, drugstores, and millinery shops. Down through the years, it featured several cafés such as the one pictured here photographed in the early 1920s.

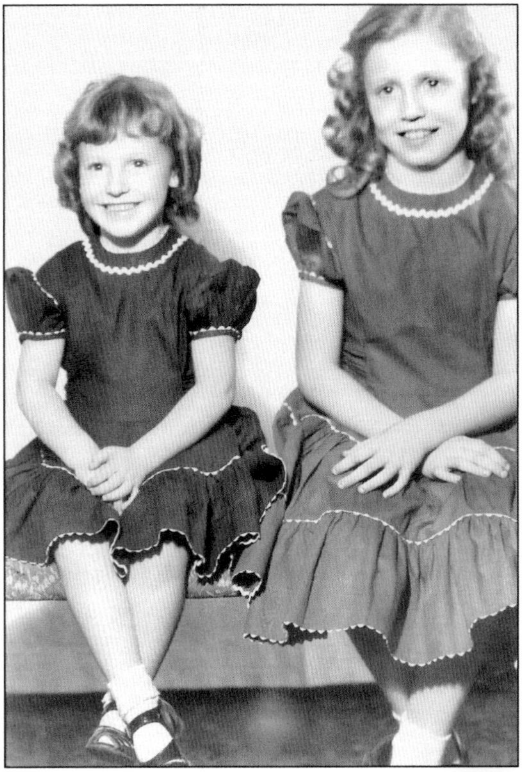

In this photograph taken in 1952, sisters Khyva Lynn (Stubblefield) Starkey (left) and Glenda Sue (Stubblefield) Cantrell are pictured sporting newly made dresses sewn by their aunt Mary Stubblefield. Daughters of Velma Starkey and J. P. Stubblefield, the family lived in the Irving College Community, where the girls graduated from the Irving College School.

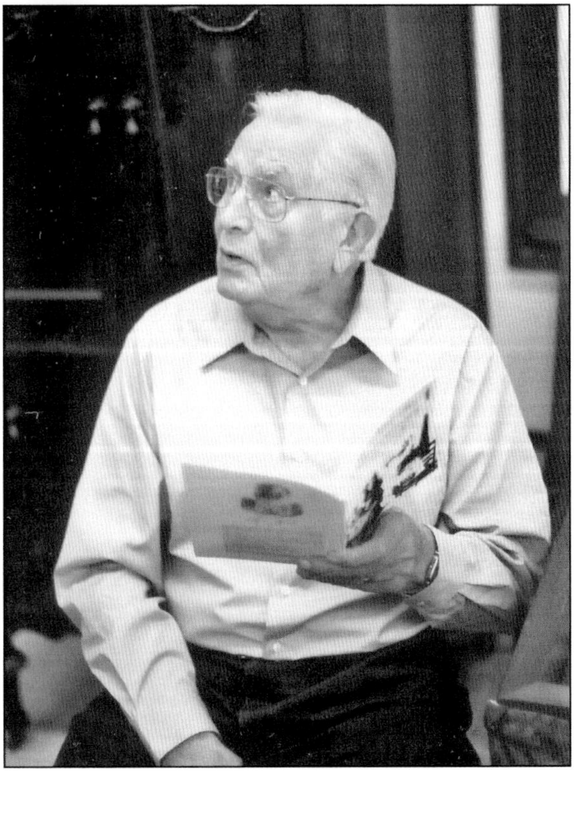

Renowned Vanderbilt University author-Professor Emeritus Herschel Gower is pictured in this photograph, reading from his book, the *Beersheba Springs Diaries of L. Virginia French*, during a visit in the summer of 2006 to the Southern Museum and Galleries of Photography, Culture and History in McMinnville. The Civil War diary, edited by Gower, was published in 1986 by the Beersheba Springs Historical Society.

The daughter of Charles Faulkner Bryan and Edith (Hillis) Bryan, Betty Lynn (Bryan) Haslam (1941–2004) was born in McMinnville and grew up in Falconhurst, the house built by Asa Faulkner. Betty married John Battle Haslam in 1962. Two sons, John Bryan Haslam and Mark Hamilton Haslam, were born. The Haslams lived in Ashville, North Carolina. This photograph captured Betty Lynn sitting on the front steps of Falconhurst in the fall of 1991.

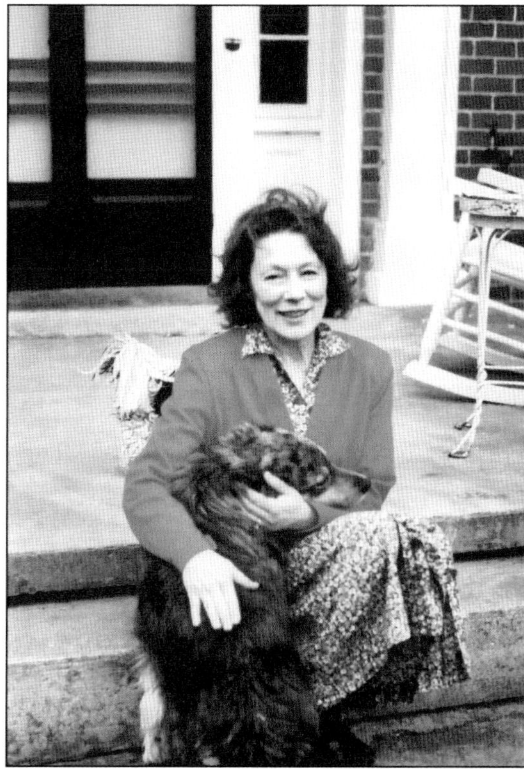

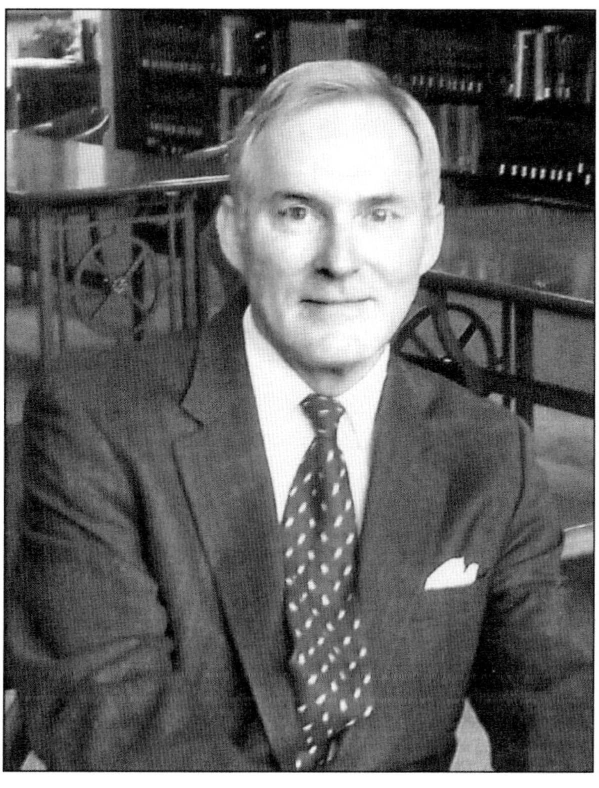

This is a recent portrait of Charles Faulkner Bryan Jr., born December 10, 1946, in McMinnville. He later graduated from the Virginia Military Institute. With a master's degree in history from the University of Georgia and a Ph.D. in history from the University of Tennessee, he has served since 1988 as president and CEO of the Virginia Historical Society, which in 2006 named its new $16-million wing in his honor.

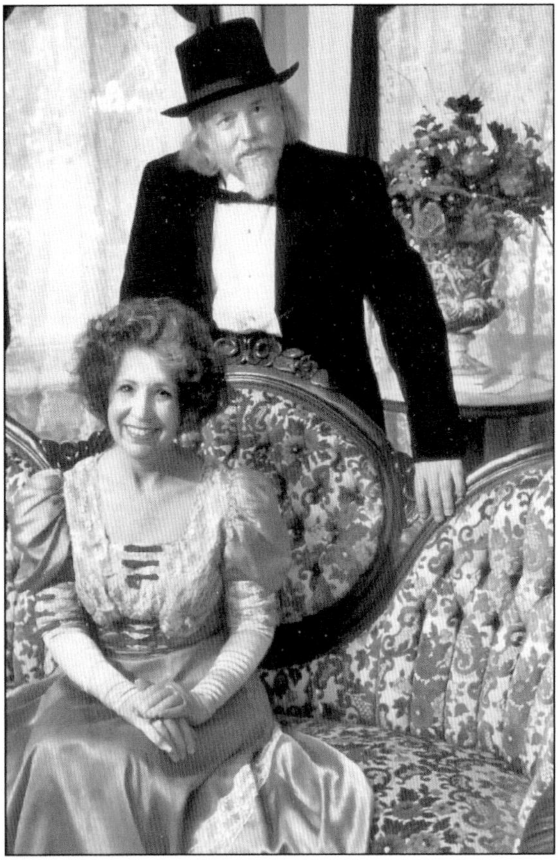

In 1997, George and Charlien McGlothin were awarded first prize in the National Trust for Historic Preservation Awards for their splendid work in preserving and restoring Falcon Rest, the Queen Anne–style house built from 1896–1897 by manufacturer Clay Faulkner. The home was placed on the National Register of Historic Places in 1992, and in 1996, the mansion was designated as a Tennessee history trail site by the State Department of Tourist Development. Today the mansion and its recent additions of carriage house, dining rooms, and gift shops, along with bed-and-breakfast cottages, make the institution one of the leading tourist attractions in the southeastern United States. In the photograph at left, the McGlothins are seen dressed in period costumes, which they often wear for the myriad educational and cultural events they present at the mansion.

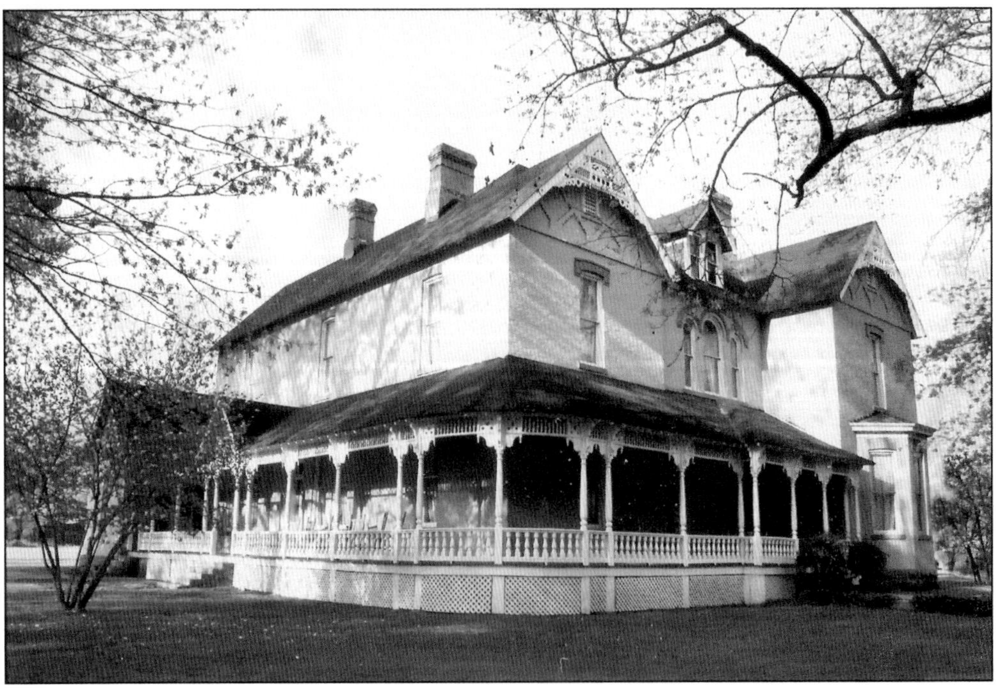

Three

McMinnville

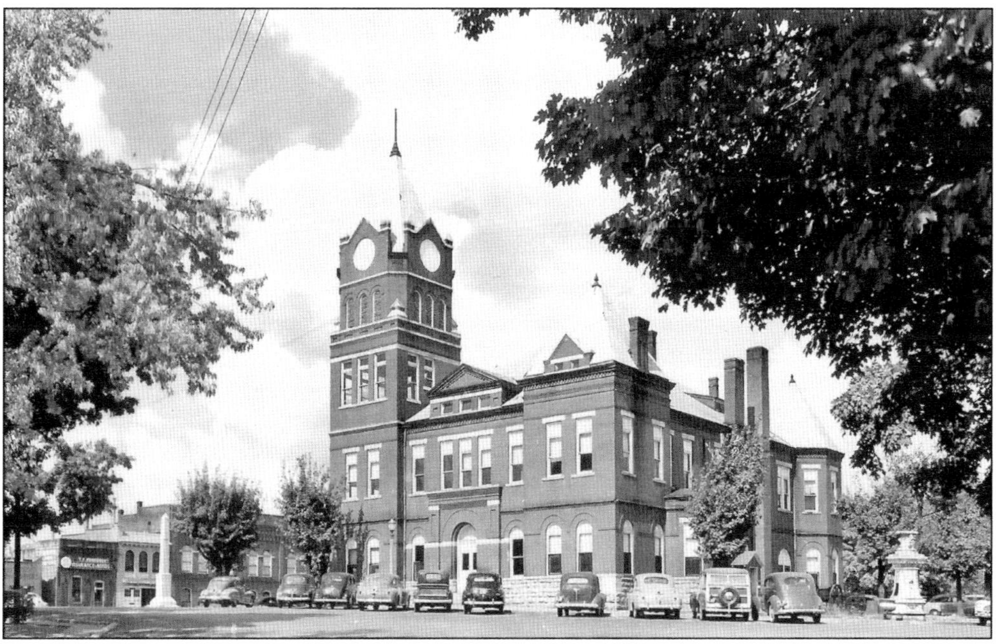

The magnificent edifice, which is the fourth and current Warren County courthouse, is pictured in a 1930s postcard. In the late 1970s, the building was changed somewhat, with an added wing to its west side and the clock towers removed. Standing near the building, left front, is the obelisk erected by John H. Savage as a monument to those men who served under his leadership during the Civil War.

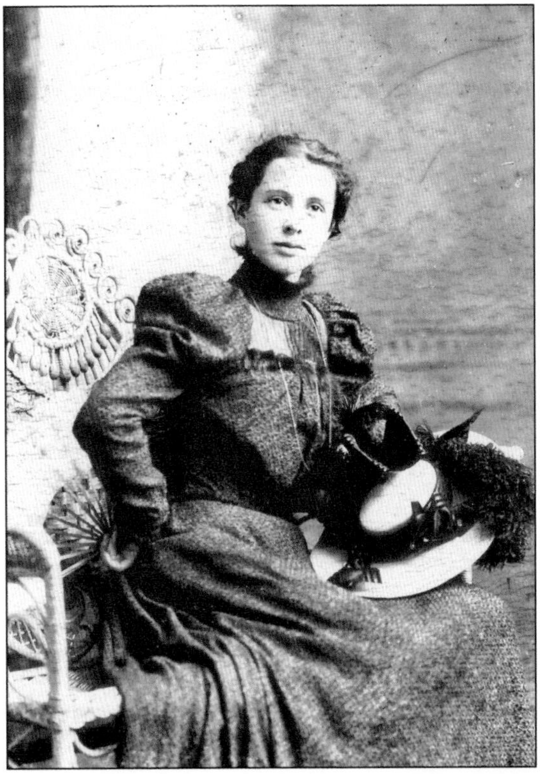

Miranda Jane Hillis is pictured in this 1900 portrait by photographer William Spencer Lively of McMinnville. She was born in McMinnville May 23, 1882, at the home of her parents, Isaiah Thomas and Miranda Jane (Moore) Hillis. She married James William Hunter December 18, 1901, after which two sons and a daughter were born. Miranda died at age 54 on April 9, 1934.

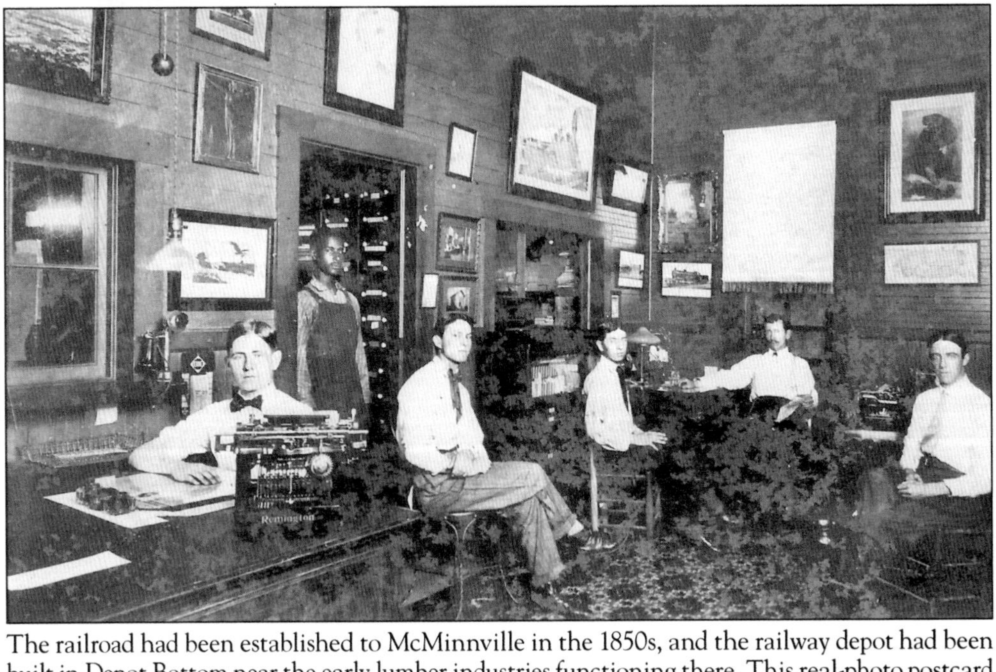

The railroad had been established to McMinnville in the 1850s, and the railway depot had been built in Depot Bottom near the early lumber industries functioning there. This real-photo postcard depicts the depot force at work in the main office. Pictured from left to right, are clerk Mitchell, John Crowder, Frank Montgomery, clerk Holt, and Otis Tidwell. The young African American man standing in the doorway is not identified.

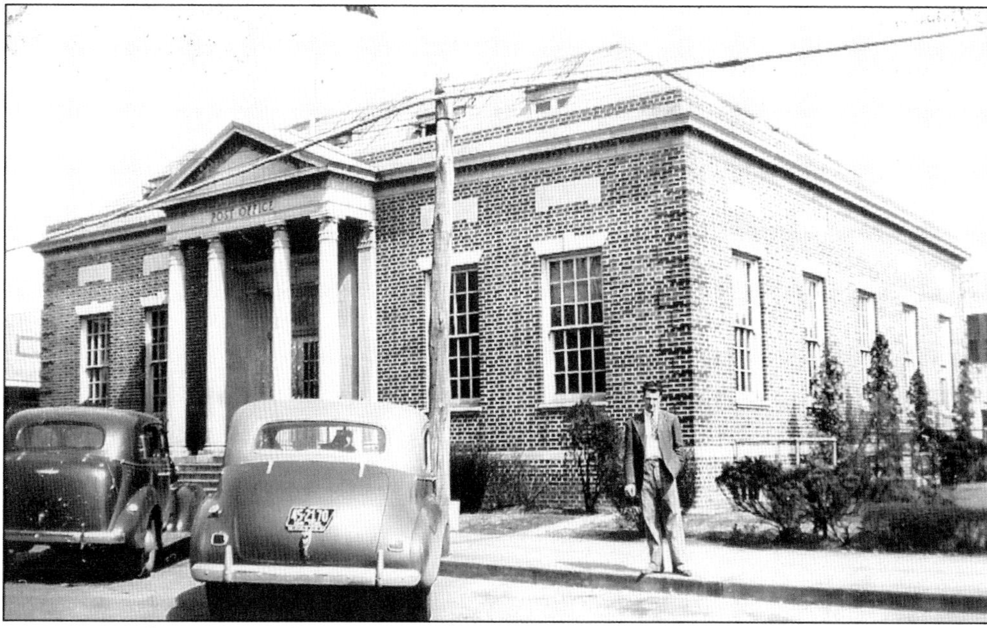

In May 1811, the McMinnville post office was established, with Joseph Colville as its postmaster. The office occupied several different locations in its early years, and later moved into the Jesse Walling building which Hargrove Office Supply now occupies. The present building, built in 1931, is pictured in this 1942 photograph with John Davis (1917–1985), who was associated for some 40 years in downtown McMinnville's H. G. Hill Company grocery store.

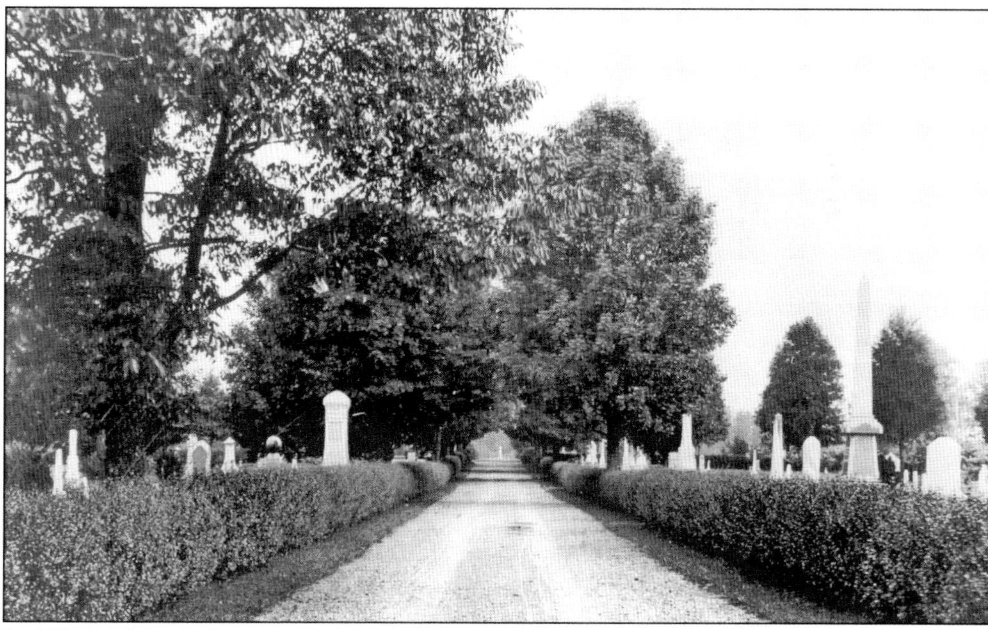

In 1878, McMinnville mayor H. H. Faulkner and the Board of Aldermen purchased property for a new cemetery from Maj. James Powell Thompson. It was located in Depot Bottom south of the railroad above the flood plain near the Barren Fork River. On September 5, 1878, Rev. William D. Chadick became the first to be buried there. In 1905, the Memorial Circle named it Riverside Cemetery, by which it is still known.

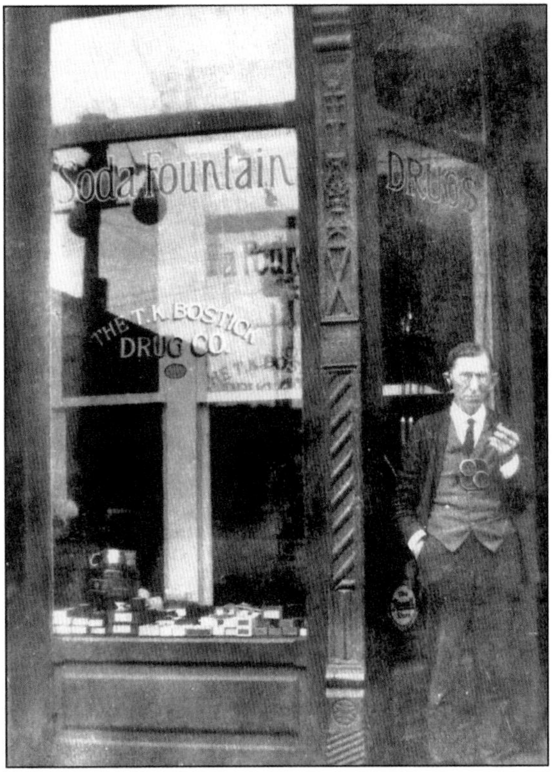

The Bostick Brothers drugstore was opened in 1896 by brothers Thomas King Bostick and James Peay Bostick on the corner of Main and South Springs Streets in McMinnville. Sometime later, James P. Bostick established his own grocery business. This early-1900s photograph pictures Thomas King Bostick standing in front of his store, the T. K. Bostick Drug Company, which was operational until 1937. The building burned in the early 1950s.

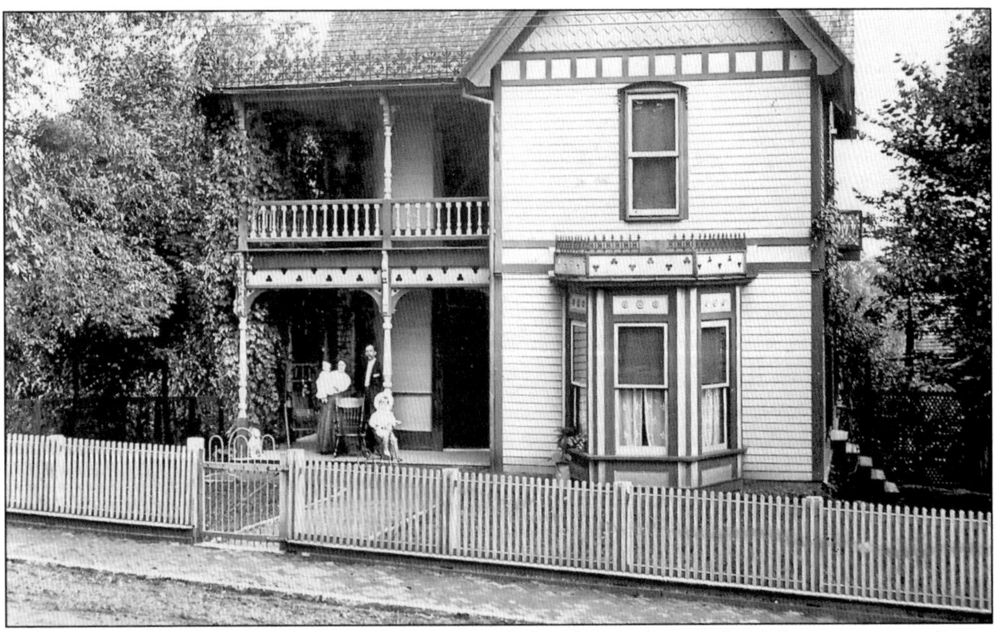

This photograph captures the James Peay Bostick family on the porch of their two-story frame home located on the south side of West Main Street, near Lind Street, in McMinnville. Pictured in this early-1900s photograph are, from left to right, Roberta (Clark) Bostick (holding son Charles), husband James Peay Bostick, and son, James Thomas Bostick. The house has been owned and occupied since the early 1970s by John Douglass.

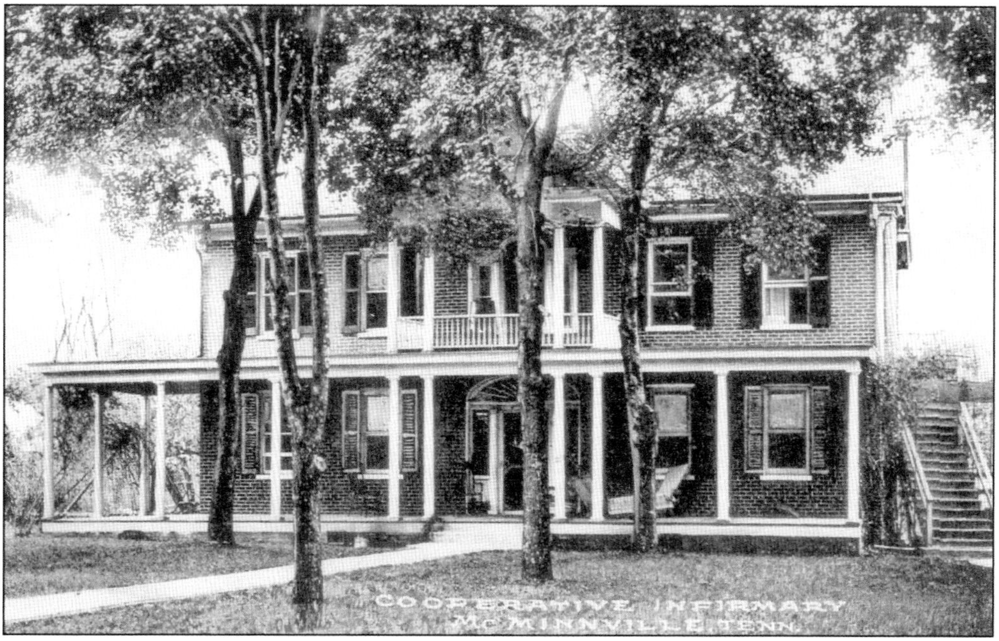

The house pictured is located on West Main Street near the old Cumberland Presbyterian Church and was built by William Washington Brittain in the early 1800s. Dr. T. O. Burger established a hospital in the house in 1911. In 1915, it was being operated by Dr. E. E. Northcutt and Dr. T. E. Bates as the Co-operative Infirmary. In 1916, Dr. R. L. Maloney purchased the building and ran it as Maloney Infirmary until 1940.

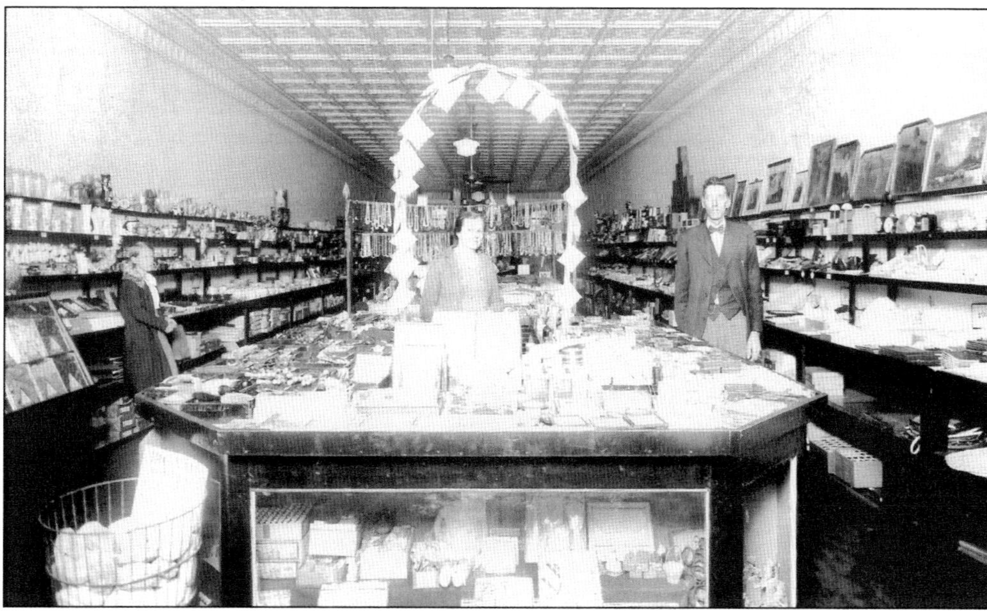

Locke's 5 and 10 Store was successfully opened in McMinnville in 1926 by Will and Sophia Williams Locke. It was effectively run by Sophia Locke after the death of Will Locke, until 1981. Son Howard Estes Locke served as proprietor of the store until the business was closed in 1994. In this 1932 photograph of the interior, an unidentified young customer is seen, at extreme left, with employee Callie Cantrell, center, and owner Will Locke, to the right.

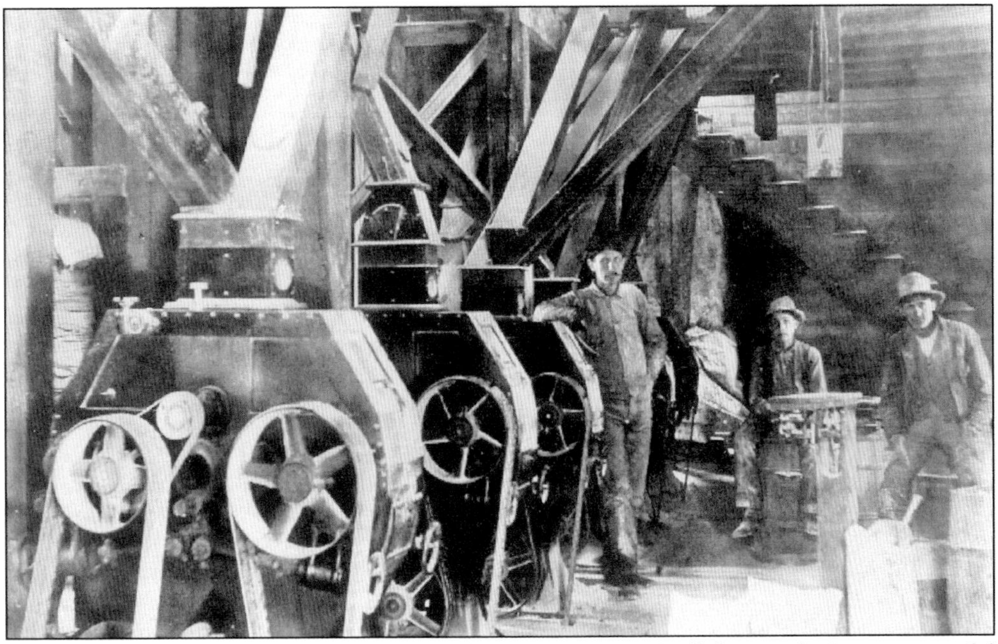

This photograph taken around 1900 inside the Annis Cotton Mill depicts the heavy, powerful machinery which the mill utilized in its manufacturing processes, as some of the workers pose beside the machines. During the 1902 flood, waters inundated the building and rose to the sills of the second floor windows. Several outbuildings and residences which stood in the vicinity of the mill were washed away in the devastating flood.

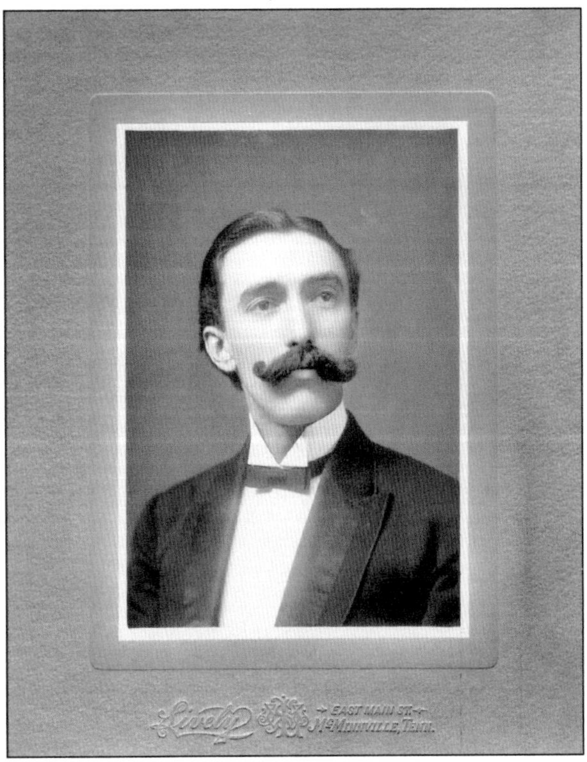

Former banker and world traveler William H. Magness Jr. (1865–1936) was a wealthy financier and philanthropist who is remembered for having deeded the property on the corner of Main and Chancery Streets in McMinnville for the erection of an imposing Greek-style library building which was dedicated in 1931, and stands today as one of McMinnville's most spectacular buildings, with Magness having been its greatest benefactor.

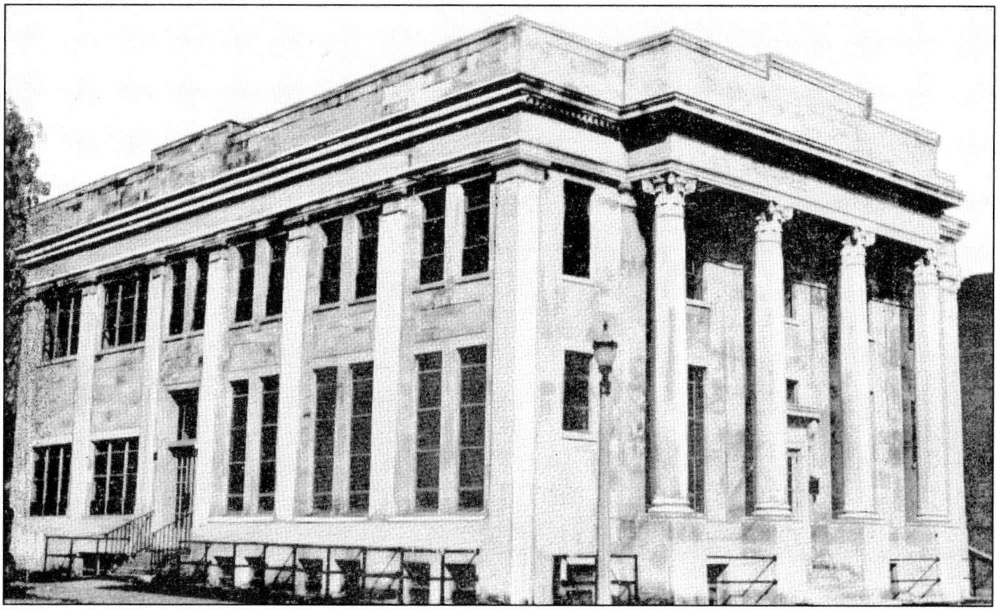

This is a 1930s postcard view of the building known from its inception as the W. H. and Edgar Magness Community House and Library, which has been listed for a number of years on the National Register of Historic Places. A groundbreaking ceremony was held in 2006 in the vacant lot behind the library for a major addition to the building. At the time it was built, an apartment for Mr. Magness was created on the top floor, and quarters to house the librarian were created elsewhere in the building. Shown below is the original program for the dedication ceremony on June 15, 1931.

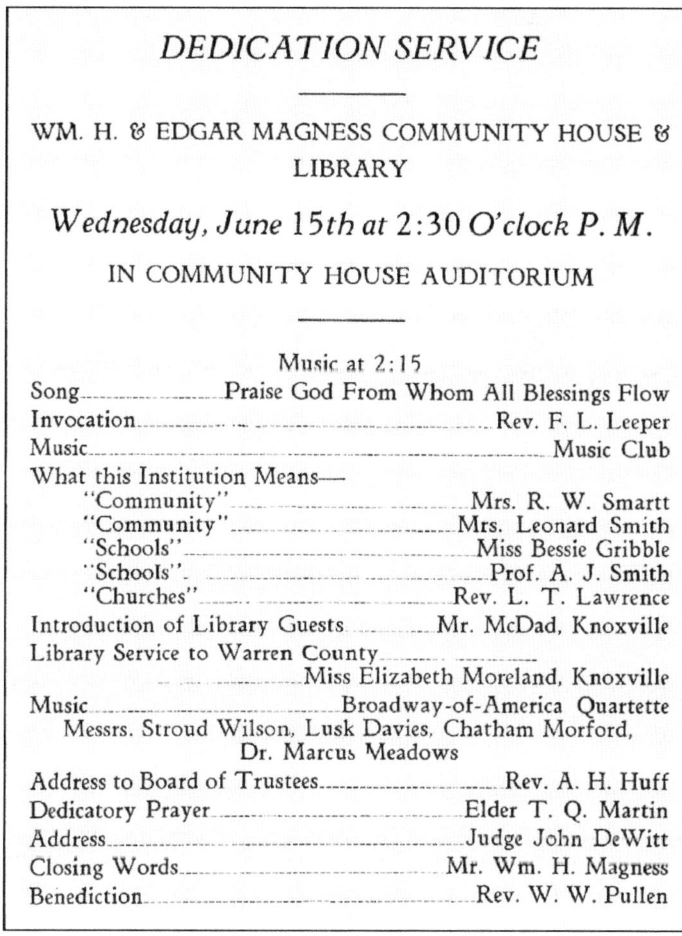

DEDICATION SERVICE

WM. H. & EDGAR MAGNESS COMMUNITY HOUSE & LIBRARY

Wednesday, June 15th at 2:30 O'clock P. M.

IN COMMUNITY HOUSE AUDITORIUM

Music at 2:15

Song............Praise God From Whom All Blessings Flow
Invocation............Rev. F. L. Leeper
Music............Music Club
What this Institution Means—
"Community"............Mrs. R. W. Smartt
"Community"............Mrs. Leonard Smith
"Schools"............Miss Bessie Gribble
"Schools"............Prof. A. J. Smith
"Churches"............Rev. L. T. Lawrence
Introduction of Library Guests............Mr. McDad, Knoxville
Library Service to Warren County............
............Miss Elizabeth Moreland, Knoxville
Music............Broadway-of-America Quartette
Messrs. Stroud Wilson, Lusk Davies, Chatham Morford,
Dr. Marcus Meadows
Address to Board of Trustees............Rev. A. H. Huff
Dedicatory Prayer............Elder T. Q. Martin
Address............Judge John DeWitt
Closing Words............Mr. Wm. H. Magness
Benediction............Rev. W. W. Pullen

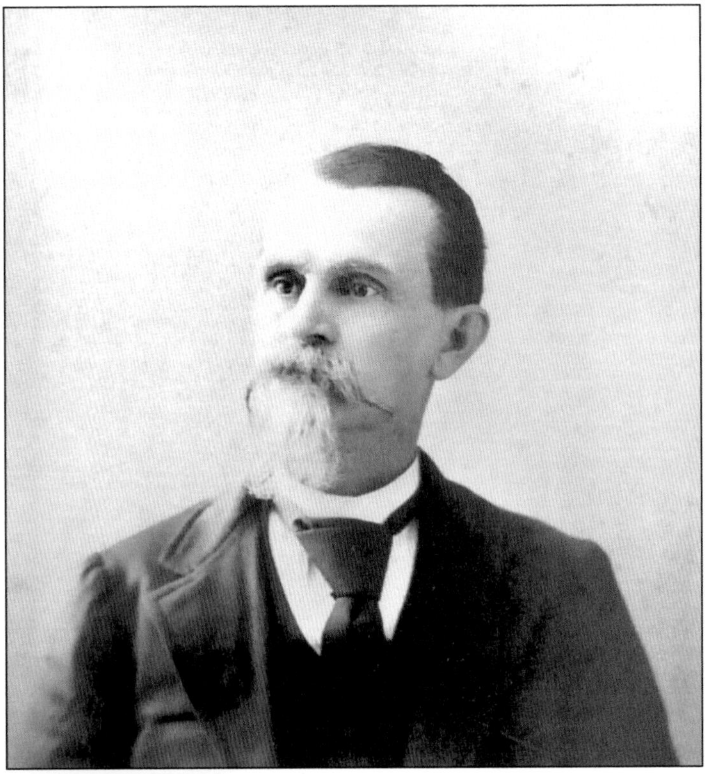

Dr. Thomas Black was the son of a McMinnville merchant who, at the time of the Civil War, was attending medical school in Nashville. He enlisted in 1861 in John H. Savage's 16th Tennessee Regiment, and during the Civil War was in charge of various hospitals. After returning from the war, he began his medical practice in the town, which he continued up until the time of his death in 1904.

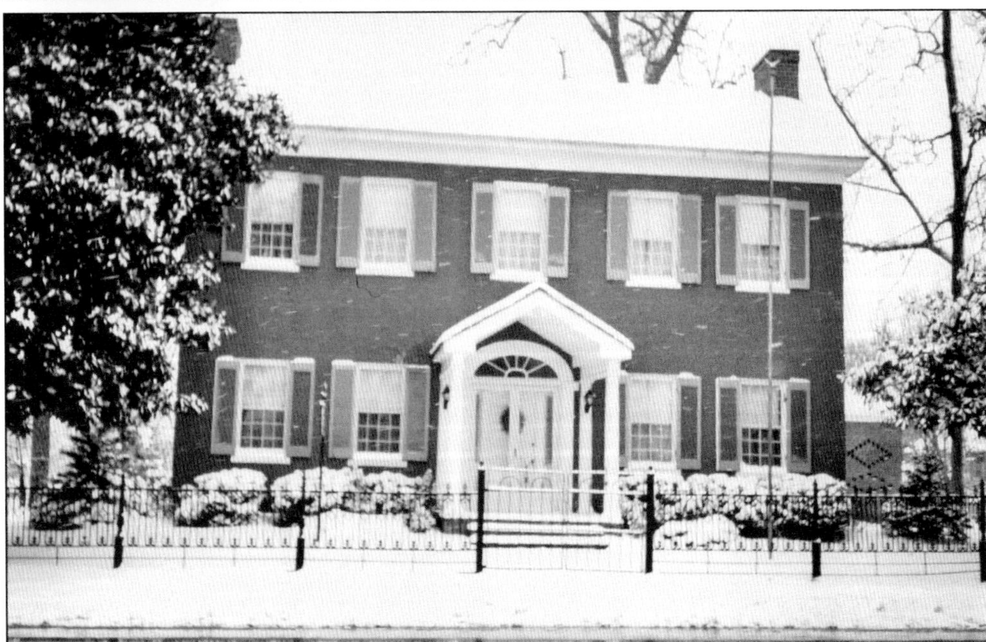

The oldest house remaining in McMinnville, the Black House, was erected by Jesse Coffee in 1825. The home, located on the corner of West Main Street and High Street, received its name from its occupation for many years by the family of Dr. Thomas Black. Thomas Black was elected mayor of McMinnville on May 24, 1884, and served on the board of education in 1886.

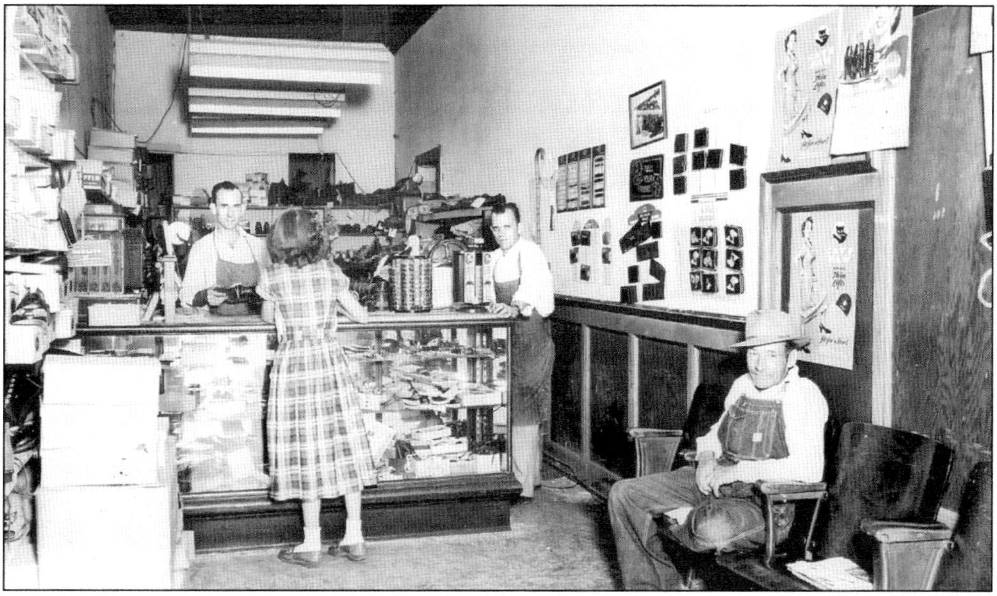

In the 1940s and 1950s, Cantrell's Shoe Shop was located in the Brown Hotel building, which was located near the corner of Main and Sparta Streets in McMinnville. This photograph, taken in 1950, shows an unidentified customer sitting while waiting for his shoe to be repaired. Another unidentified customer stands at the counter with Franklin "Brackett" Cantrell (left), and Cecil Cantrell (behind the counter).

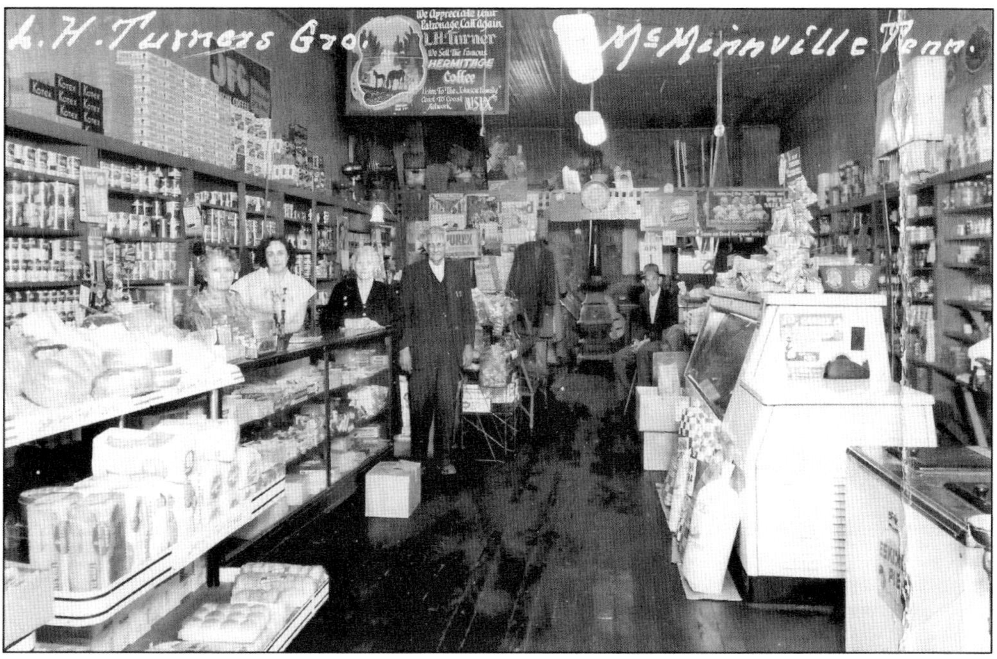

Spring Street was named for the town spring, located at the south end of the street. The L. H. Turner Grocery Store, located on North Spring Street, was one of many such stores serving the bustling community in McMinnville in the 1940s, 1950s, and 1960s. This photograph, taken sometime in the 1950s, shows, from left to right, Florence Blair, Mabel Bess, Delia Turner, and Hezikiah Turner, inside the family-run business.

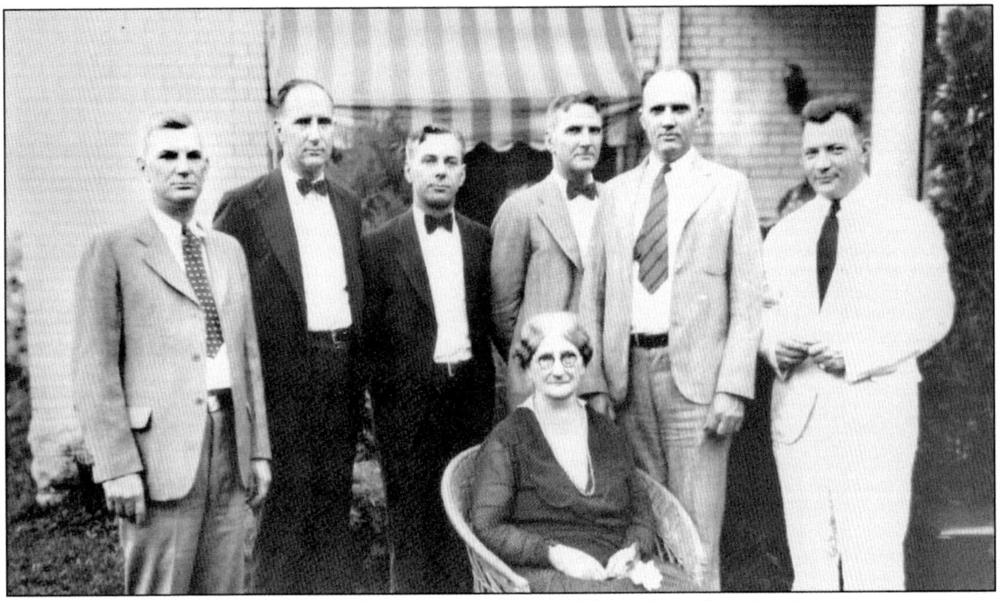

This photograph of Susan (Smoot) Henegar (1856–1943), and her family of grown-up sons was taken in 1931 or 1932 at the family home on College Street in McMinnville—one of the town's prominent civic- and business-minded families. Pictured from left to right are Edgar Henegar (1886–1933), Frank Henegar (1887–1986), Elric Henegar (1891–1960), Ernest Henegar (1893–1965), Harold Henegar (1894–1978), D. Porter Henegar (1897–1979), and, sitting in front, mother Susan Smoot Henegar.

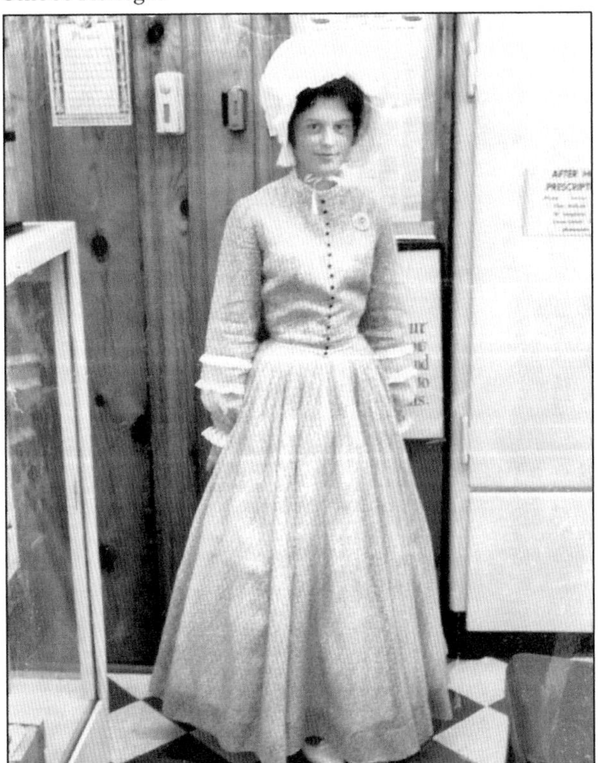

This photograph of Betty Joyce Higginbotham was taken at the popular Crouch Drug Store, located for many years adjacent to the Park Theater on the south side of West Main Street in McMinnville. She is wearing a dress and bonnet, which she made and wore for McMinnville's sesquicentennial celebration, which was held throughout the town during 1960.

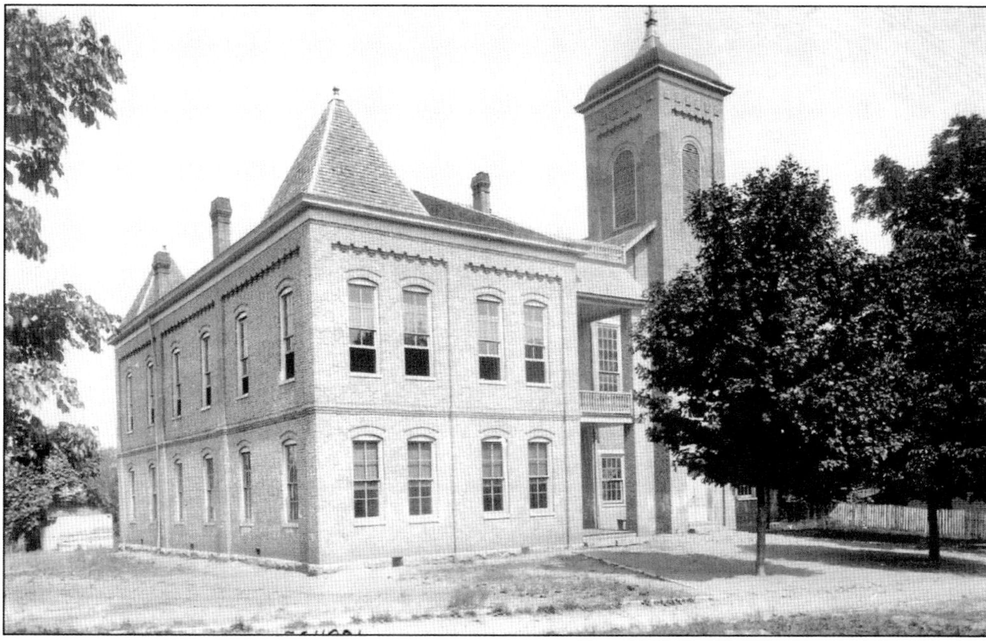

This brick, two-story building was McMinnville's first high school, located on the west side of College Street near the courthouse. The Methodist Episcopal Church erected this building in 1867, and, in about 1870, it was deeded to the black Methodist congregation. In 1886, it was deeded to the city of McMinnville for use as a high school. The building burned in 1914.

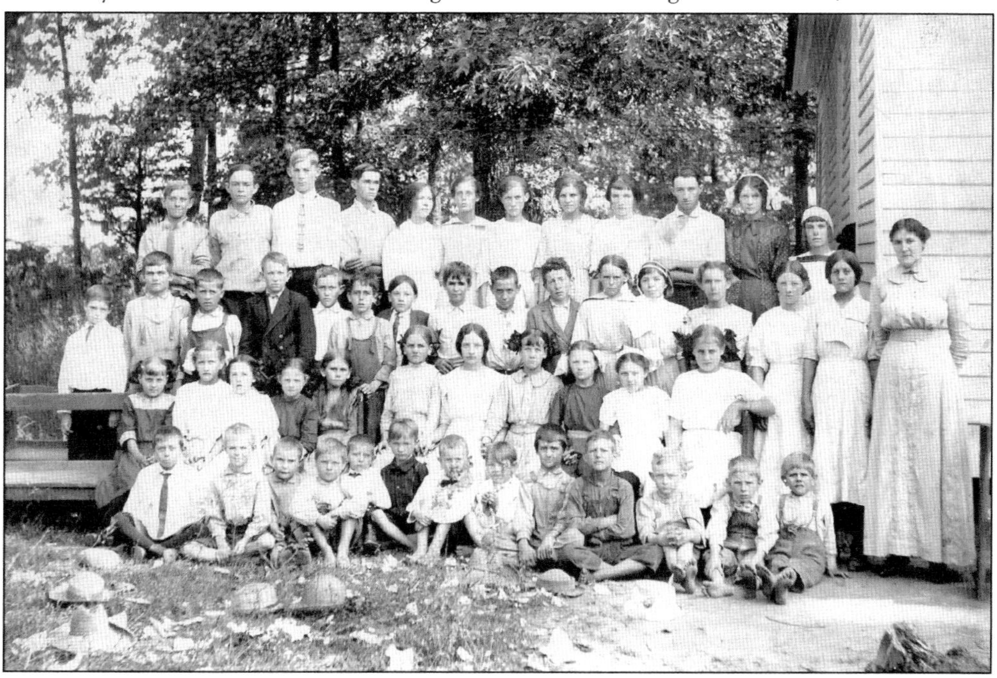

In the early 1900s, there were some 80 schools distributed in the various outlying communities of Warren County. One such school was the Lone Poplar School located in the Pleasant View Community, which was off Highway 30, a few miles northeast of McMinnville. This 1913 photograph depicts 51 students at the school with teacher, ? Bass (right).

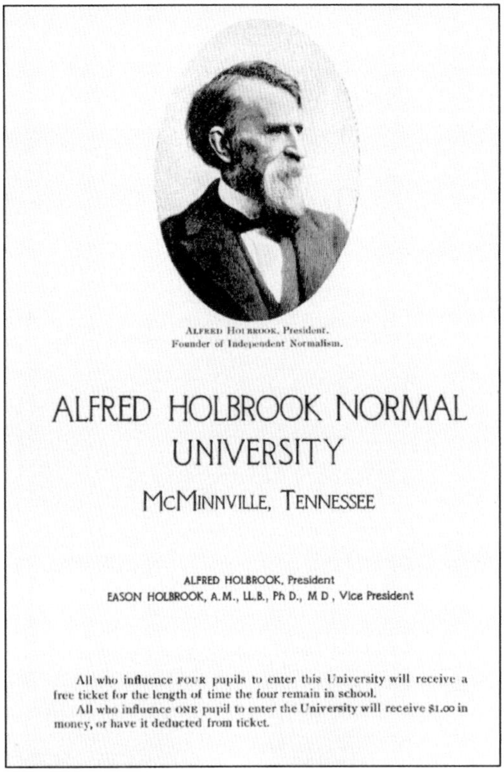

ALFRED HOLBROOK, President.
Founder of Independent Normalism.

ALFRED HOLBROOK NORMAL UNIVERSITY

McMINNVILLE, TENNESSEE

ALFRED HOLBROOK, President
EASON HOLBROOK, A.M., LL.B., Ph D., M D , Vice President

All who influence FOUR pupils to enter this University will receive a free ticket for the length of time the four remain in school.
All who influence ONE pupil to enter the University will receive $1.00 in money, or have it deducted from ticket.

The Alfred Holbrook Normal University was chartered in September 1900 and opened at that time in the old Cumberland Female College building in McMinnville. Among the numerous teachers employed, one from McMinnville was Octa Smartt. Seen here is the title page from an early Holbrook Normal University catalog featuring a portrait of its founder. The school was only in operation for about three years.

This photograph, taken in July 1979, depicts Warren County native J. R. "Peanut" Cantrell (1897–1991) playing the large hammer dulcimer at the Fiddler's Jamboree in Smithville, Tennessee. The dulcimer was made by him (at age 14) and his father, George Lawrence Cantrell. J. R. Cantrell married Jackie Arnold Cantrell (born 1899) in 1919, and they had two sons, Grady and Kenneth.

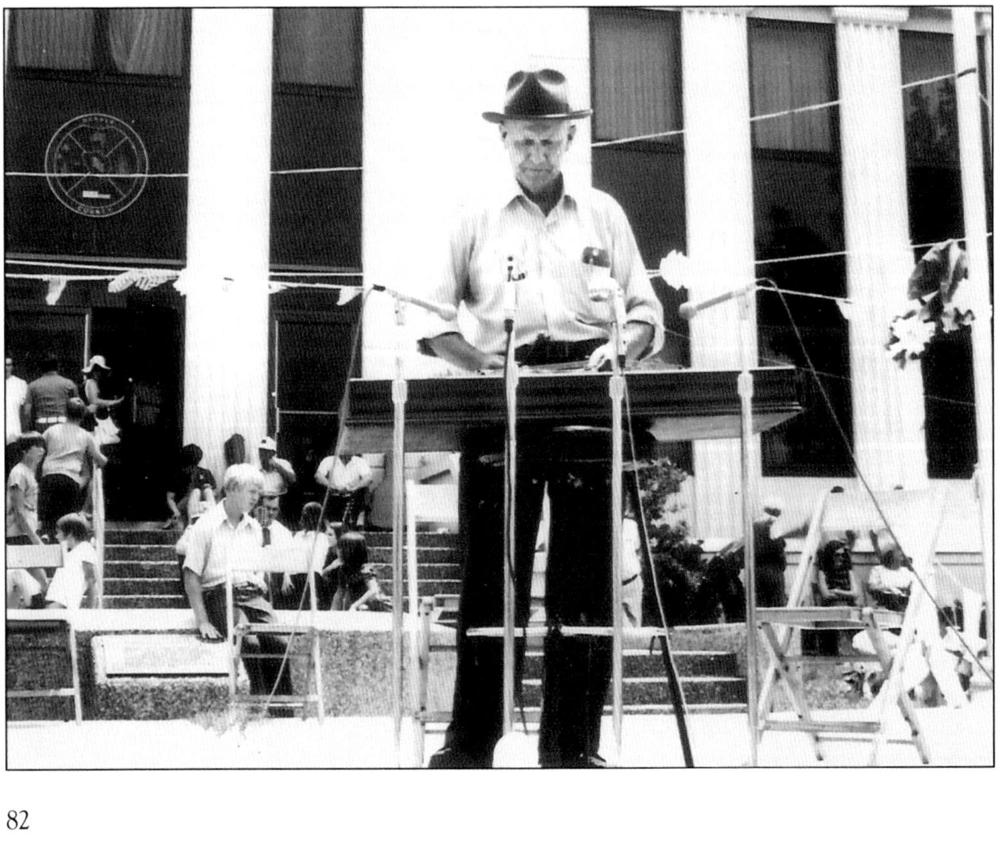

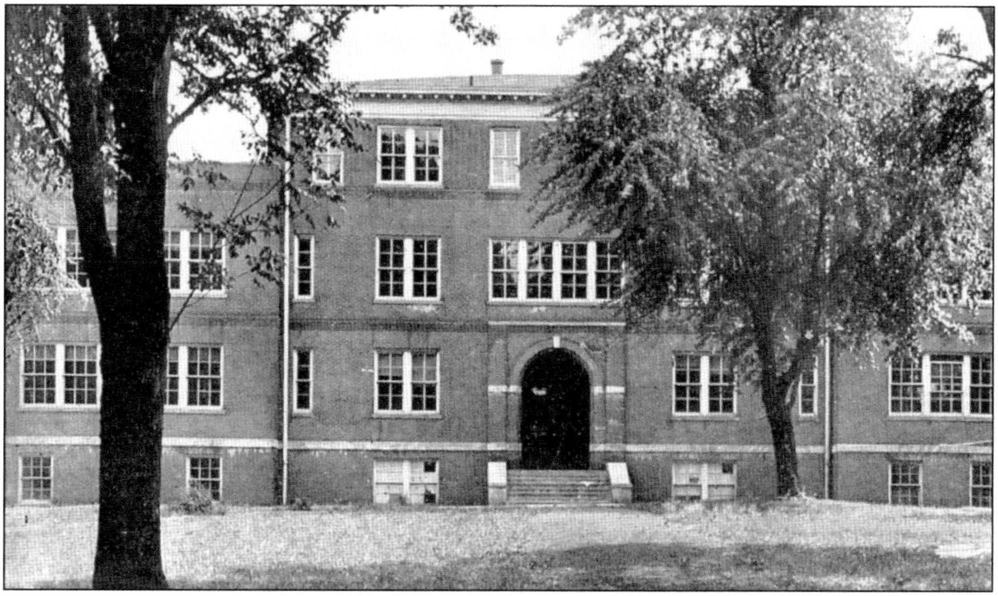

In 1916, this building, which is now the McMinnville City Hall, was added to and converted, as the McMinnville City Grammar School, and served as the high school building until Central School was erected in 1928. In 1978, the building underwent another renovation and was rededicated as the Franklin P. Blue Municipal Building.

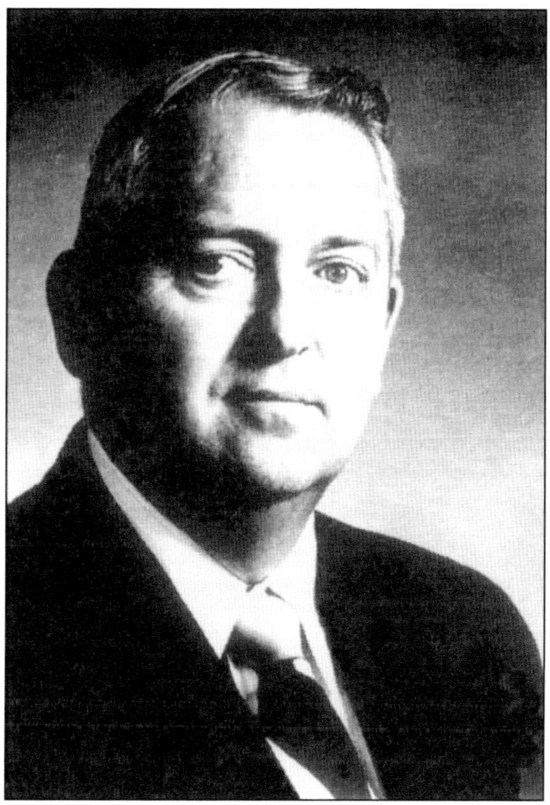

Since 1978, James A. Dillon Jr. has officially served as Warren County Historian. He is descended from Irish ancestry and grew up and attended schools in McMinnville before earning a bachelor of science degree in agriculture engineering in 1950. He took over his father's insurance business in 1965 and has been active in civic and community activities through the years.

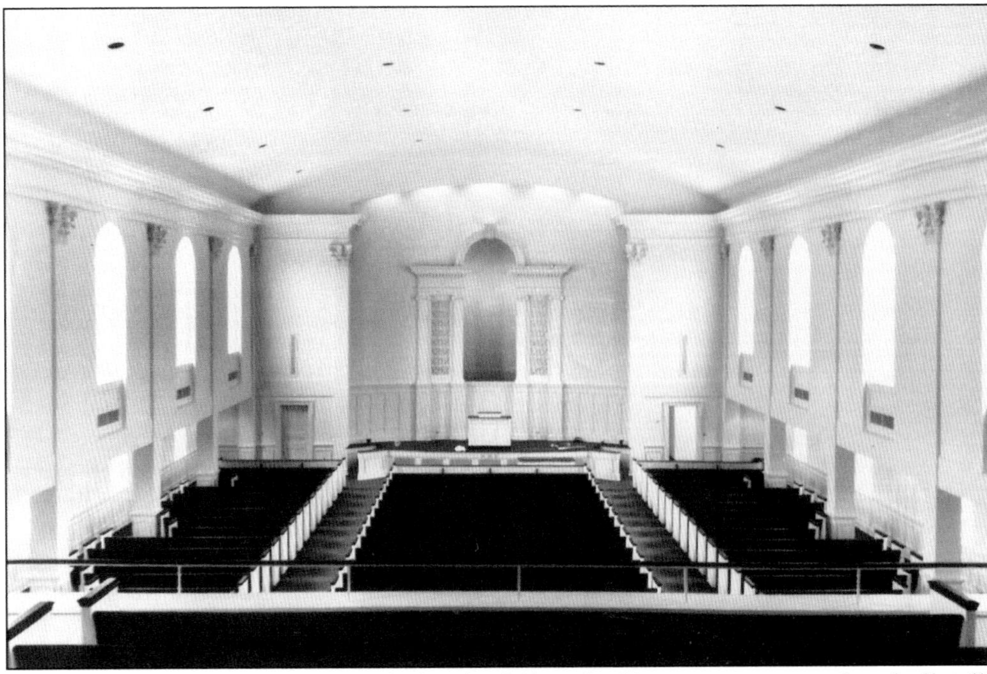

In 1972–1973, McMinnville's Central Church of Christ building was constructed, and officially occupied on October 7, 1973, after having used the former building in that location since its erection in 1928. This Charles Cassetty photograph of the sanctuary, which seats approximately 1,000 worshippers, was made in October 1973. As the congregation grew progressively through the years, a new, larger building became necessary.

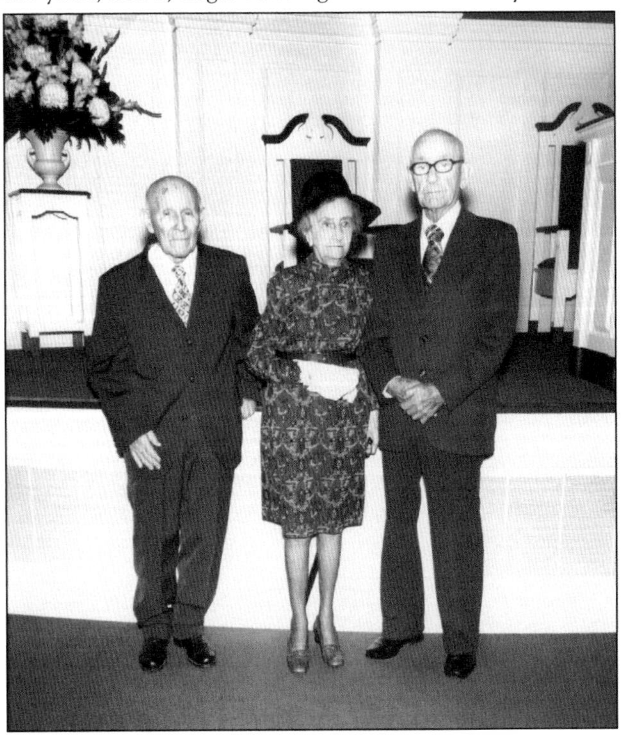

At the open-house dedication of the new Central Church of Christ in October 1973, Charles Cassetty photographed these three oldest members of the congregation. They are, from left to right, J. L. Gilbert, Nettie Drake, and O. L. Hammer. McMinnville photographer Charles "Steamboat" Cassetty and Mrs. Evelyn Cassetty were longtime members of the Central congregation.

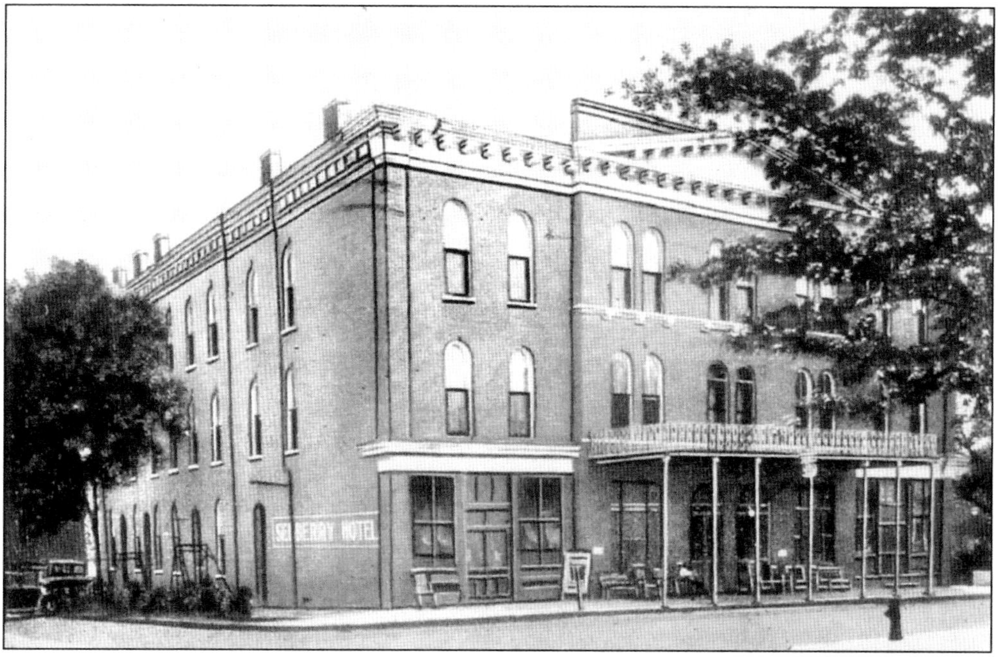

In its heyday, McMinnville's Sedberry Hotel was a nationally recognized institution. Oceana Tucker Sedberry (1871–1930) with daughters Connie and Erby, came to McMinnville and, in 1913, leased the old Warren House, which became known as the Sedberry Hotel after they purchased the property in 1920. Widely known for its delicious Southern cuisine and gracious hospitality, it operated until 1954 when it closed its doors and was sold at auction. Connie Sedberry Moore (1895–1958) was the more attractive of the two Sedberry daughters. After they arrived in McMinnville in 1913, she was considered to be the most beautiful woman in the town. Just prior to their arrival, she had been chosen by the Kentucky Traveling Association to represent the organization in the "An American Beauty Rose" convention in Jackson, Tennessee. This portrait of Connie was made sometime around 1925.

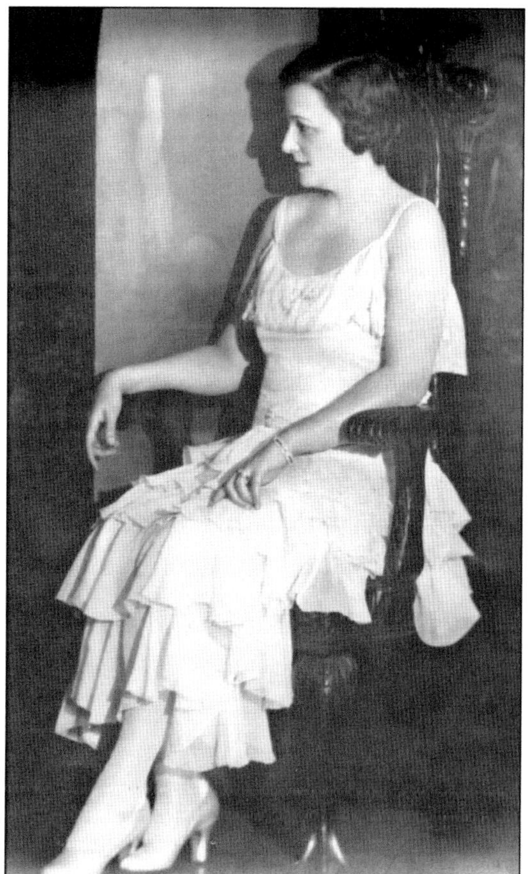

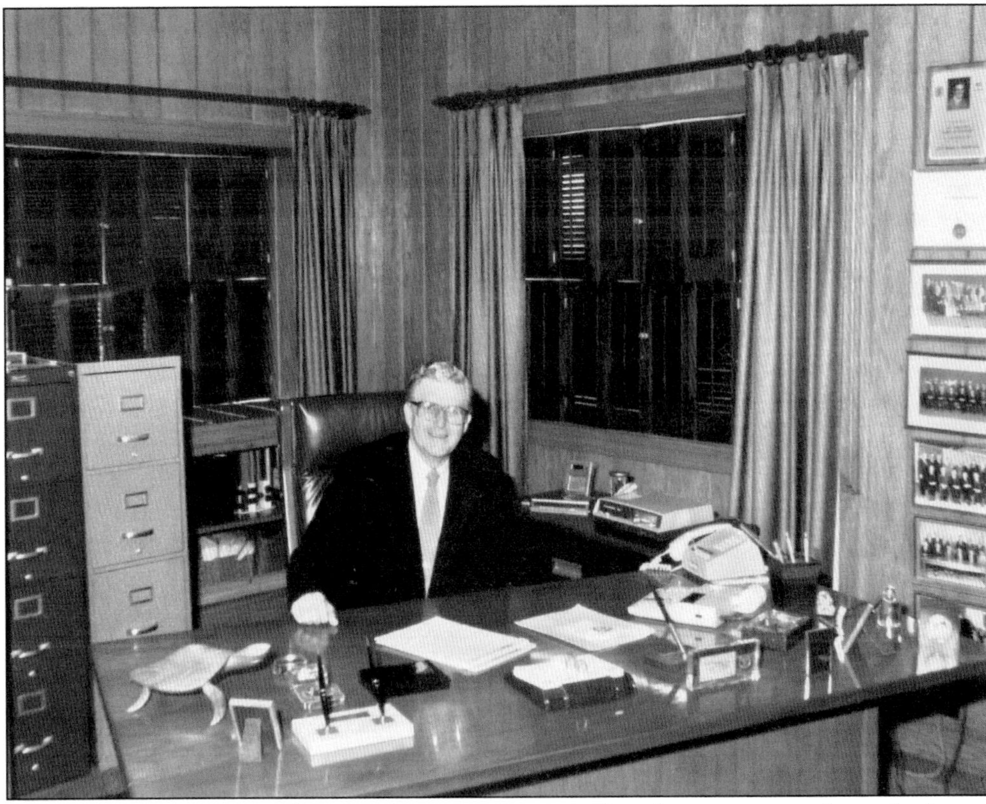

Begun in 1894, McMinnville Manufacturing Company has, for many years, been the largest producer of hardwood flooring in the United States. Originally an early sawmill operation, it began producing hardwood flooring, interior trim, and other items after 1912. After 1924, it became a family-owned-and-operated enterprise run by Tom Mullican and sons Bill, Mike, and Jim Mullican. This photograph of its president, Tom Mullican, was taken in 1982.

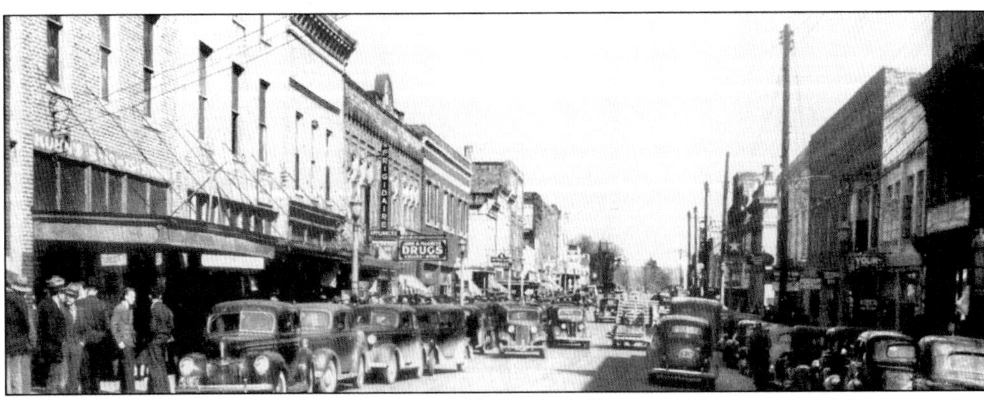

This view of a bustling downtown McMinnville in 1940 illustrates the activity of the town when every store building and shop offered a multitude of services for the citizens of Warren County, who came from miles around to shop. In 1940, McMinnville was regarded as the richest city in the entire Upper Cumberland region, based on population.

Pictured is Georgia Etter-Huggins who was photographed at an October 2006 awards banquet by *Southern Standard* newspaper writer-photographer Margaret Hobbs honoring Warren County Women of Achievement. Announced as the Woman of Achievement winner for 2006, Huggins was cited for her determination to educate her two children whom she raised as a single mother under adverse circumstances. She went on to train for a nursing career to help ensure that both her son and daughter received a formal education and subsequently earn doctorates.

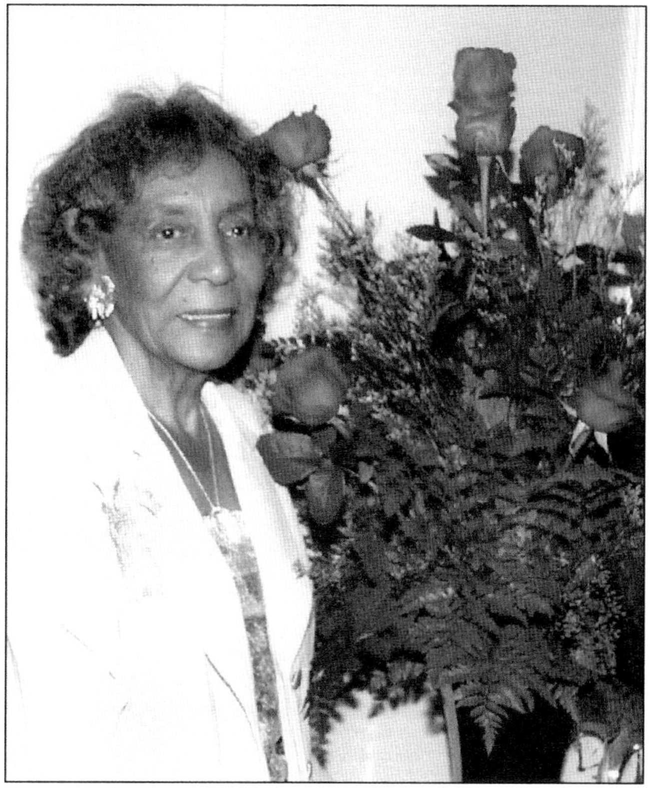

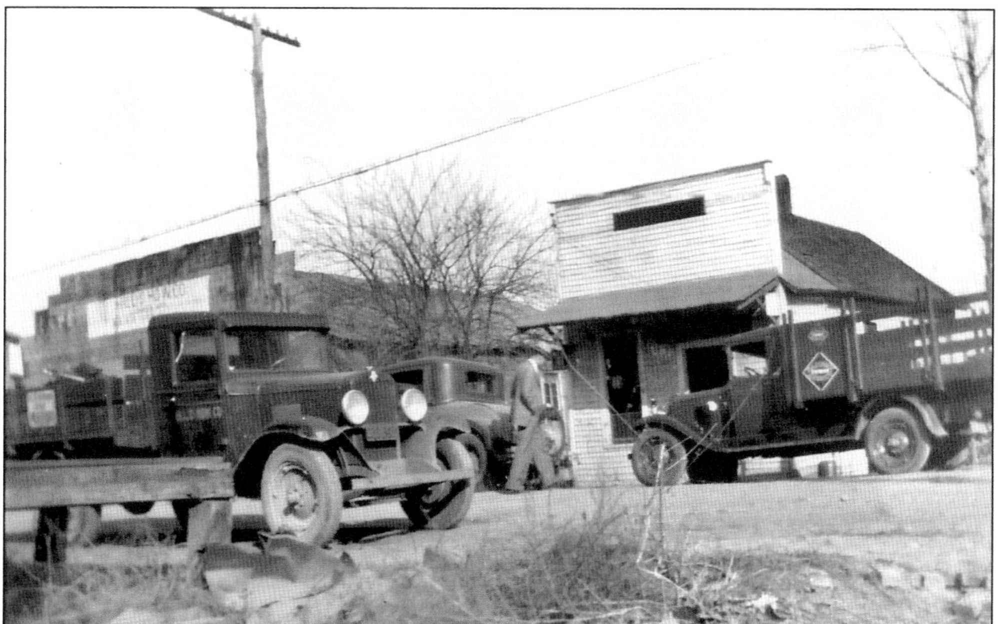

After his association from 1917 to 1923 with the Warren County Mercantile Company, Iver H. Hillis founded the Hillis Hardware Company on Spring Street in McMinnville. In 1926, he moved the firm to a building on the north side of East Main Street. Pictured is a 1920s photograph of the hardware store's Depot Bottom branch, showing the firm's delivery trucks in front of the store.

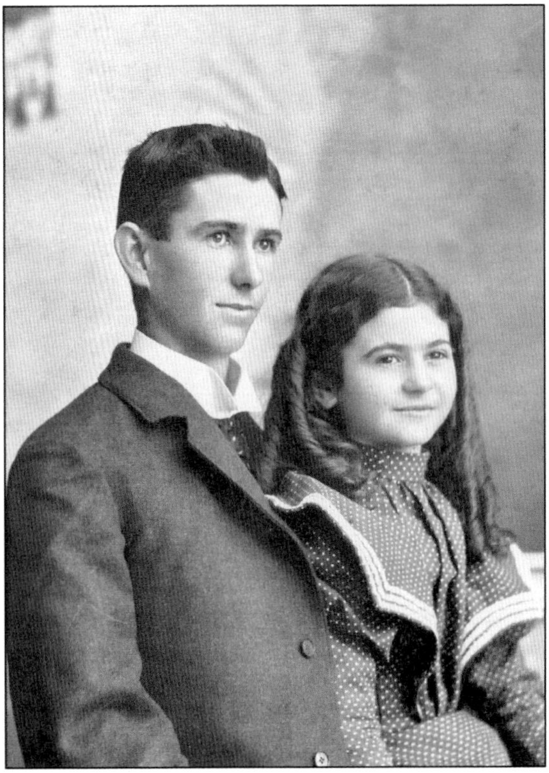

This portrait of Stokley Donalson Rowan and his sister Elsie Rowan was made about 1899 by "Lively's Art Gallery," McMinnville, Tennessee. Born in 1875 in Warren County, Stokley Rowan was married to Jennie Emmaline Higginbotham and had three children. With an innate interest and ability in engineering, he was elected chief engineer of the city waterworks and electric light plant. He died in 1911.

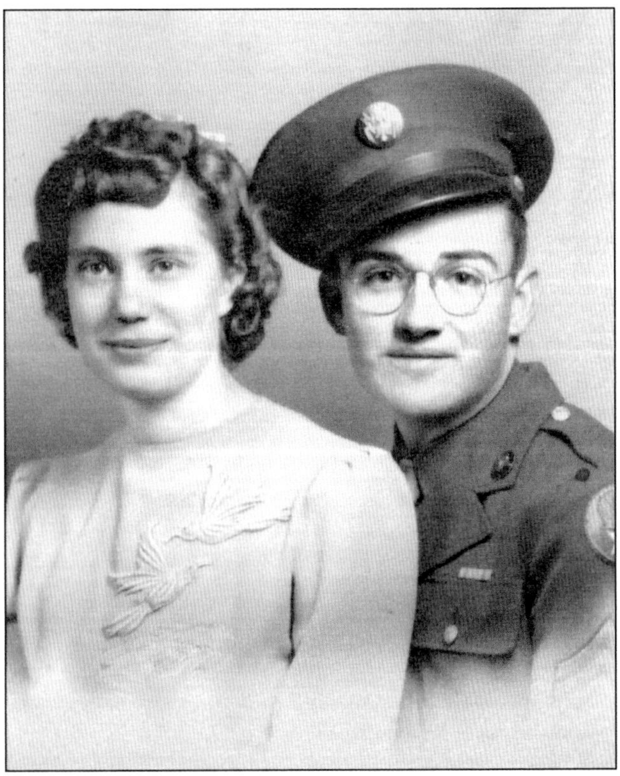

Beloved McMinnville couple George and Robbie Beaver were married in February 1943. They have two children, daughter Robbie Sue (Beaver) Pichon and son George Mason Beaver Jr. George Beaver, born in 1920, practiced law in McMinnville from 1947 until he retired in 1989. Robbie, born in 1922, was active as leader in the Cub Scout movement, and was a longtime volunteer at the Magness Memorial Library.

Frank C. Martin (1921–2005) is a fondly remembered McMinnville businessman who, in the 1940s, was a partner in the Martin and Durham Furniture Store. Later he became president of the Tullahoma Freight Line and spent the last years of his life in the freight business. Martin and lovely Helen P. (West) Martin, born in 1927, are pictured in their wedding portrait taken in January 1947. They have three sons.

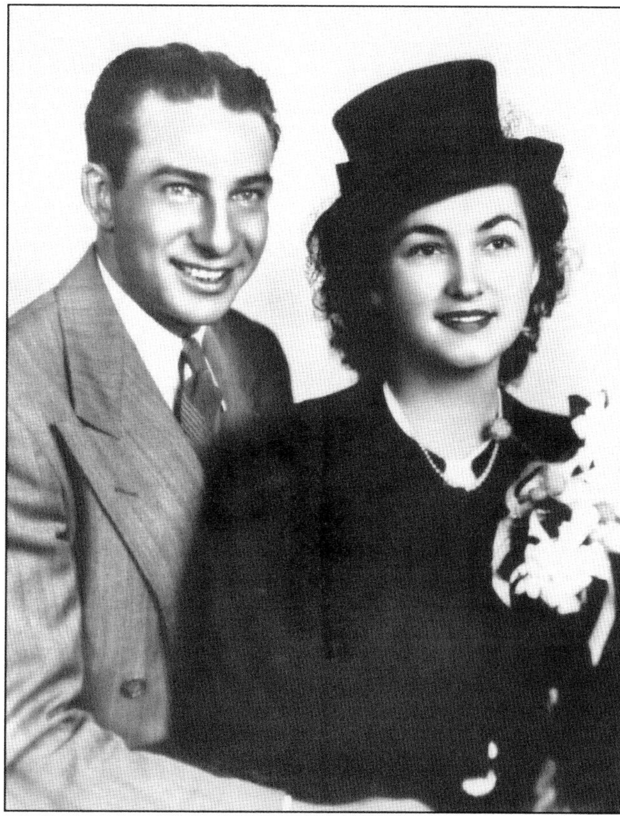

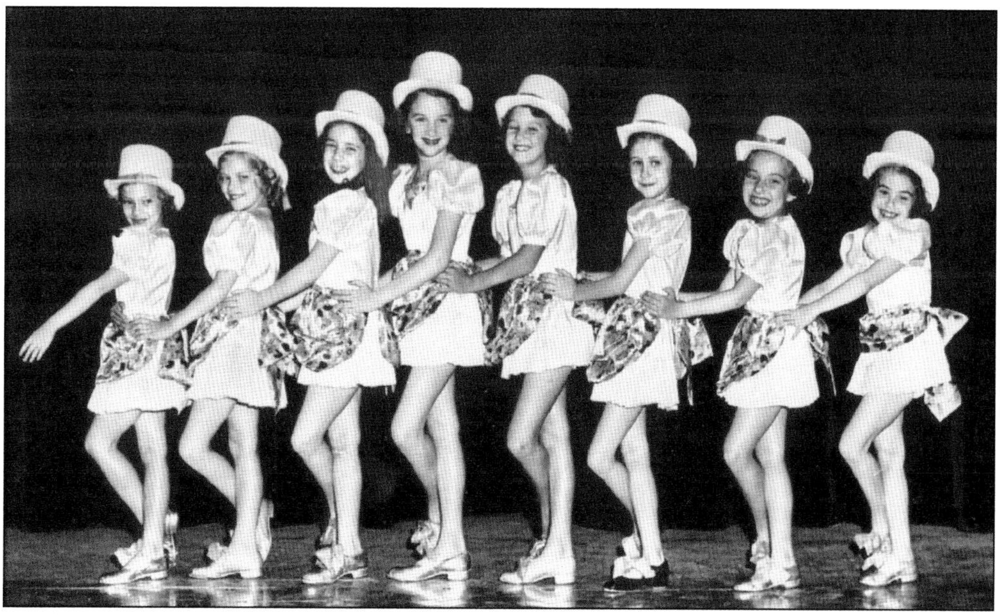

Teacher Valerie Moody's second-grade dance class review presented at the city elementary school, the Southside School, in McMinnville in 1952 is pictured in one of the girls' dance routines. Shown from left to right are Sandy Farless, Lucia Cordell, Kathy Smoot, Cynthia Womack, Betty Boyd (a third-grader), Jane Whitson, Patty Powell, and Ann Lewis.

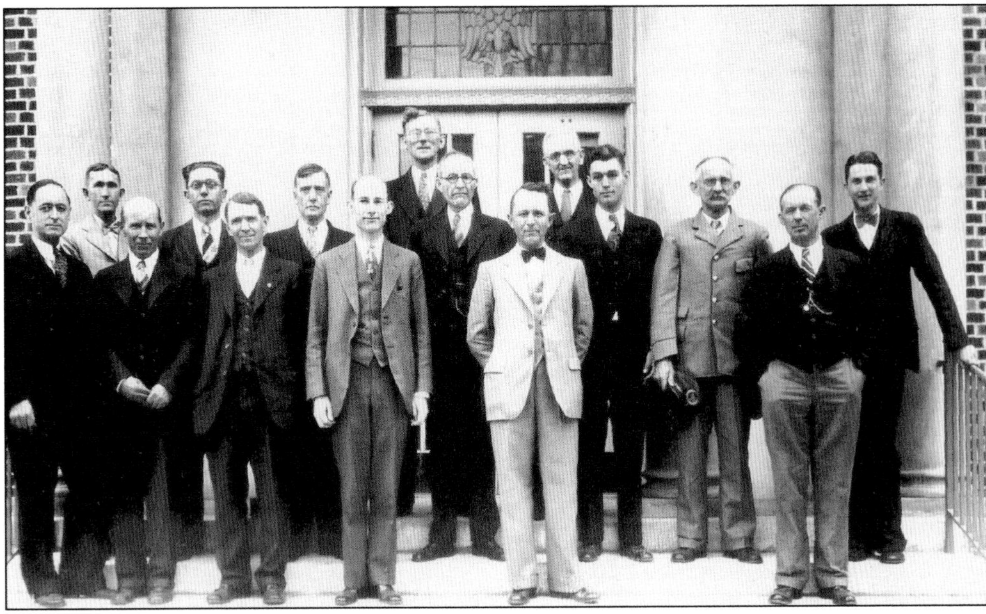

The new McMinnville Post Office was completed and dedicated in May 1937. Pictured in this 1937 photograph are the post office officials and construction engineers. From left to right are the following: (first row) three unidentified men, Brown Oliver, Jessie Lee Gilbert, and Ike Grizzell; (second row) Paul Frazer, unidentified, ? Dotson, George B. Beaver, unidentified, ? Gaffin and George Trail; (third row) Rice Hancock, and ? Crisp.

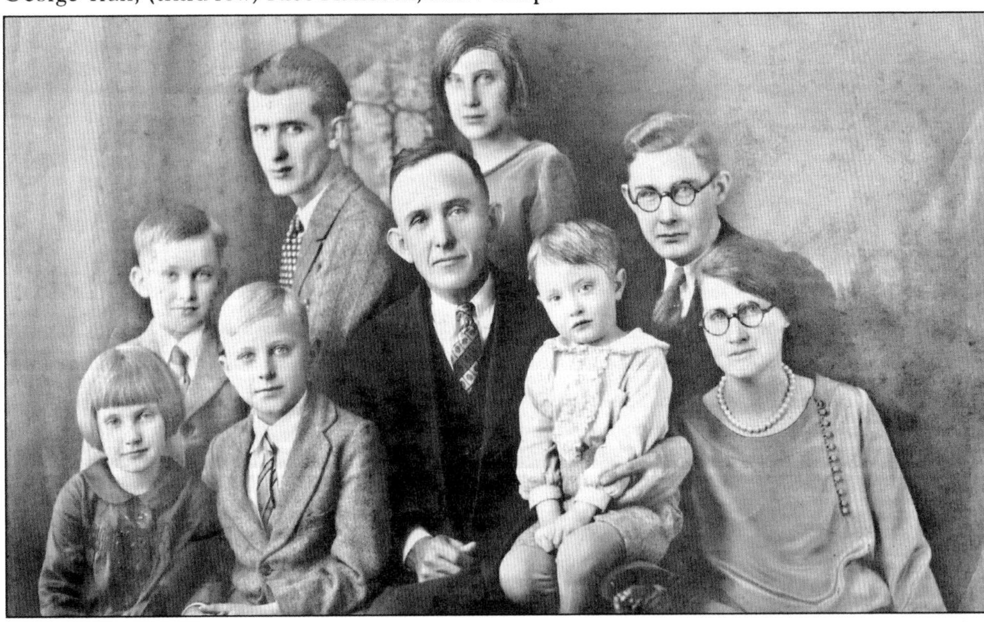

John Wesley Nelms came to Warren County as a young man to work for the Otis Lumber Company. He married Hallie Pearl Wanamaker on September 15, 1907. They are pictured in about 1928 with seven of their eight children. From left to right are the following: (first row) Hallie Lillian, John Wesley Jr., John Wesley (holding Clifford), and Hallie; (second row) William Hall, Charles Harold, Mildred Inez, and Morris Otis. Daughter Dorothy Jean was born after this portrait was taken.

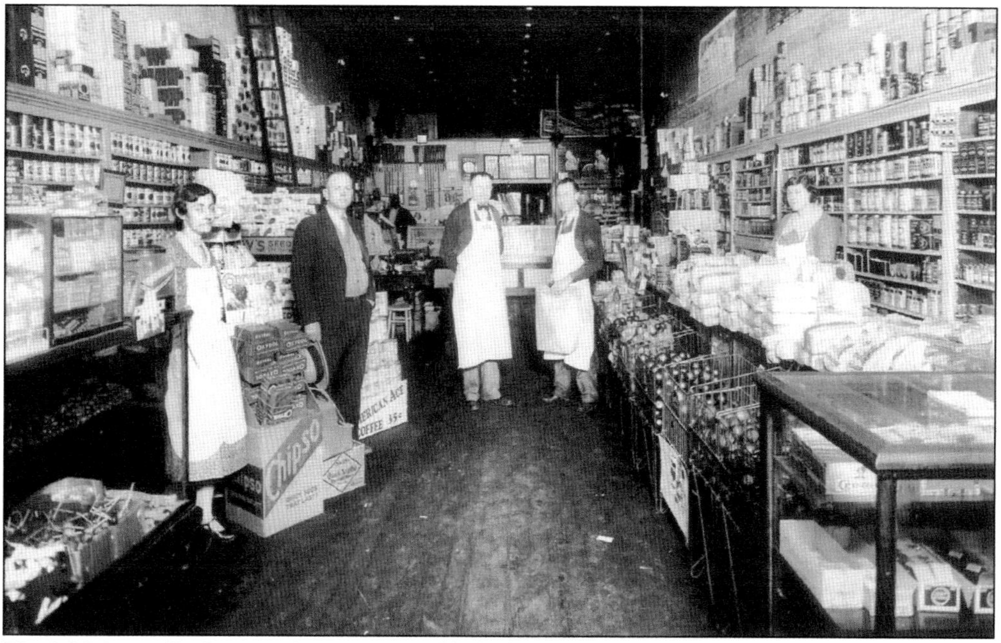

The McMinnville Grocery Company, established in 1925 by Frank and Origen Williams, was in operation until 1941 and was located on the north side of East Main Street. Pictured in this 1920s photograph of the interior of the store are, from left to right, Jackie Kell, unidentified, Oscar Kell, Frank Williams, and, at extreme right, Origen Williams.

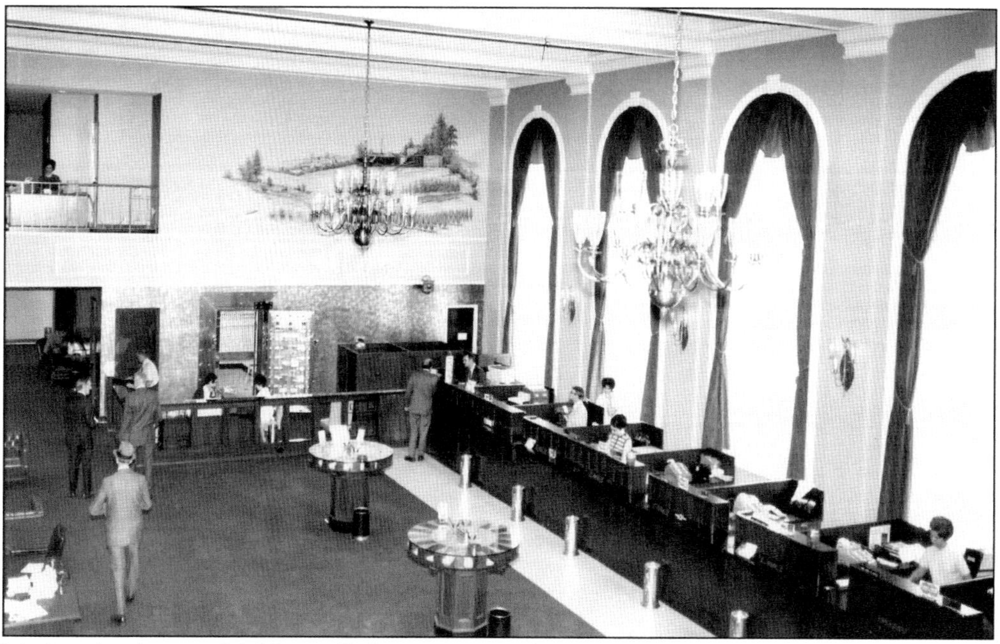

Modern banking in McMinnville began on October 30, 1874, with the establishment of the National Bank of McMinnville. In 1905, it was reorganized as the First National Bank, with J. N. Walling acting president. McMinnville's first National Bank building was constructed in 1923 on the southeast corner of Main and Spring Streets. This Charles Cassetty photograph of the bank's lobby was taken about 1975, before renovations and expansions.

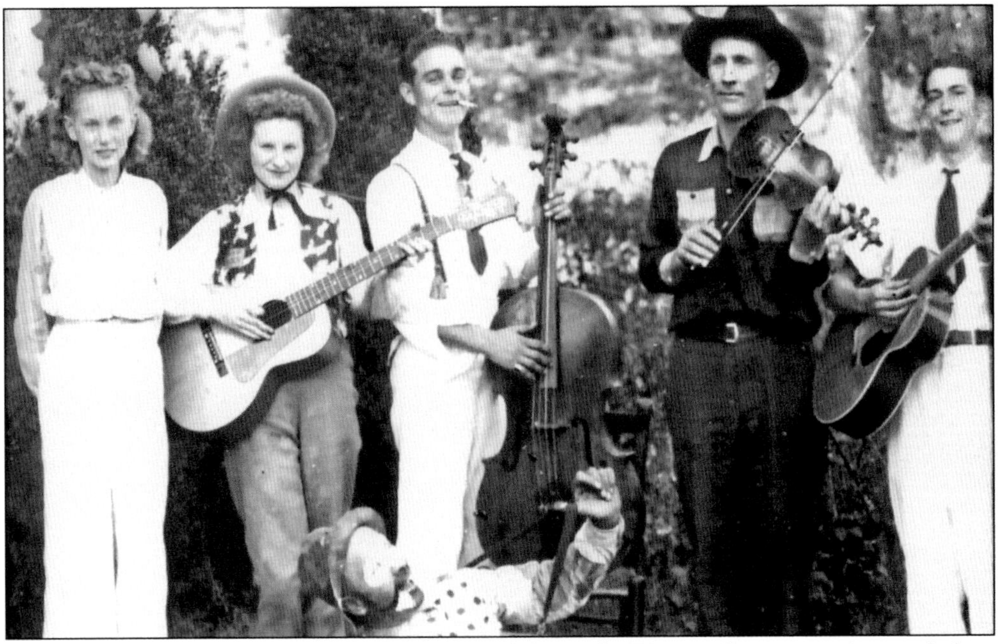

Music played an important role in the lives of the early Warren County settlers and their descendants. This 1940s photograph captured a string hand that entertained at social functions, and often got together in the homes of friends and neighbors to play their music. Pictured from left to right are Lucy Emma "Tooter" Barnes, Lola Wanamaker, Ted Cagle, Ernest Wimberly, Willie B. Nunley, and Guy Moffitt (the reclining clown).

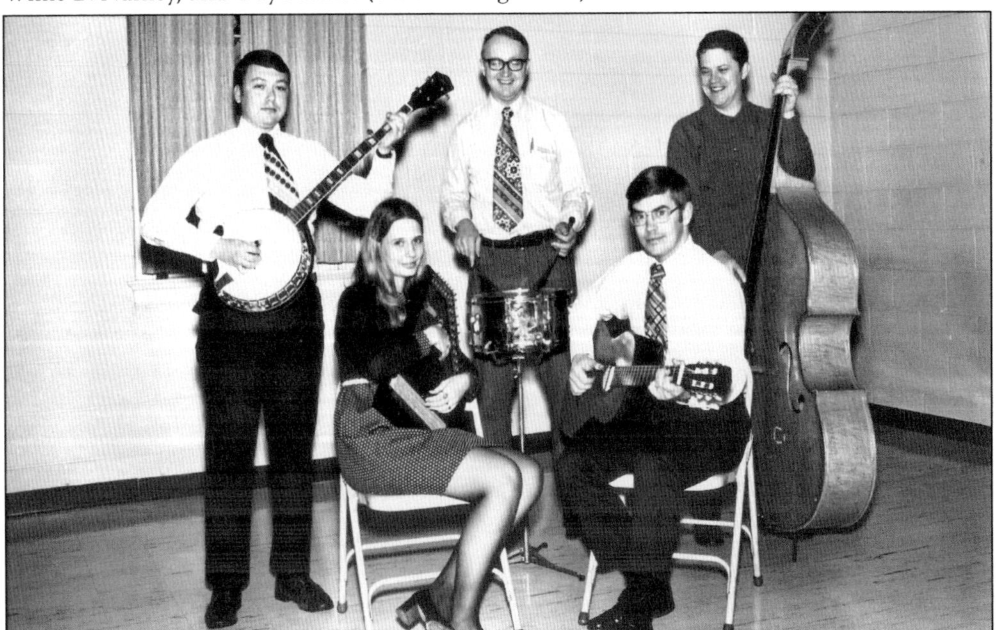

This musical group, made up of members of McMinnville's Central Church of Christ congregation, is pictured during the group's heyday. Pictured in this *c.* 1975 photograph are, from left to right, (first row, seated) Susan Bryant and Doug Cantrell; (second row, standing) Eben Gilbert (with banjo), pastor Julian Goodpasture (on drums), and Jeffery Golden (with bass fiddle).

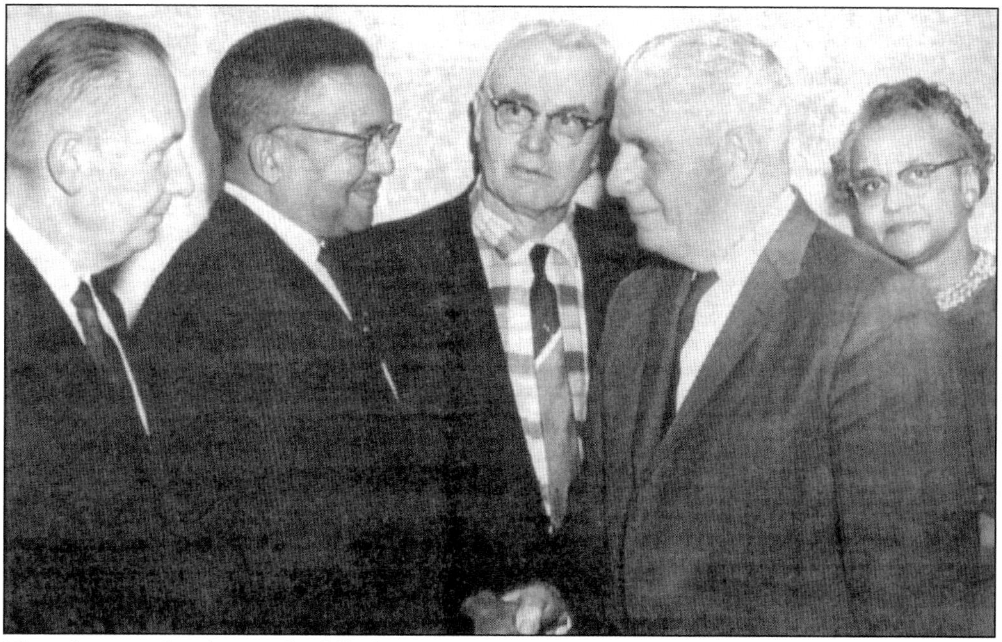

This photograph taken in the fall of 1962 captures five distinguished citizens of Warren County who are assembled for the purpose of recognizing the outstanding work of Howard Martin, president of the Pleasant Hill Community Fair held in 1961. Pictured from left to right are as follows: (first row) Jesse Safely, honoree Howard Martin, and Tom Woods; (second row) county agent H. V. Massey and Frances Bonner.

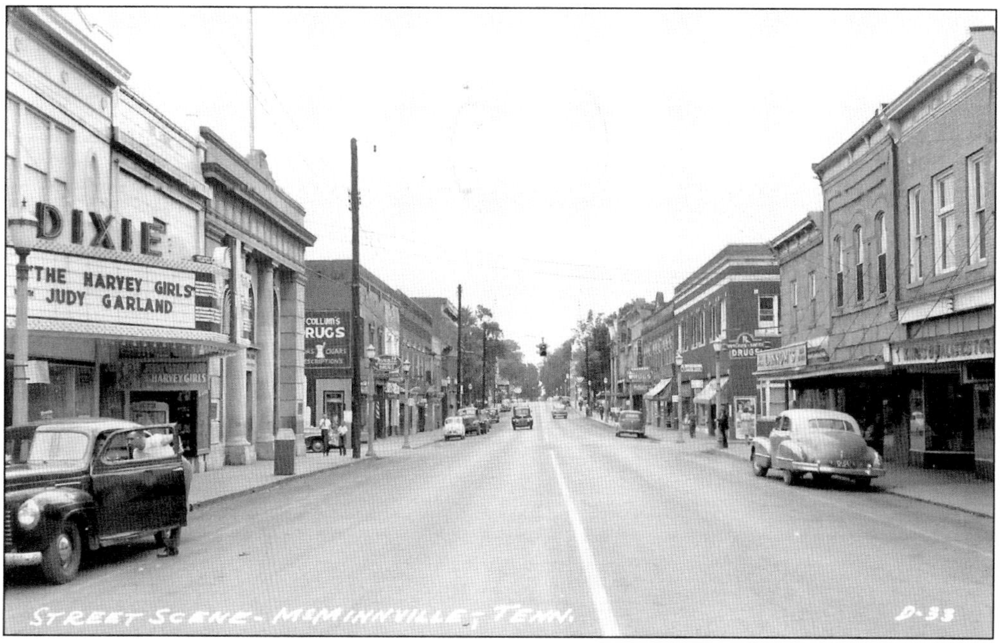

This is an early-1960s postcard view of Main Street McMinnville to the tree-lined city park in the distance. The First National Bank building is pictured at left. At that time, the Dixie Theater, left, forefront, was one of three theaters in operation in the town. A drugstore, at right, had operated on the corner of Spring and Main Streets, since before the Civil War, until 2006.

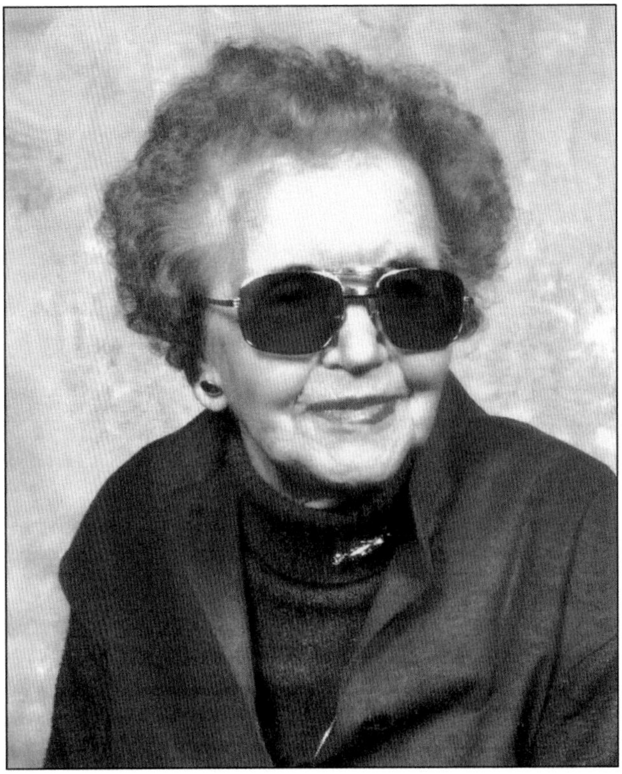

Sophia Jane (Williams) Locke, pictured, was a clever businesswoman ahead of her times. Her stunning good looks and independent spirit helped guarantee success for many years in running Locke's 5 and 10 Store in McMinnville. Her determination for success was so great that she changed her name during the early years of the business, signing her checks S. J. Locke.

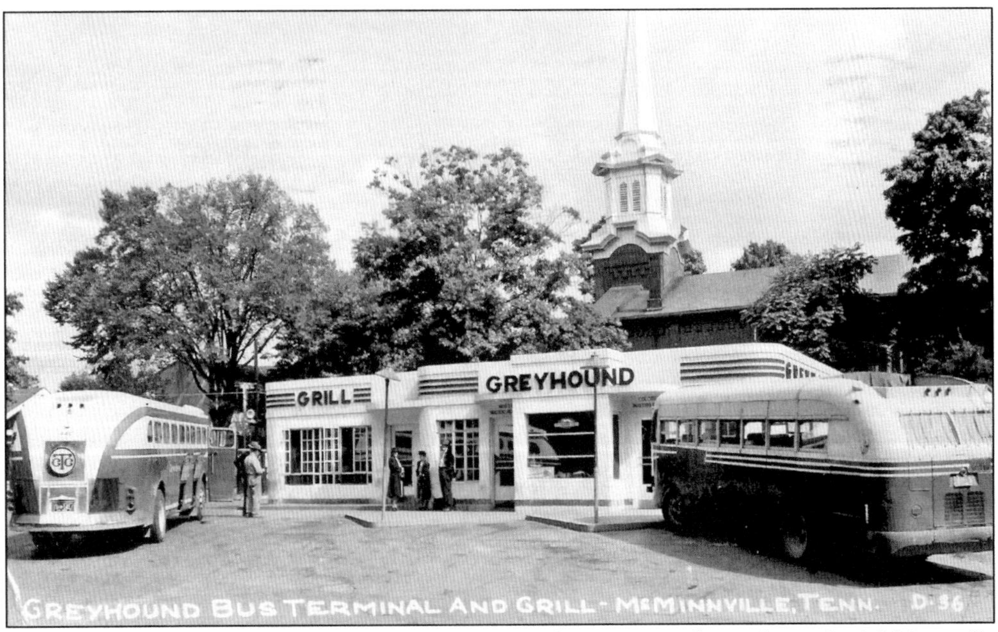

In the 1940s and 1950s, the Greyhound bus terminal and Pan-Am Grill were located in McMinnville just off West Main Street, on the southeast corner of High Street. In this 1950s postcard view, the Cumberland Presbyterian Church is visible directly behind the bus terminal. For several generations, Greyhound and Trailways bus service were a popular mode of transportation, after the discontinuation of rail service to the county.

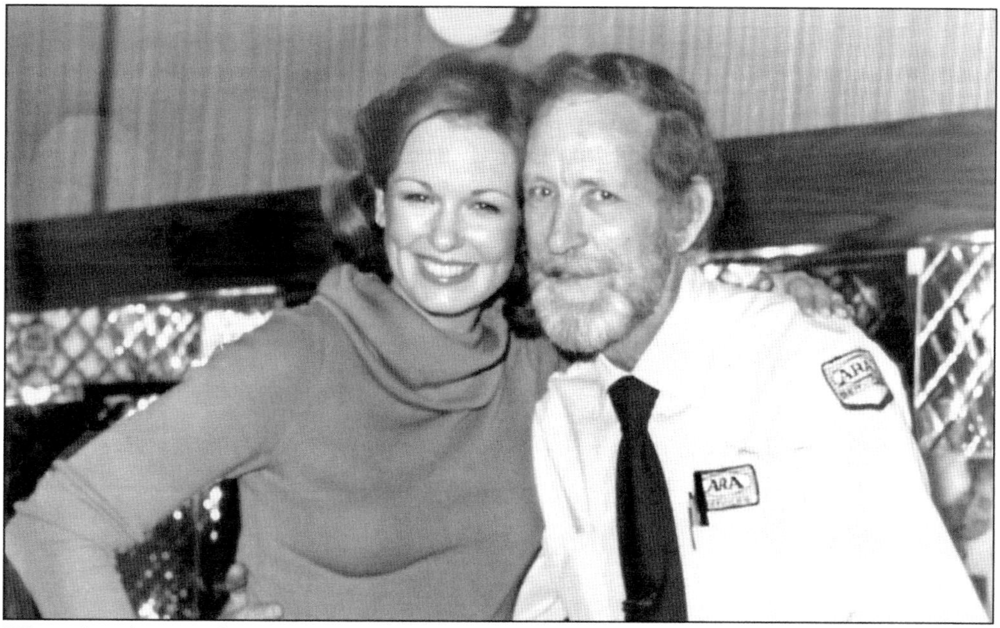

When this photograph was made in 1978, Hubert Graham was working for ARA servicing vending machines at the John Oster Manufacturing plant in McMinnville. Phyllis George, former Miss U.S.A., visited the plant and spent the day visiting and speaking with the admiring employees. The John Oster Manufacturing Company was sponsoring her CBS television network program at that time.

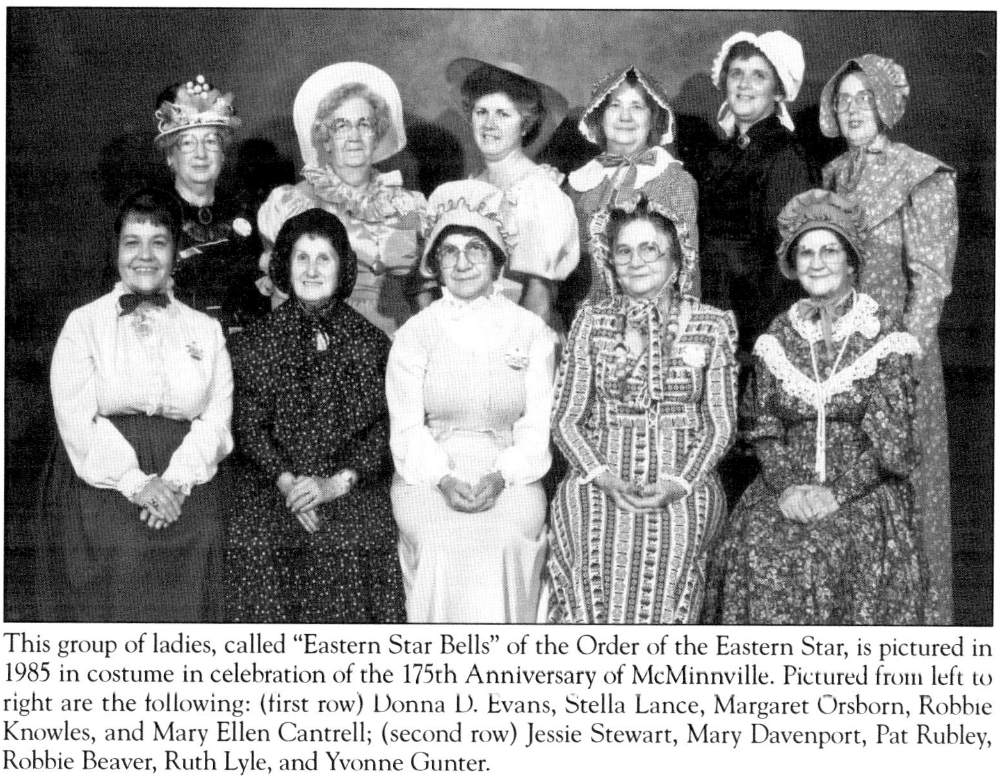

This group of ladies, called "Eastern Star Bells" of the Order of the Eastern Star, is pictured in 1985 in costume in celebration of the 175th Anniversary of McMinnville. Pictured from left to right are the following: (first row) Donna D. Evans, Stella Lance, Margaret Orsborn, Robbie Knowles, and Mary Ellen Cantrell; (second row) Jessie Stewart, Mary Davenport, Pat Rubley, Robbie Beaver, Ruth Lyle, and Yvonne Gunter.

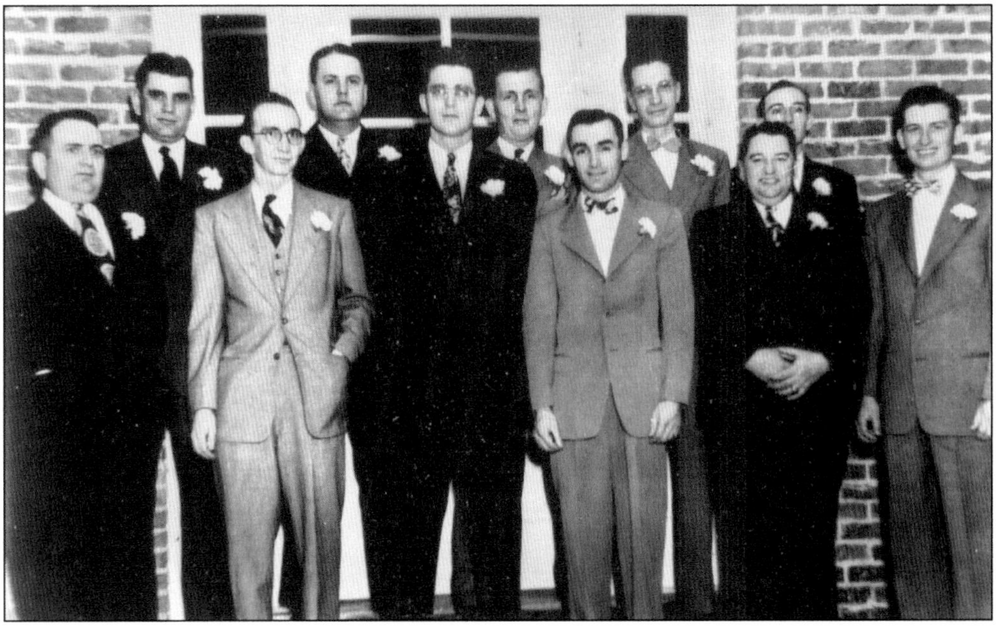

This photograph was taken at a McMinnville Junior Chamber of Commerce Banquet in 1947, with 1947–1948 chamber members in attendance. Pictured left to right are the following: (first row) Robert Greer, James Dempster, Tom Mullican (president), Robert Boyd, "Fat" Henderson, and Everett Brock; (second row) Ray Southern, Chick Brown, Bill Strick, Jack Hennessee, and Mason Beaver.

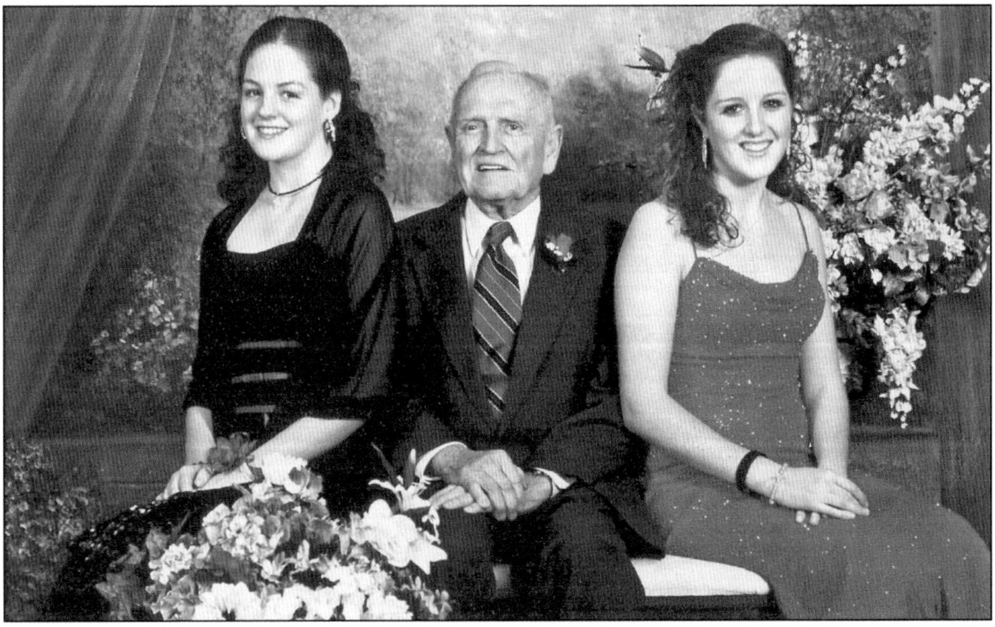

Born in 1918, prominent McMinnville community leader Marvin Campen loyally served on the Magness Memorial Library Board and was a member and past president of McMinnville Noon Rotary. Married to Cynthia Brady Campen, he was the father of two daughters seen here with their father in 2005. Pictured at left is Daisy Elizabeth, born in 1991, and, at extreme right, Kathleen Rebecca, born in 1989. He died February 20, 2006, in McMinnville.

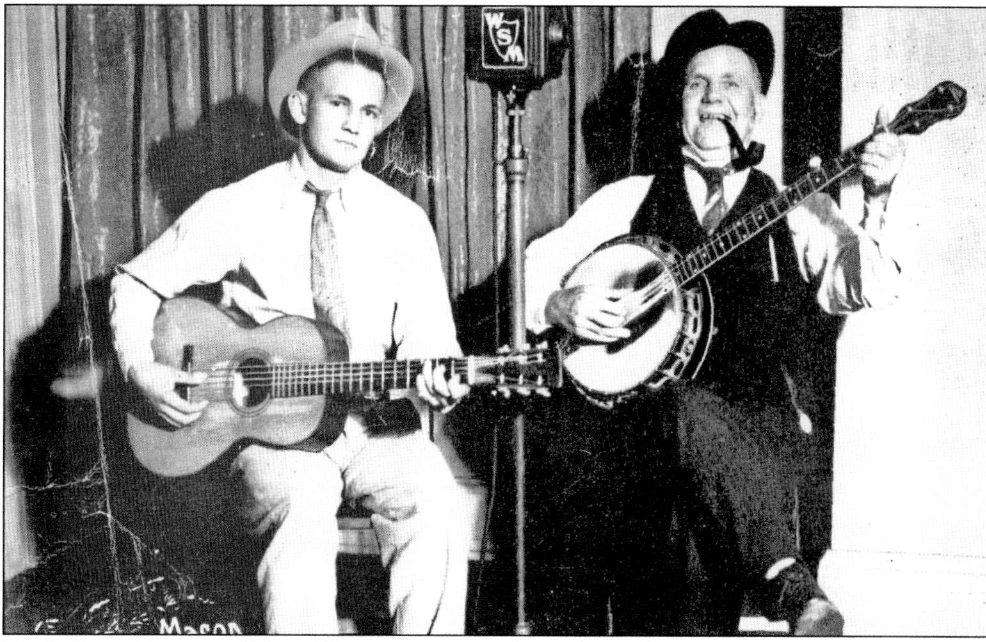

Uncle Dave Macon (1870–1952), pioneer music legend, was born David Harris Macon in the Smartt Station Community of Warren County and at an early age became interested in folk music and learned to play banjo. He was one of the two original performers in 1925 on the first Grand Ole Opry broadcast. This 1930s photograph pictures Macon with his son, Dorris, as they appear on WSM in Nashville.

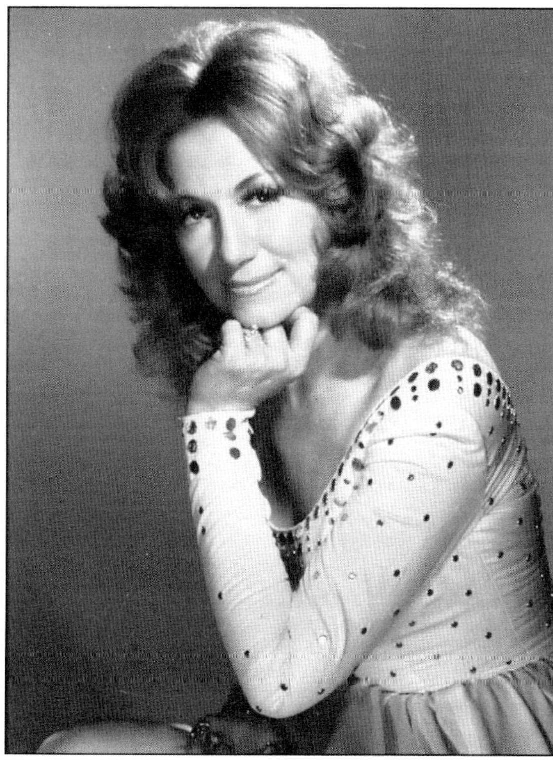

Country music superstar Dottie West was born Dorothy Marie Marsh, in 1932, in the Dibrell Community of Warren County. After graduating in 1951 from McMinnville's Central High School, she earned in 1956 a bachelor of arts degree in music from Tennessee Tech University. A coveted member of the Grand Ole Opry, she, in 1964, was the first female ever awarded the Grammy. She died in an automobile accident in 1991.

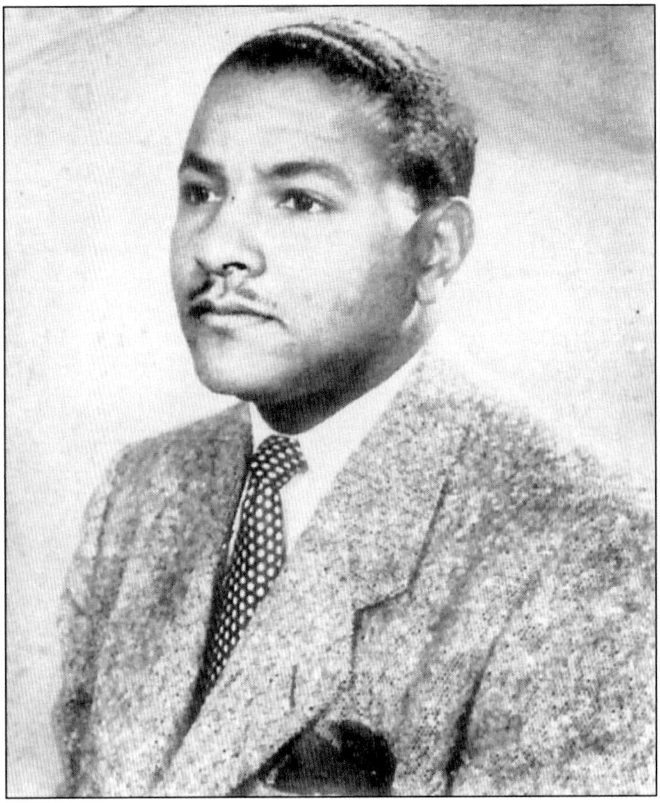

Renowned columnist, author, and statesman Carl Thomas Rowan (1925–2000) grew up in McMinnville. He attended Oberlin College and the University of Minnesota School of Journalism then worked for 13 years as journalist for the *Minneapolis Morning Tribune*. He served as ambassador to Finland and, in 1964, was appointed head of the U.S. Information Agency by Pres. John F. Kennedy. Rowan is pictured in the 1950s.

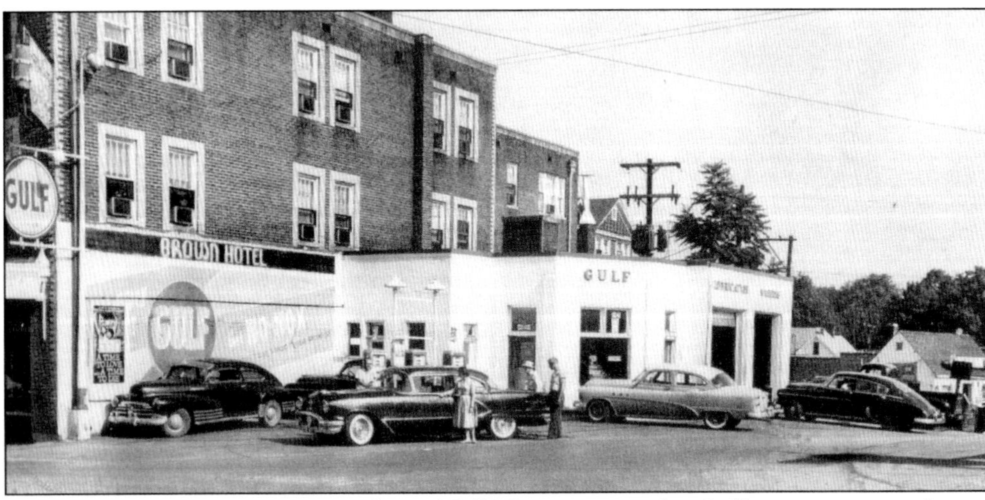

In the 1930s and 1940s, Herman Gillis and Bill Thompson ran this Gulf service station adjacent to the Brown Hotel on the north side of East Main and Sparta Streets in McMinnville. The hotel was established in 1923 when J. B. Brown purchased the old Tate House on the site and renamed it the Brown Hotel, which operated into the 1980s. Remnants of the service station were demolished in 2004.

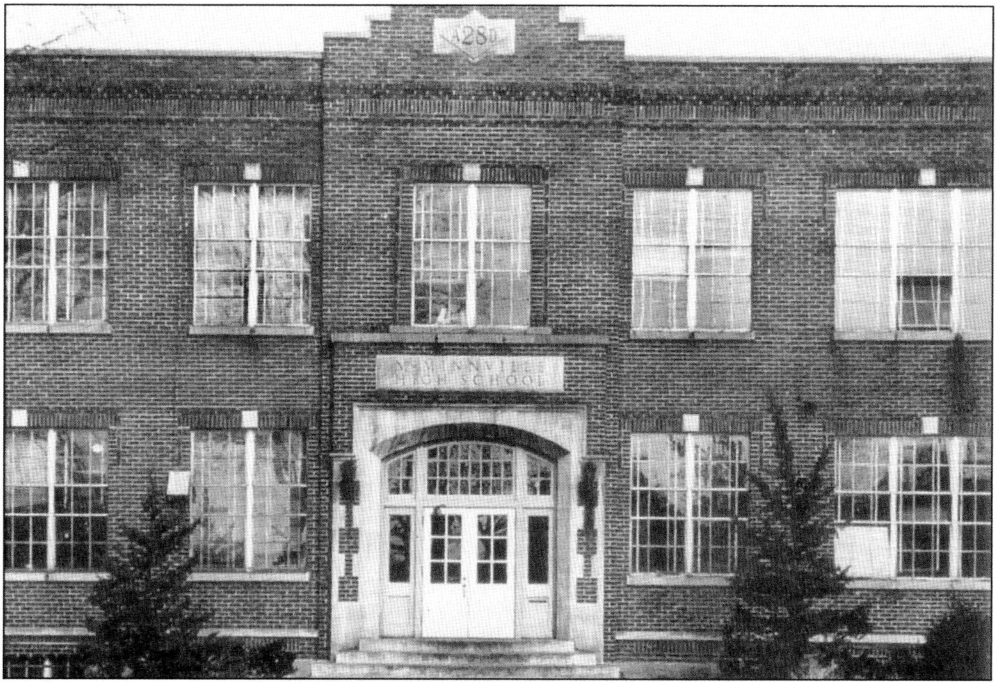

Up until 1928, the three-story building, later called the Blue Building, had served as the McMinnville City School. At that time, a new school building was built on Chancery Street. The school, pictured shortly after it was built in 1928, officially became the McMinnville Central High School at the site now occupied by Bobby Ray Elementary School. In 1974, a fire destroyed the building, which had recently become a junior high school, with damage from the fire estimated at over $1 million. Photographer Charles Cassetty captured the building as it burned in 1974.

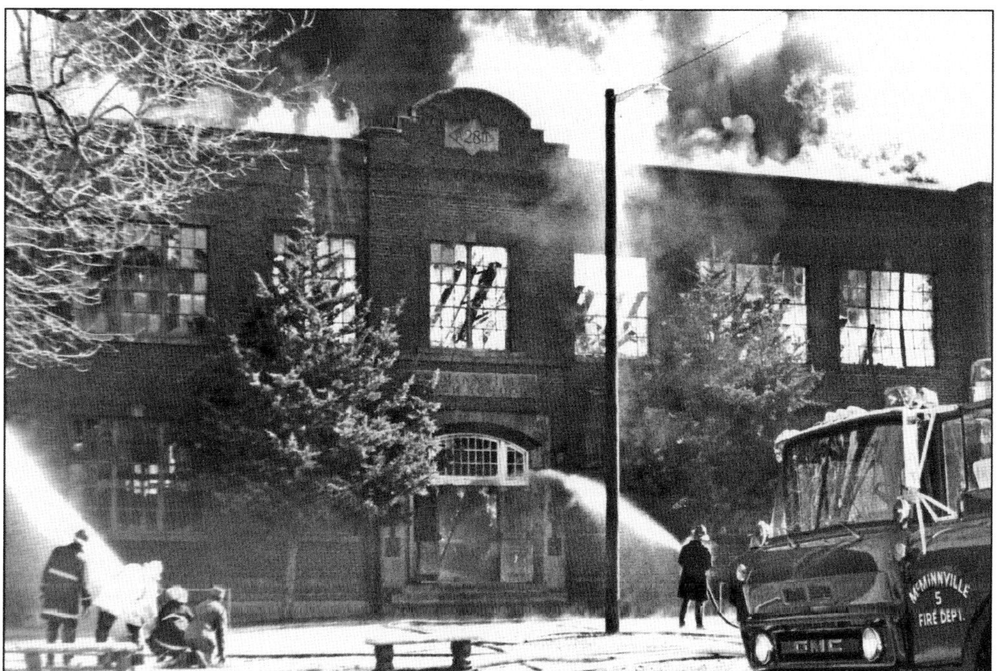

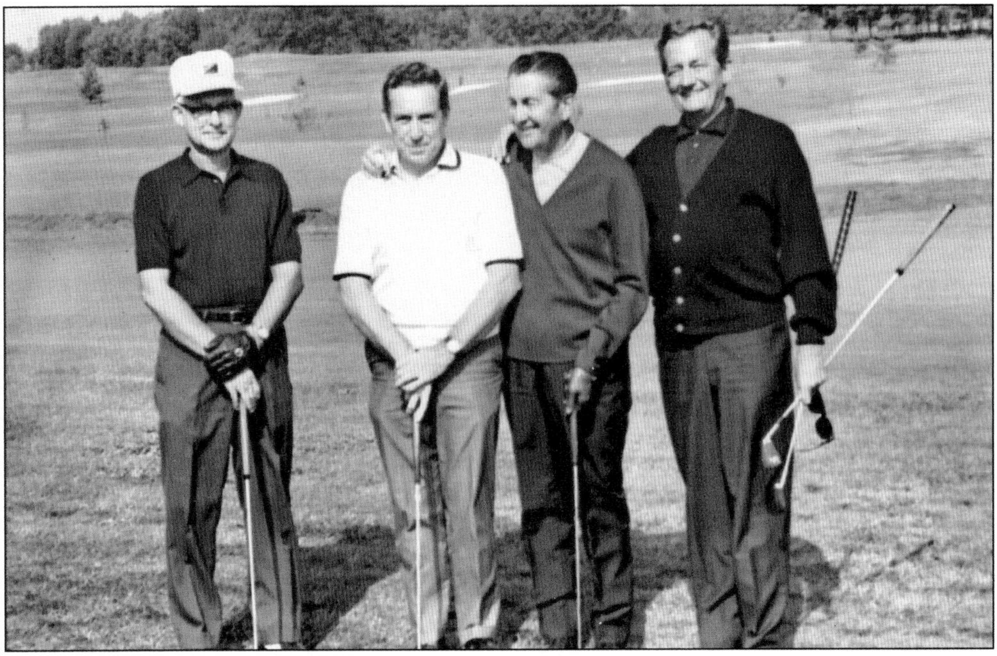

Popular entertainer and band leader Laurence Welk had ties to Warren County through his friendship with Morrison native Randy Wood, who established the Dot Record Company in the 1950s. Pictured in this photograph, taken at the McMinnville Country Club golf course in the early 1980s, are, from left to right, Sam Cordell, Randy Wood, Laurence Welk, and Don Fedderson.

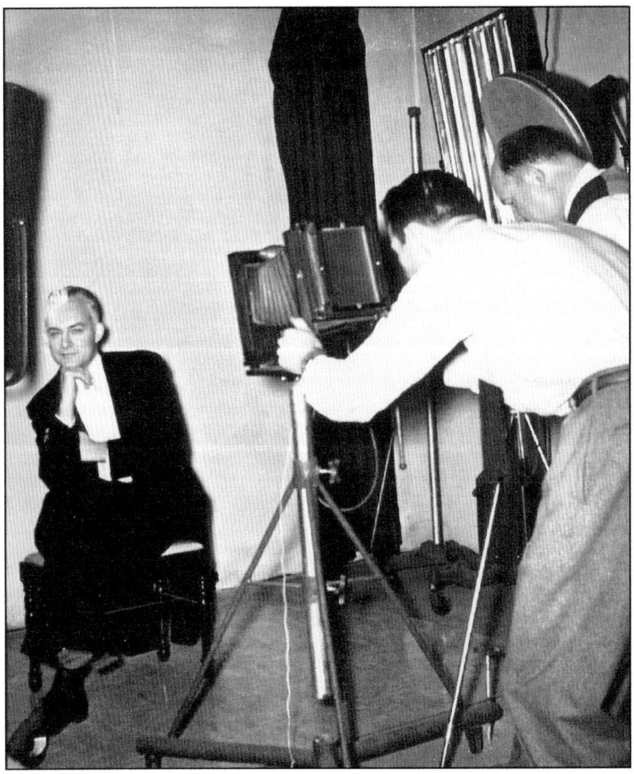

Esteemed local citizen and jeweler Samuel "Sam" Cordell is a man of multiple talents who has been active in community affairs and cultural activities in McMinnville and Warren County. In 1952, he organized the Community Choral Society of McMinnville and Warren County, which he directed. Sam is seen here being photographed in 1955 for a magazine article related to the chorus. Born in 1916, he celebrated his 90th birthday on January 23, 2006.

Distinguished McMinnville citizens William Spencer Lively Jr. and Betty (Yager) Lively were married on February 27, 1943, in San Diego, California, and sat for this portrait the day before he was to be shipped out to Europe by the U.S. Military the following day. William "Billy" Lively, born March 17, 1922, is the son of William Spencer "Dad" Lively and Ethel Cook Lively of McMinnville. Betty was born May 18, 1923. Her parents operated the Yager Grocery on East Main Street for some 30 years beginning in the 1920s. Billy Lively, operated the Lively Drug Store from 1958 to 1984 in downtown McMinnville. He served some 20 years as city alderman. The couple was photographed by Monty Wanamaker in February 2006 in the Southern Museum and Galleries of Photography, Culture and History in McMinnville.

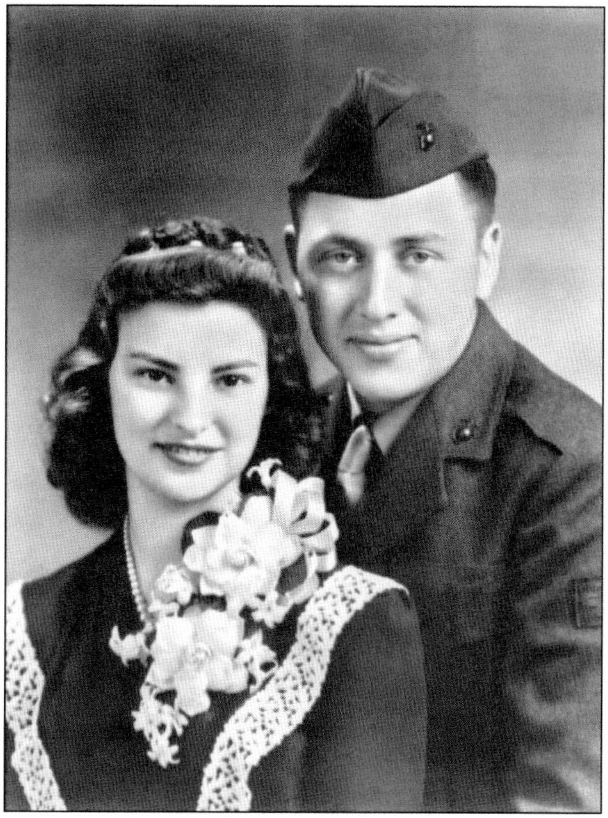

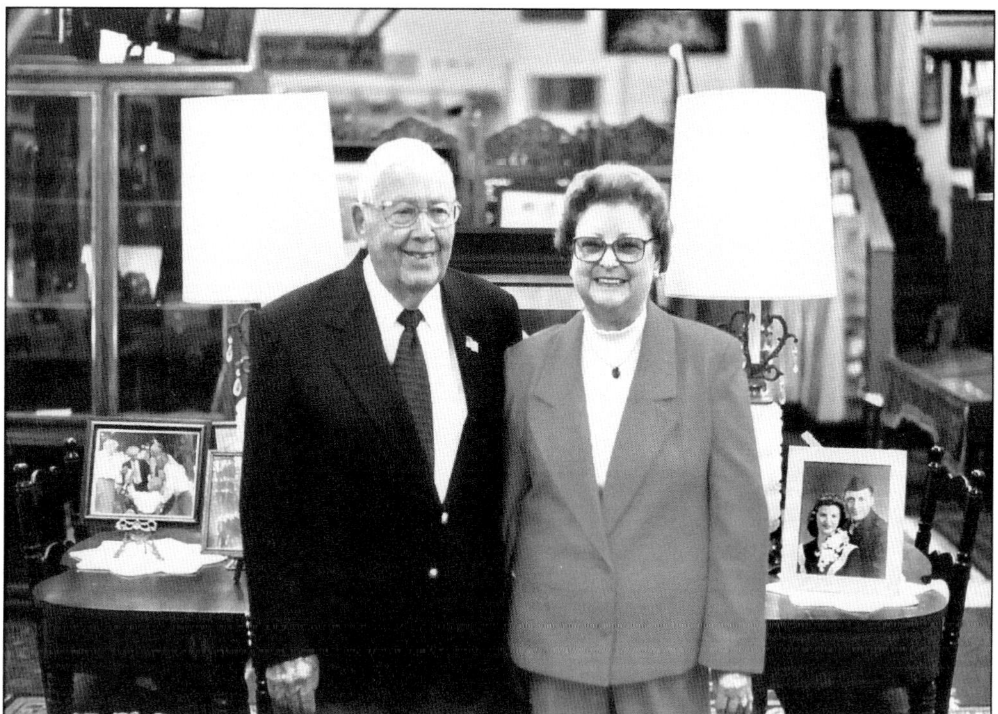

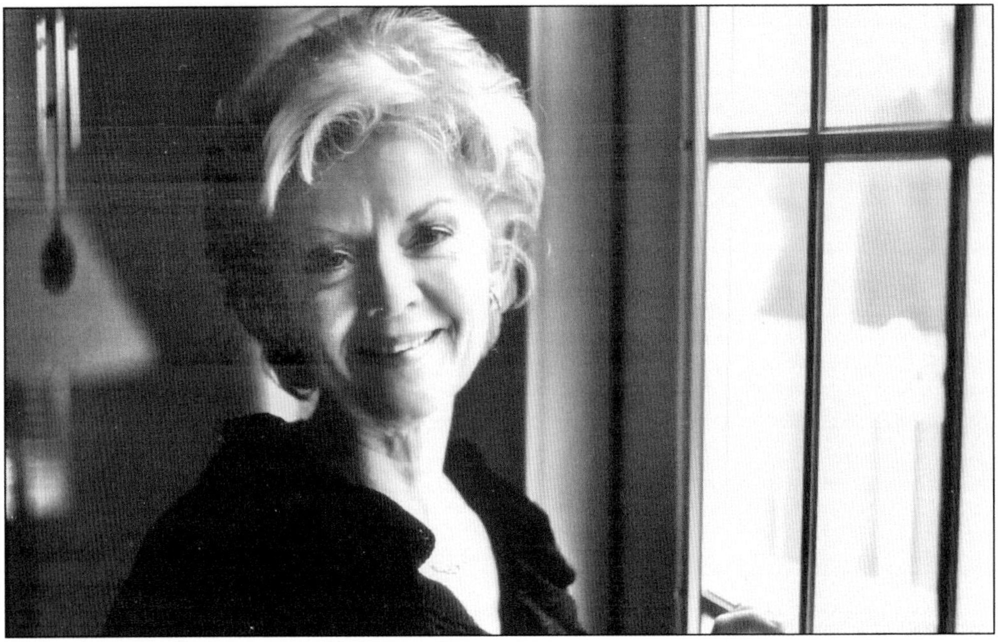

Lucia Cordell Getsi, poet, Fulbright Scholar, professor of English and comparative literature at Illinois State University, grew up in McMinnville, the daughter of Georgia (Bragg) Cordell and Sam Cordell. She has published three volumes of poetry—the first in 1968—and is currently writing a novel influenced by memories of her childhood. Monty Wanamaker took this photograph of her in 2004.

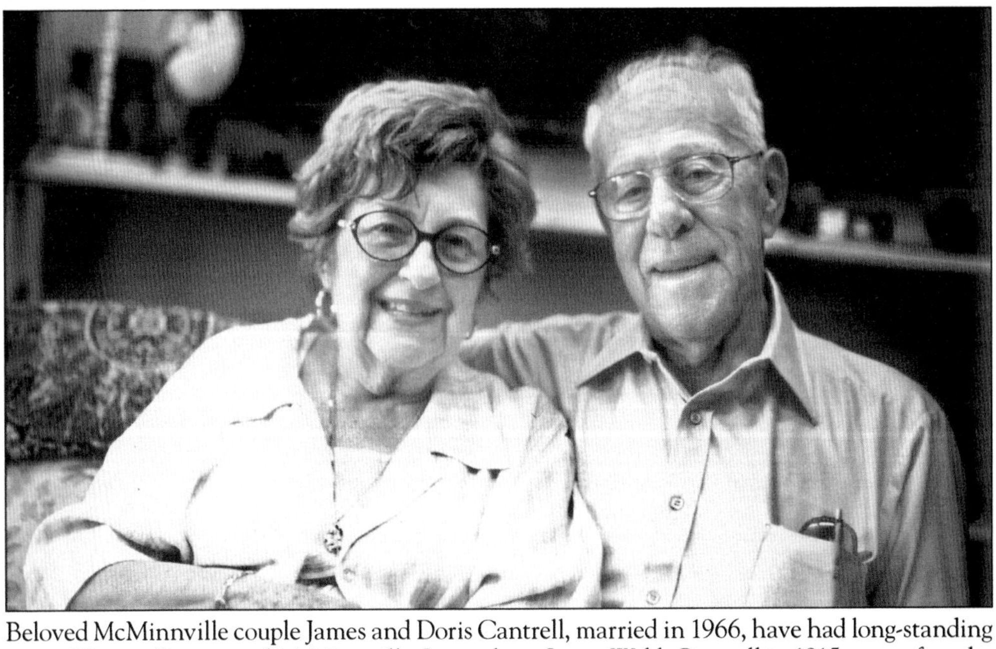

Beloved McMinnville couple James and Doris Cantrell, married in 1966, have had long-standing ties to Warren County and McMinnville. James, born James Webb Cantrell in 1915, was cofounder of Love-Cantrell Funeral Home, which opened in 1950 in McMinnville. Doris (Powell) Julian Cantrell, born in 1925, is the only child of Jess H. and Mildred (Stepp) Powell. James died in October 2005.

Beloved McMinnville mayor Franklin Porter Blue served seven terms—a total of 17 years—as mayor of the city, beginning in 1963. A compassionate and civic-minded citizen, he had the honor of having the first McMinnville city hall building, the former Southside School Building, named in his honor in 1978—the Franklin P. Blue Municipal Building, which is still utilized by the City of McMinnville.

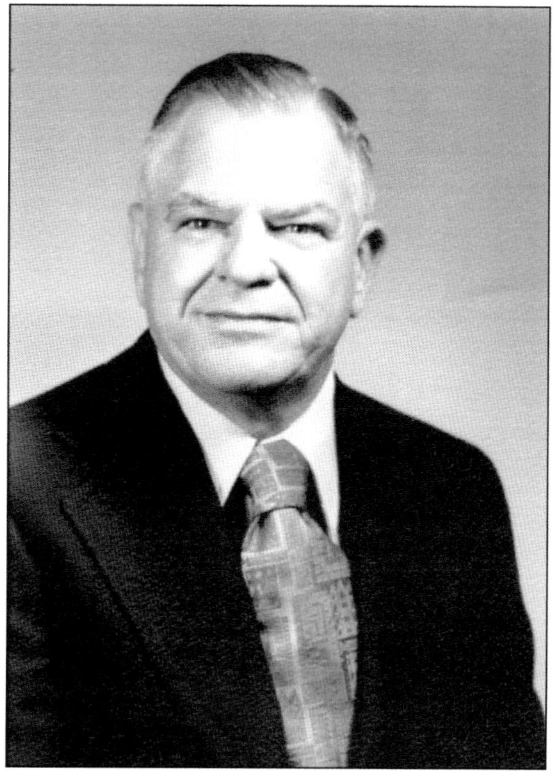

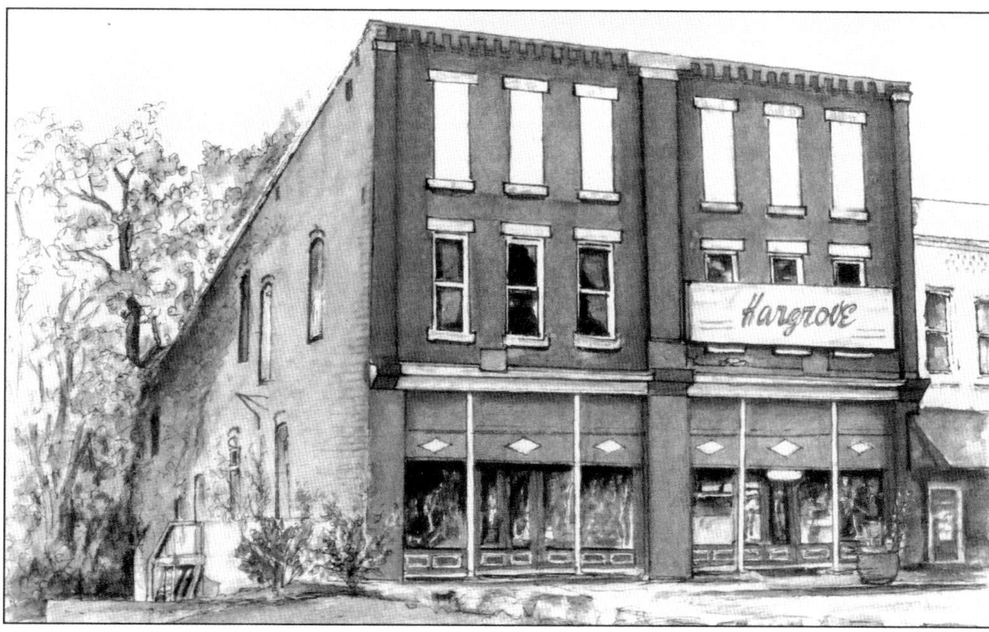

The South Court Square location of Hargrove Office Supply was the site of the first residence in McMinnville, a log house built in 1810 by Charles Sullivan. The present building was erected by Jesse Walling in 1910. Neil Hargrove came to McMinnville in 1950 and opened an office supply business, Hargrove Office Supply, pictured in this 2004 pen-and-ink drawing by Monty Wanamaker. Since his death in 1996, the business has been in operation by family members.

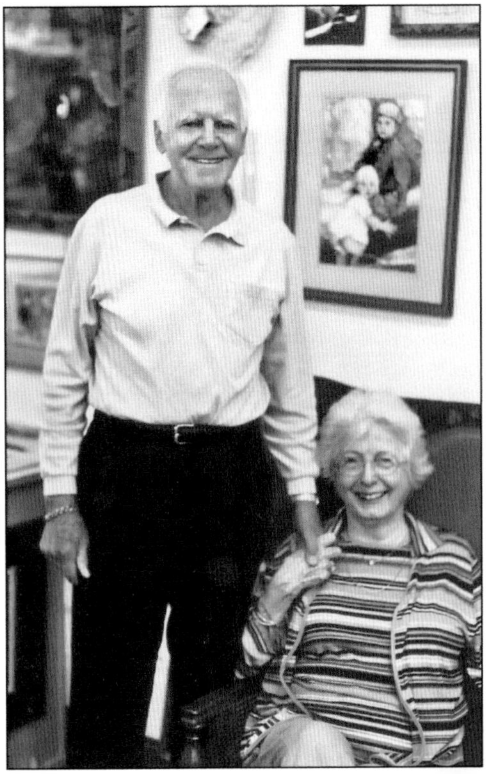

No living citizen of McMinnville is more venerated than Howard Estes Locke, who, in 2006, celebrated his 86th birthday. His memories go back to the early years when he worked as a lad in his family's store, Locke's 5 and 10, on Main Street. Locke is pictured here, photographed in 2005 by Monty Wanamaker, with his wife, Louise (Womack) Locke, whom he married in 1992.

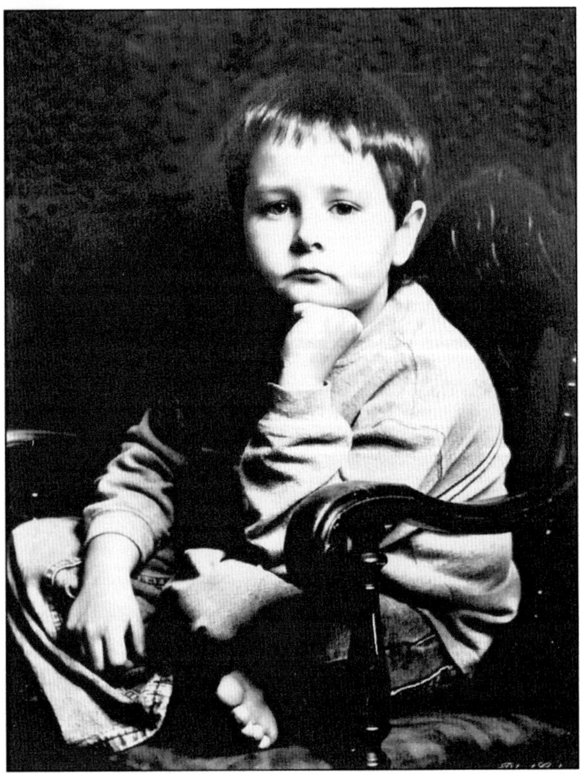

In 1994, portrait photographer and artist Deborah (Humphrey) Good came with husband Dr. Michael Good and young son Spencer Clay Good to live in McMinnville, where she opened the Deborah Good Photography Studio in 1998. Her portraits reflected the powerful influence of the work of photographer William Spencer Lively when she photographed her son Spencer, featured in this 2002 portrait.

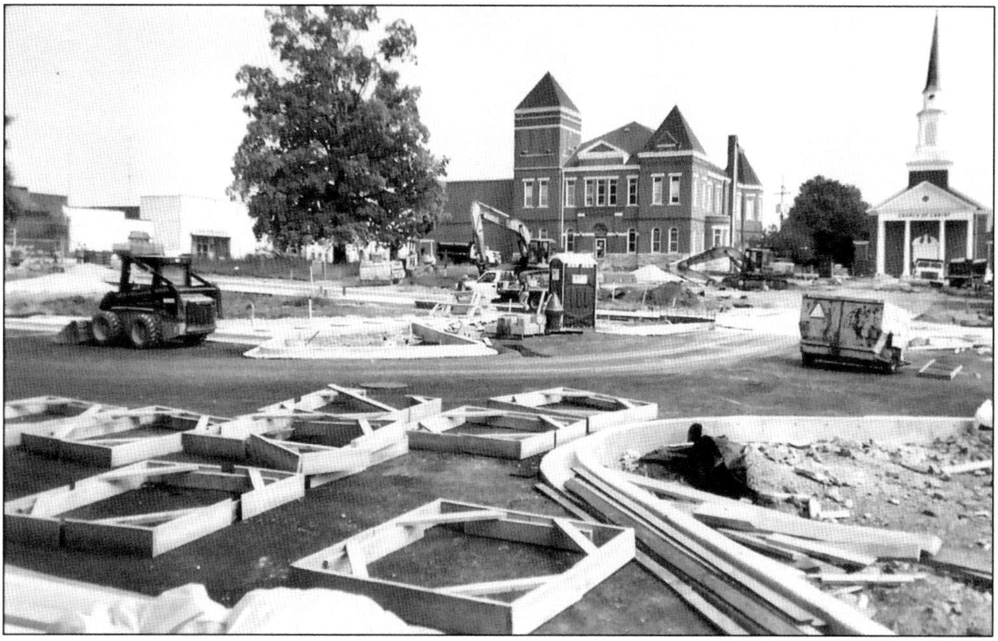

In August 2004, ground was officially broken for the McMinnville Main Street Renovation project, which was designed to totally resuscitate the downtown historical district. Pictured in the above photograph are the Warren County Courthouse and City Park area during the latter stages of repaving and restructuring of the sidewalks and streets. The Central Church of Christ is visible at far right in the photograph. The $5 million project was completed, and the street through the center of the park reopened the week before the Christmas holidays in 2005. In the lower photograph, the courthouse and park are seen, with the addition of street lights, original fountain, park benches and landscaping, photographed as the project neared completion in late spring 2006.

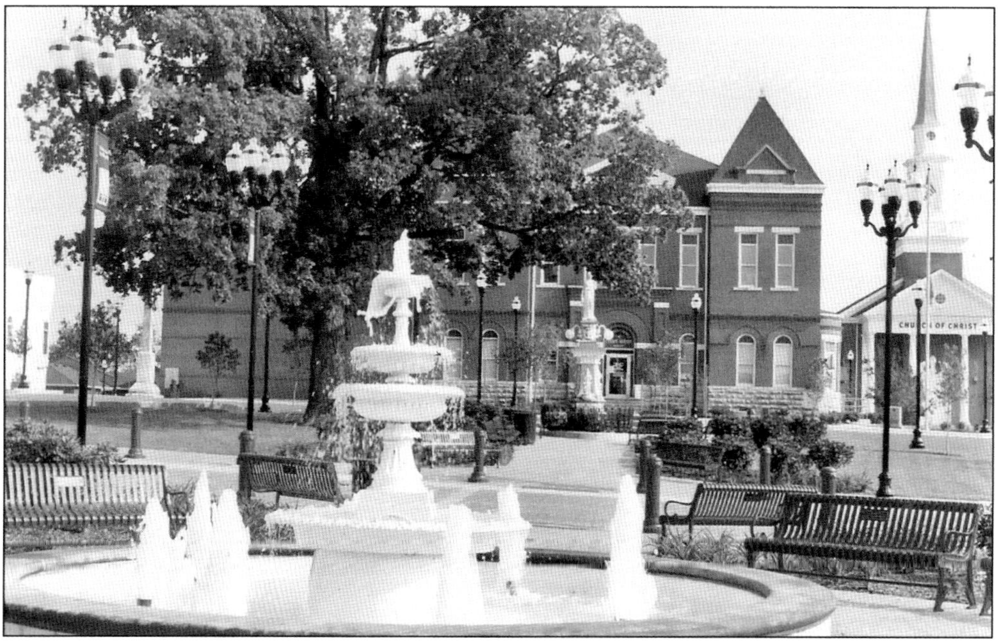

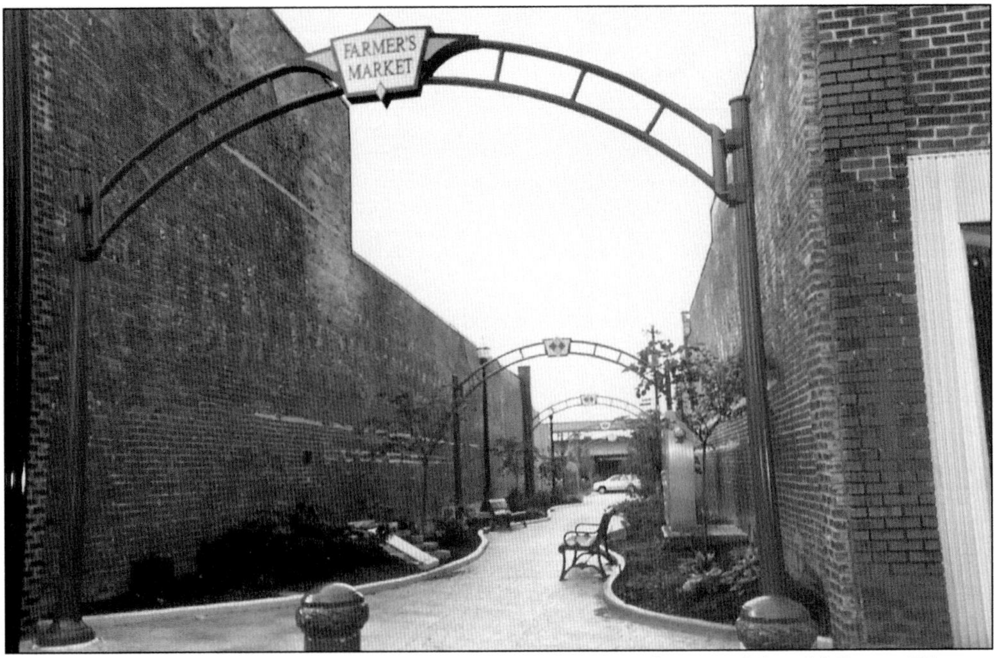

After the completion of the Main Street Renovation Project, the site of the old Center Theater on the south side of East Main Street has been transformed into a winding city mall throughway, which leads to the newly erected Farmers Market Pavilion visible in the distance. The original brick walls that formed the sides of the theater were left intact with landscaping and monuments along the sides leading to the pavilion. In the lower photograph, the completed Main Street Renovation project is reflected in this view of Main Street looking west toward the city park. In the distance, the steeples of the First Presbyterian Church can be seen at left, and that of the First United Methodist Church at far right.

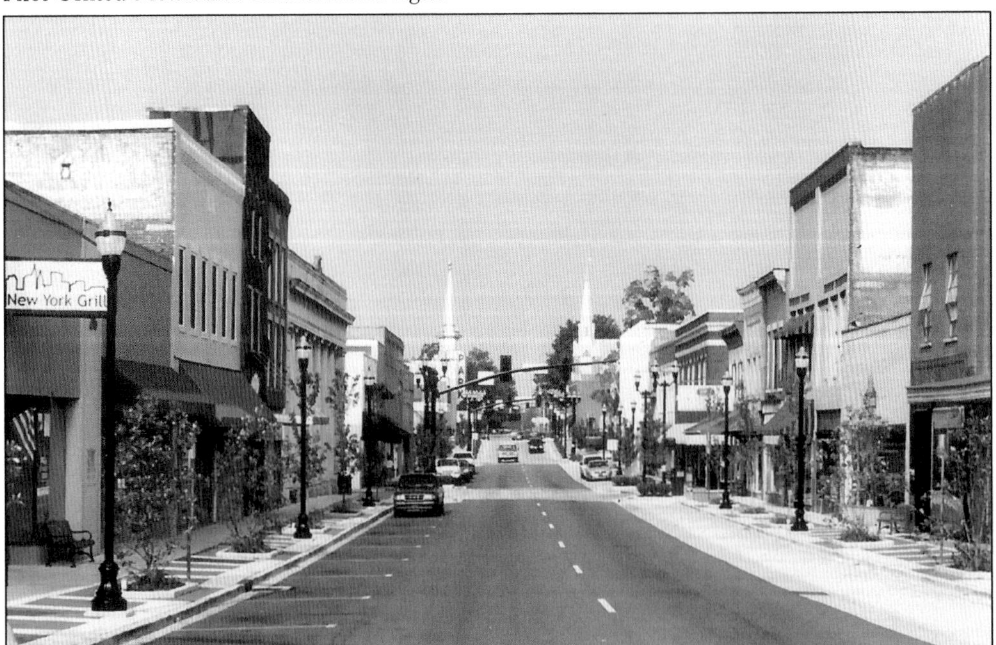

Four

SOUTHERN SCHOOL OF PHOTOGRAPHY

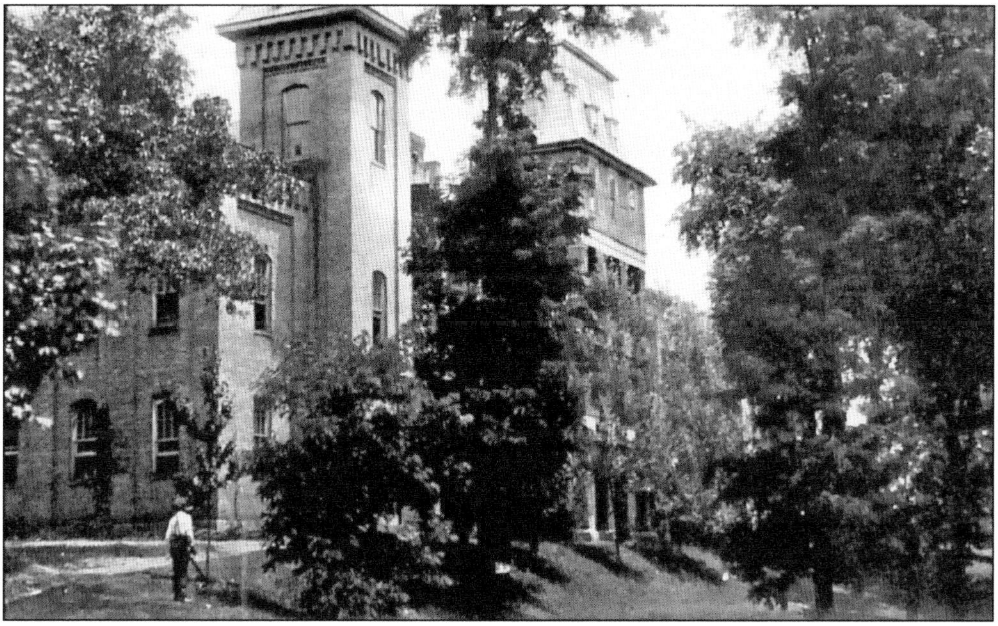

In 1903, McMinnville photographer William Spencer Lively and his longtime friend and imminent colleague W. G. McFadden, from Puducah, Kentucky, purchased what was formally the old Cumberland Female College property on the hill at the end of College Street, on Donnell Street in McMinnville. After renovating the building and installing the most modern equipment then available, the 65-room Gothic Revival brick structure was officially opened in 1904 as the Southern School of Photography—the second of only two schools of photography in the United States. It was to become legendary, and widely known as the largest and most important institution of its kind in the United States. Pictured in this photograph, looking from the west, is the school building and its lush, tree-laden grounds, taken in the early 1900s.

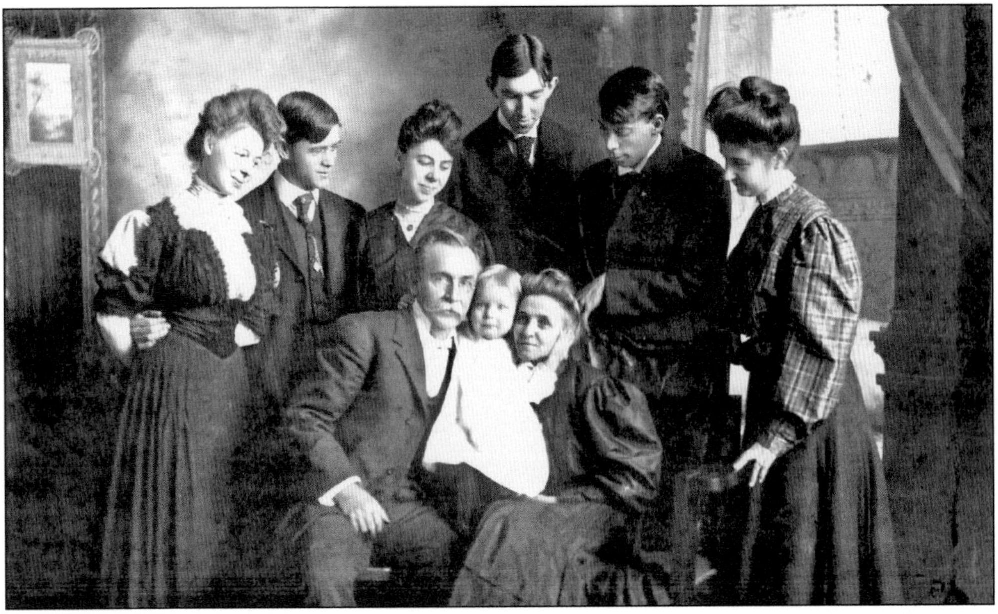

This family portrait of the William Spencer Lively family with their three children and spouses was probably taken sometime in 1907. Seated in front from left to right are the following: (first row) Lively, (first grandchild) William, and (wife) Lela Jones Lively; (second row) Lillie Pearl (Jackson) Lively (wife of son Lee Allen Lively), (son) Lee Allen Lively, (daughter) Nancy Pearl (Lively) Austin, Joseph Mudd Austin, Joseph Spencer Lively (father of young William), and (wife) Winona Lucile (Bryan) Lively.

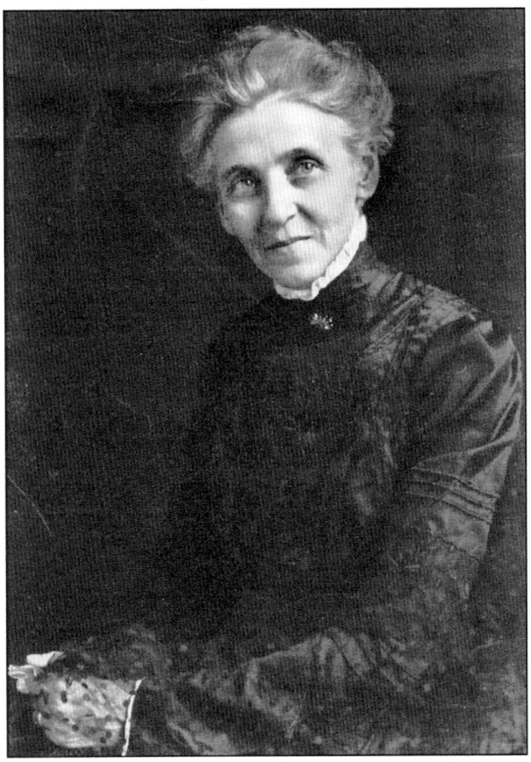

In 1878, after working in Warren County as a traveling photographer visiting each house in the different communities selling portraits of family members, William Spencer Lively moved his fledgling business to Scottsboro, Alabama. Four months later, he married Lela Jones, the daughter of a north Alabama farmer, and lived in the area for the next five years. Pictured here is Lela Lively in her later years. She died in 1920.

As his photography school became more widely known, with increased enrollment from only one individual at the beginning to several hundred in the months to come, William Spencer Lively became regarded more and more in photographic circles throughout the country as a master of the art of portrait photography, as illustrated in this stunning portrait of an unidentified young man with a fishing pole.

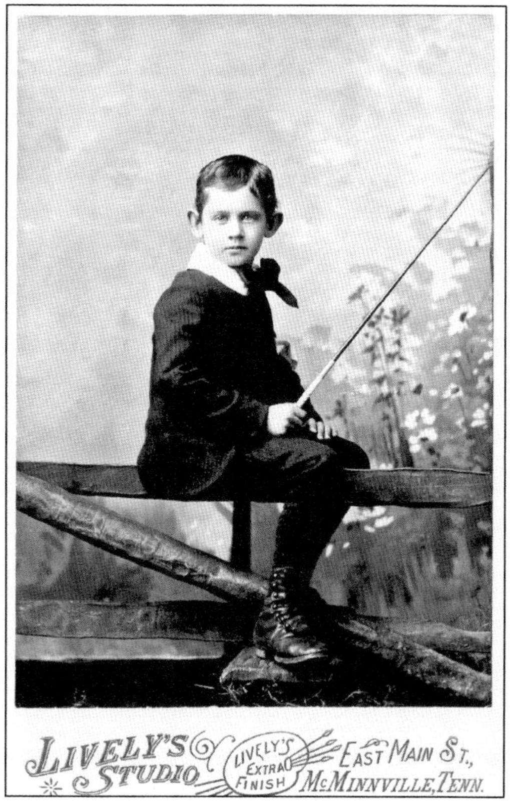

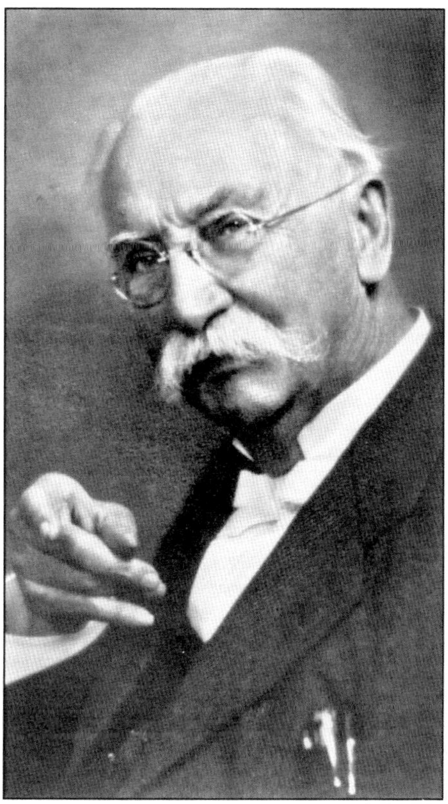

This portrait of William Spencer Lively was probably made around 1925 by one of his sons when he was 70 years old. Through the years, he was often photographed by his students as well as his sons Joe and Lee, both of whom were award-winning photographers. William sported a long mustache, even as a young man, and in later years, his snow white hair greatly contributed to his striking appearance.

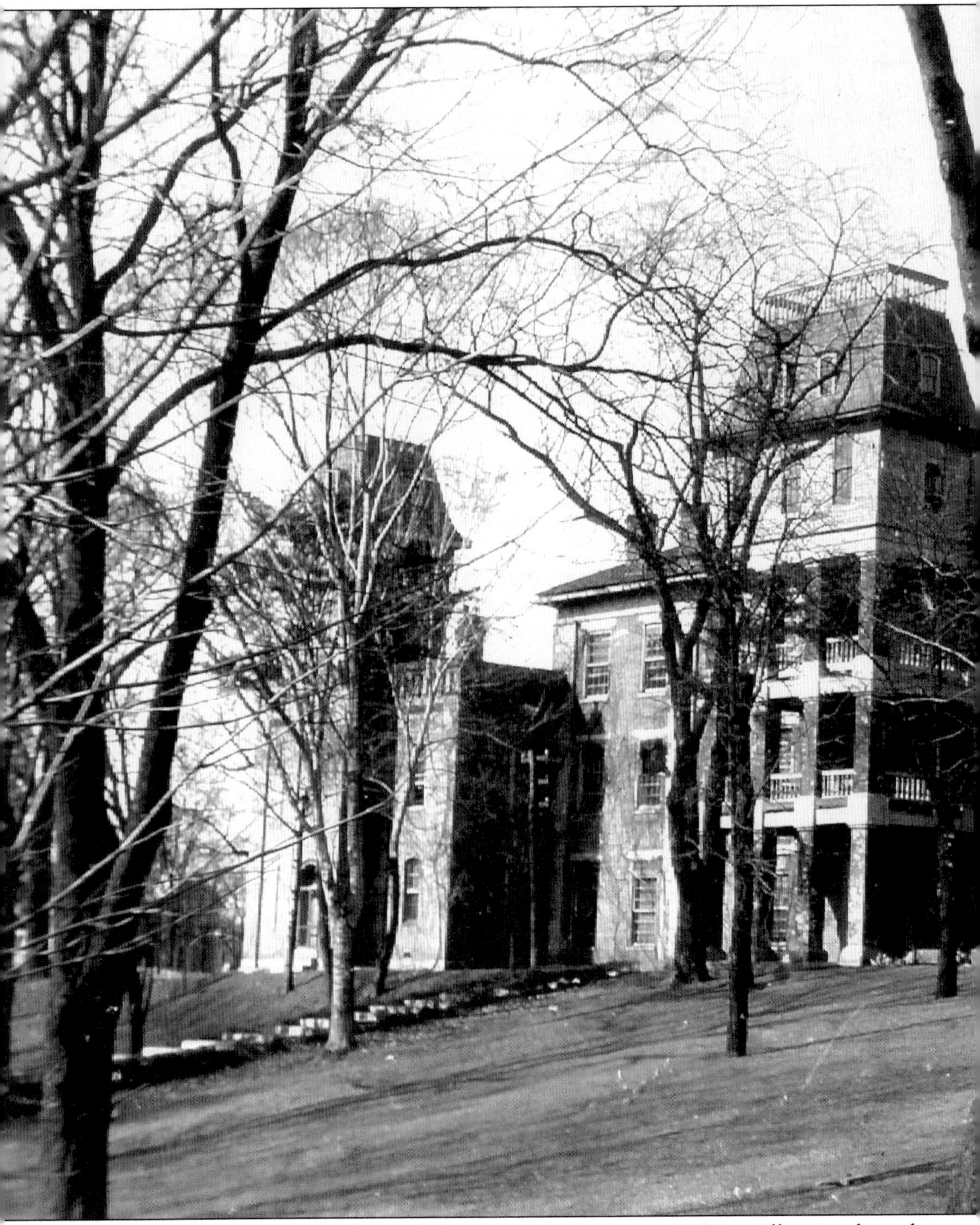

Students from every state and several foreign countries came to McMinnville to study at the Southern School of Photography from its inception in 1904 until 1928, when it ceased operations due to a fire that claimed much of the building. Because of the women's rights movement in the late 1800s, female students comprised a large percentage of the student body. One of the most

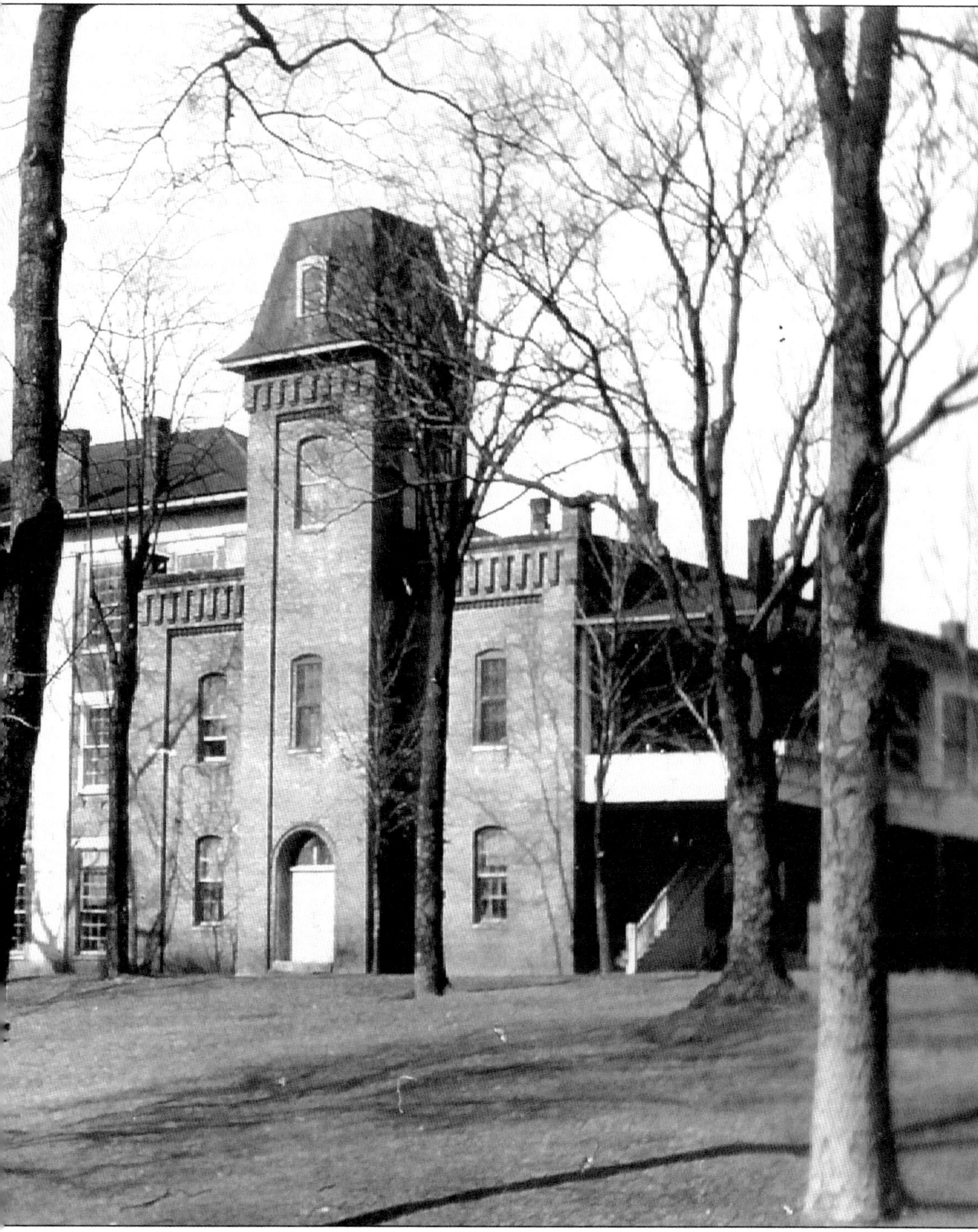

impressive and imposing buildings in all of middle Tennessee, the Gothic Revival–style edifice was magnificent, with its sloping, landscaped grounds and grand vistas of the town of McMinnville and the mystical Ben Lomand Mountain in the distance beyond.

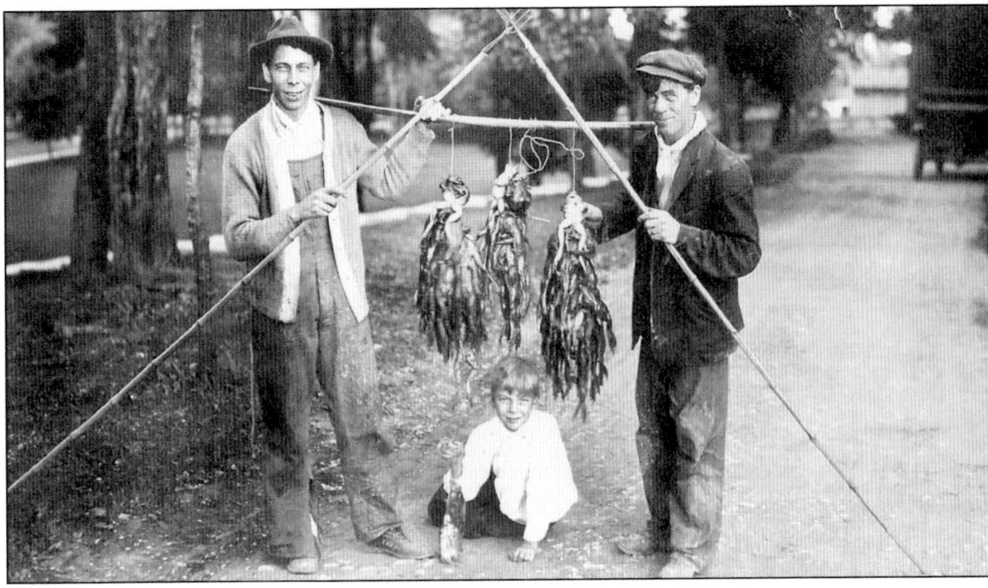

These photographs graphically illustrate the love of play, as well as the love of nature and outdoor activity often displayed by William Spencer Lively and his sons, Joe and Lee. In the above photograph, Joe (left) and Lee (right) display their catch of frogs collected from a gigging trip. Lively's youngest son, Billy, is seen sitting on the ground underneath the catch. Frog legs have long been revered in the region as a great culinary delicacy. In the photograph below, taken by photography school student Marion Kelly, Lively is pictured at the table cutting a watermelon, while students from the school and family members, indulge in eating the sliced fruit. The picture was probably taken in the backyard of the Southern School of Photography building.

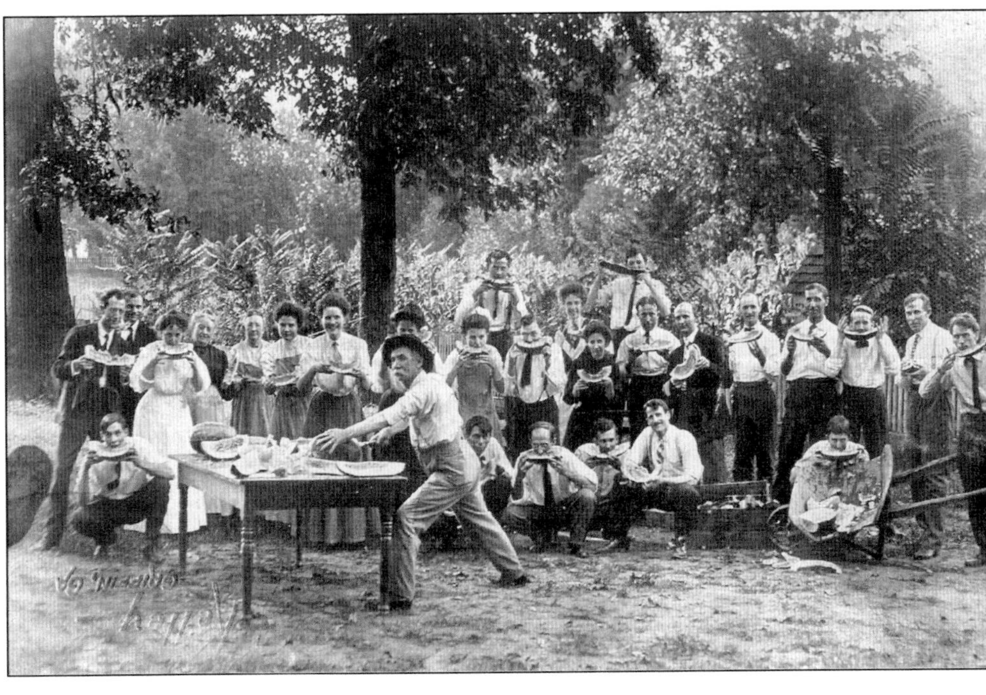

During the fledgling years of photography, after the Lumiere brothers in France had developed in 1909 the auto-chrome, the first color photographic image, William Spencer Lively began experimenting with the complex process and worked to develop and perfect a more simple way of producing the color images. Lively produced this auto-chrome portrait of Ethel Cook, the woman who would later become his second wife.

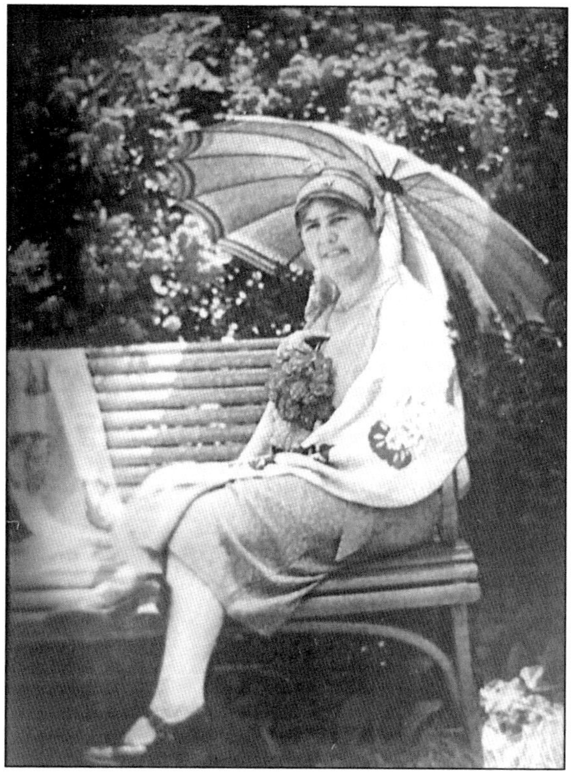

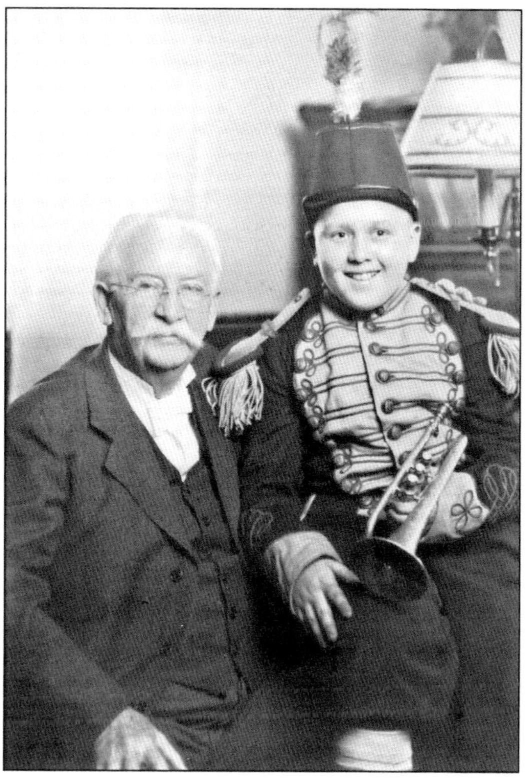

After the death of his first wife, Lela, William Spencer Lively married the young woman, Ethel Cook, who had been Lela's faithful nurse during her illness. In 1922, Ethel gave birth to his fourth child, William Spencer "Billy" Lively Jr. In this photograph, taken about 1931, Lively's son is wearing Lively's Warren House Band uniform and holding his father's coronet.

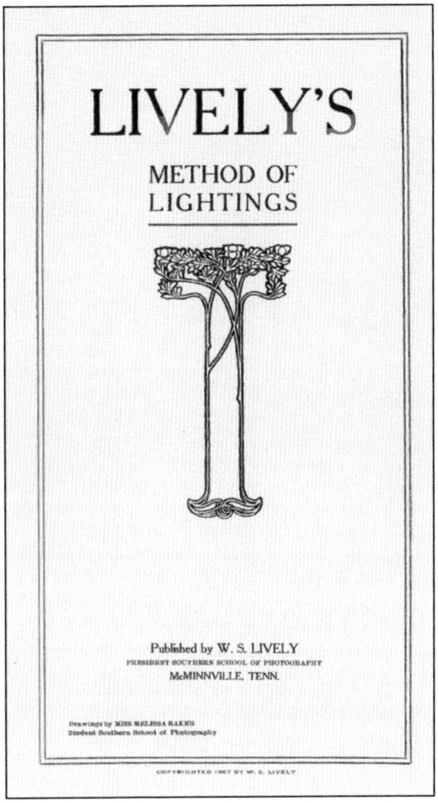

LIVELY'S

METHOD OF
LIGHTINGS

Published by W. S. LIVELY
PRESIDENT SOUTHERN SCHOOL OF PHOTOGRAPHY
McMINNVILLE, TENN.

Drawings by MISS MELISSA BAKER
Student Southern School of Photography

COPYRIGHTED 1907 BY W. S. LIVELY

In 1907, three years after he opened the Southern School of Photography, William Spencer Lively published a 60-page hardback book, titled *Lively's Method of Lighting*, which contained numerous photographic portraits and illustrations demonstrating a variety of photographic lighting techniques he had perfected. The title page of the book is seen here along with the frontispiece image in the book. One of Lively's favorite subjects was old men, usually photographed with long hair and beard. This portrait of an unidentified subject demonstrates his particular method of Rembrandt lighting. His book was reportedly an immediate success, with the entire edition sold out within a very short time. The book was used as a textbook in his photography school.

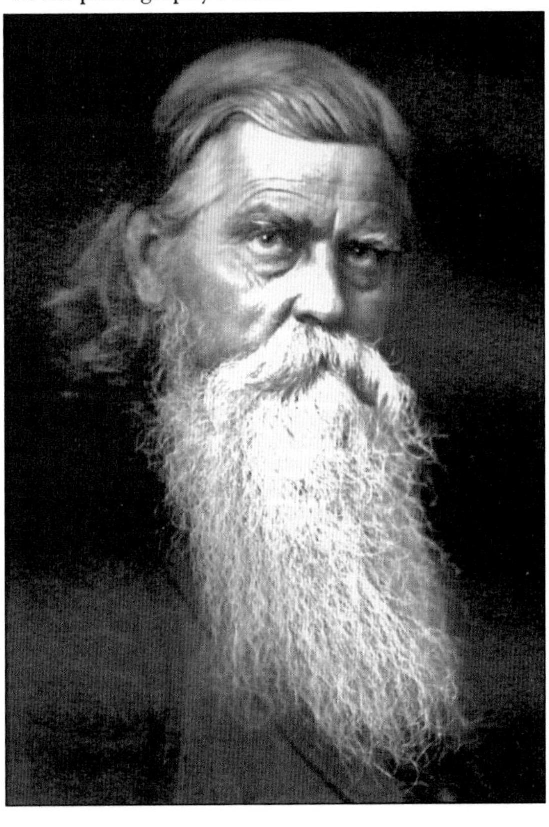

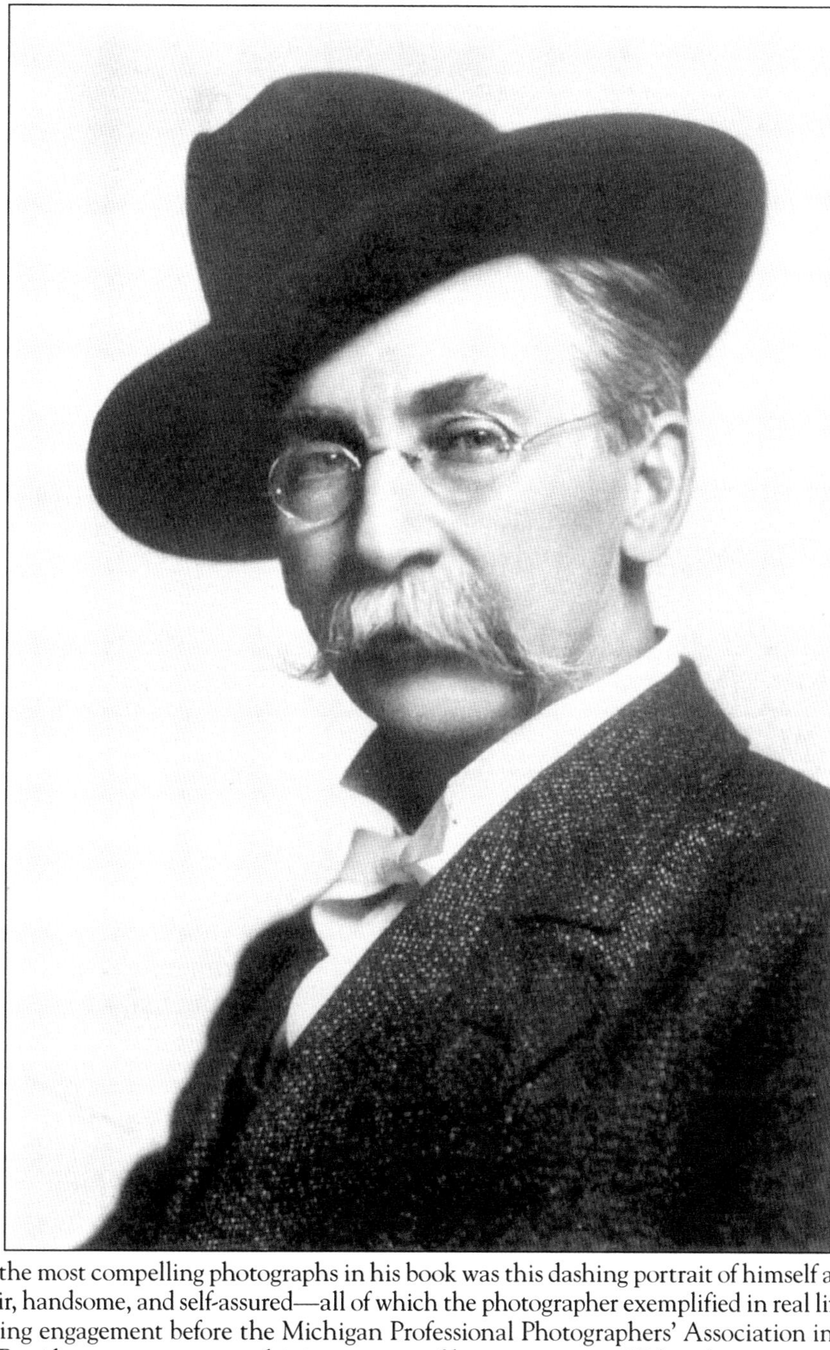

One of the most compelling photographs in his book was this dashing portrait of himself as proud, debonair, handsome, and self-assured—all of which the photographer exemplified in real life. After a speaking engagement before the Michigan Professional Photographers' Association in 1913, a Grand Rapids newspaper wrote this in a report of his appearance: "Of medium stature, a head abundantly crowned with silver locks, a sweeping white moustache that sets off a slightly aquiline face, perfectly, and gives a commanding look that is quite borne out in the general makeup of the man. All this coupled with that soft voice and purring accent of the Southern man makes a study that is mighty interesting." Lively maintained throughout his life a charming, warm disposition, one which won him early in his teaching career the appellation of "Dad" which remained as a label of affection throughout his remarkable career.

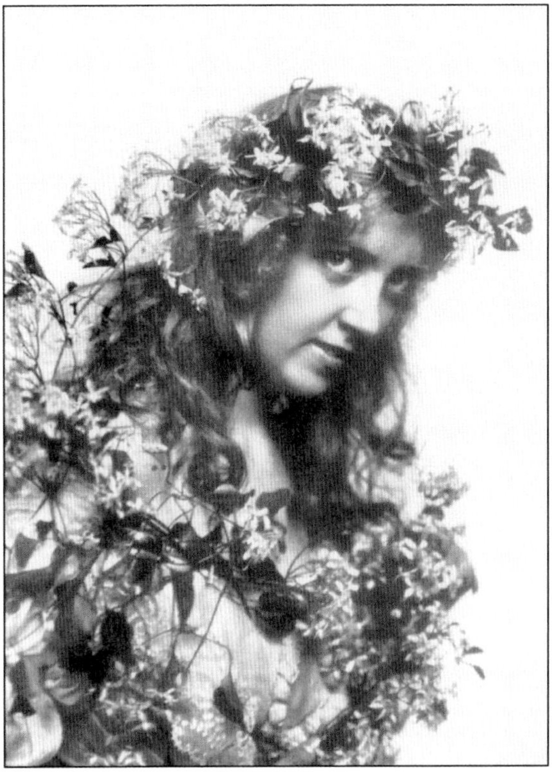

Perhaps the most unusual and creative photograph in the book is that of a young, unidentified woman wreathed in garlands of Virgin's Bower, a native clematis which grows in Warren County in the forests and is often seen blooming along the roadsides in profusion. Many of Lively's female subjects were often photographed among flowers, usually blooming in the gardens that were maintained by the photography school. The image below was the final photograph in the book on lighting, showing a semi-profile of the school building, facing west, with the road winding up to the building's entrance. The Lively family maintained a residence in this wing of the building, and continued to live in the building even after the fire in 1928 destroyed much of the west wing and central part of the building.

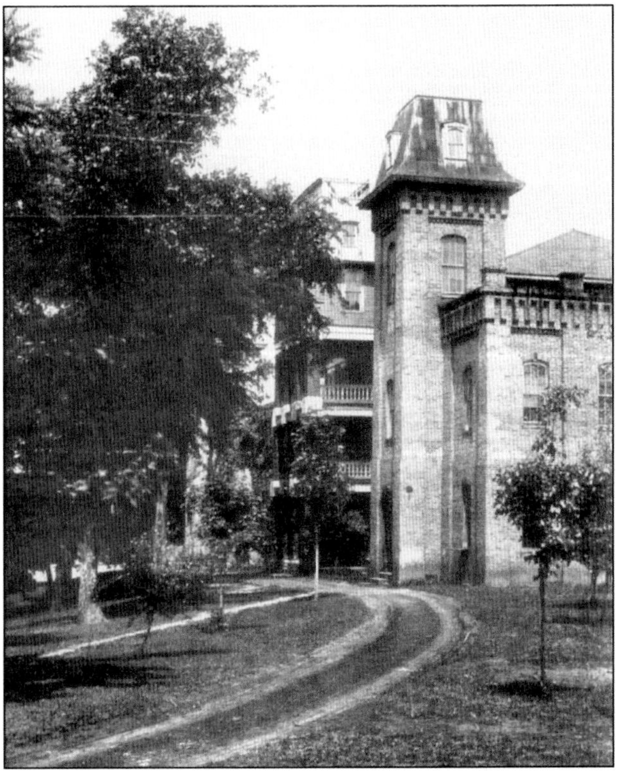

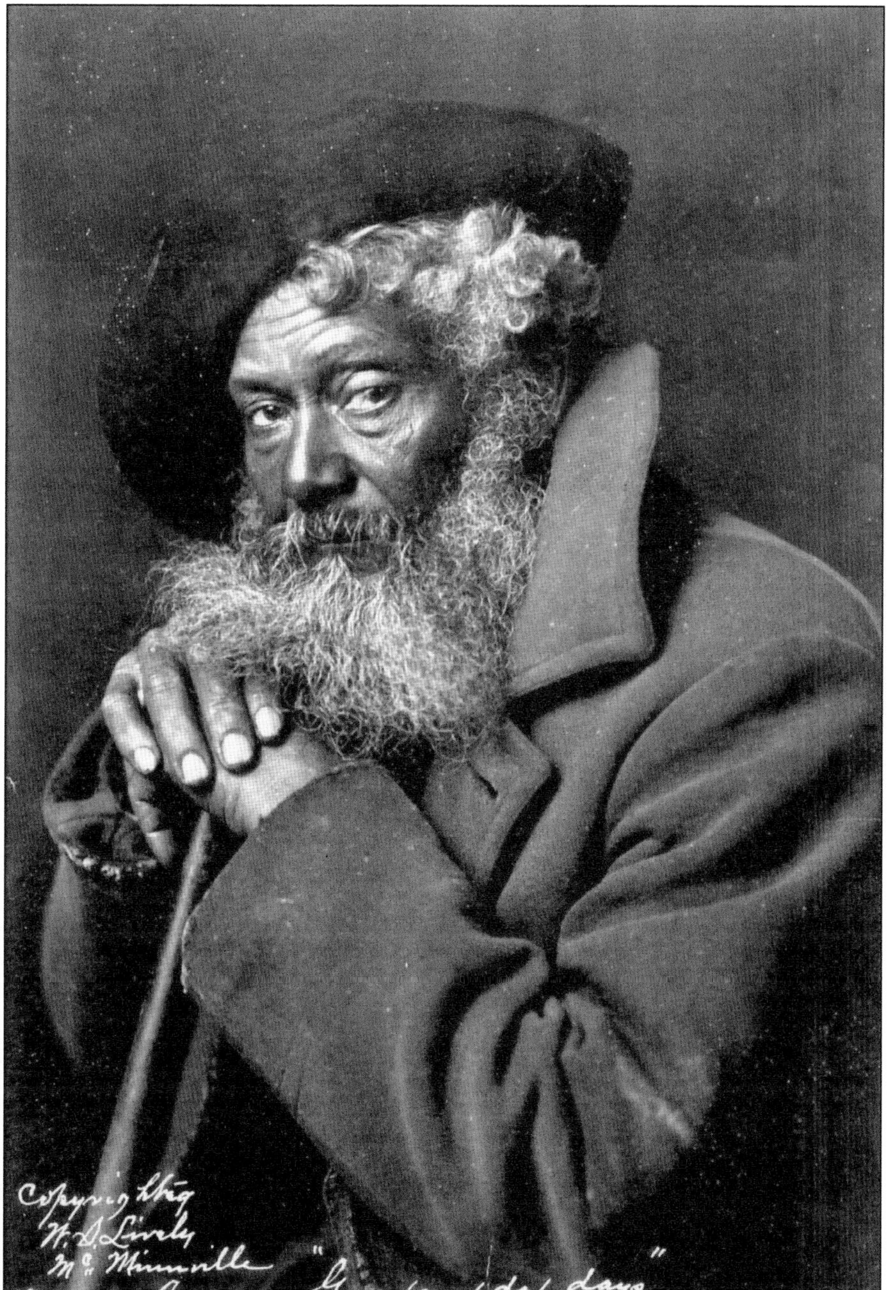

Dated 1903, this award-winning portrait study by William Dad Lively received national recognition when it was displayed throughout the country in various photography conventions in the early 1900s. Lively often asked rugged, elderly men to sit for his camera, which resulted in some of the most distinguished character studies of his career. Beginning in 1904, when he opened his Southern School of Photography, he concentrated on making pictures for competition with other photographers. From 1904 to 1909, his photographs were awarded the grand prize on more than 14 occasions, with salon honors for 10 consecutive years from the Daguerre Institute in Winona Lake, Indiana.

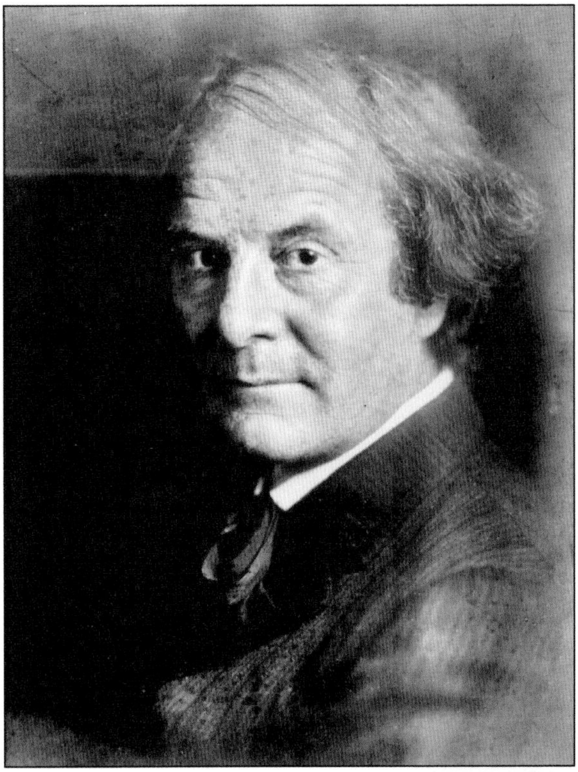

World-famous lecturer and author Elbert Hubbard, pictured, was at one time a student at the Southern School of Photography in McMinnville. He was reportedly one of the most photographed persons in the world, who, later in his career, maintained that William Spencer Lively's portraits of him were the favorites of all ever taken of him.

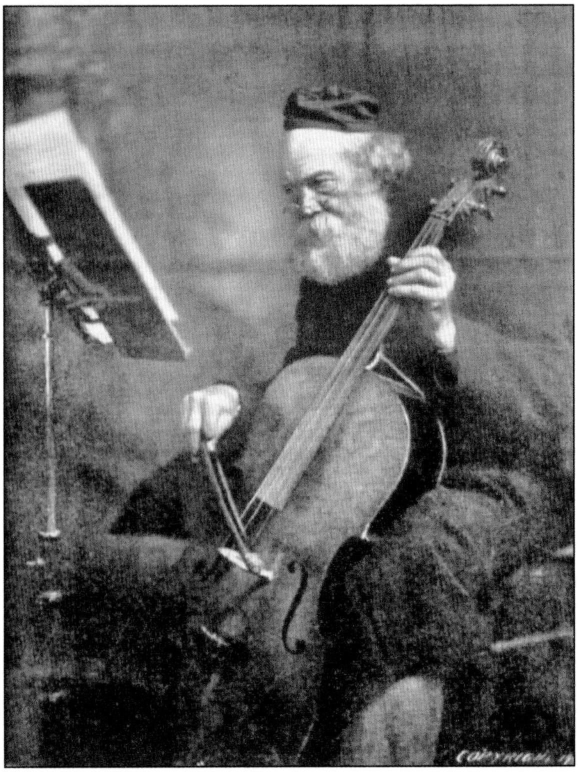

Joe S. Lively, Dad Lively's son, was also an award-winning photographer who created photographs for competitions. From the beginning of the school's existence, Joe was one of the important instructors at the institution. Joe's photograph, "Practice Hour," seen here, received the grand prize at the Tri-State Convention, Atlanta, Georgia, in 1904. It also won the highest award at Winona Lake, Indiana, in 1904, and was published in *Wilson's Photographic Magazine*.

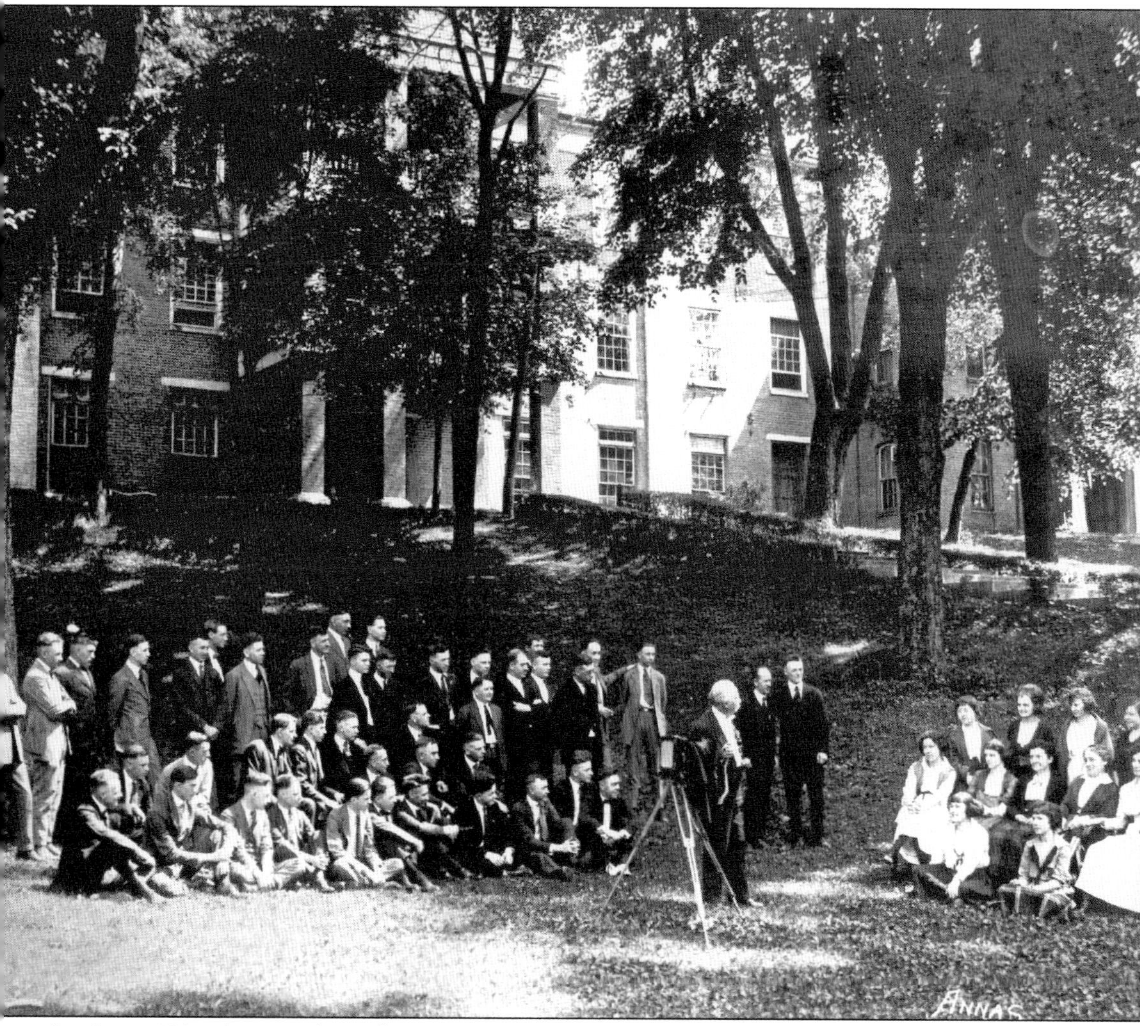

In this *c.* 1924 photograph, William Spencer Dad Lively is seen conducting an outdoor master class on the subject of "small group posing" to students on the front lawn of the school. Lively often took his students on field trips to picturesque destinations in the surrounding area to conduct his classes.

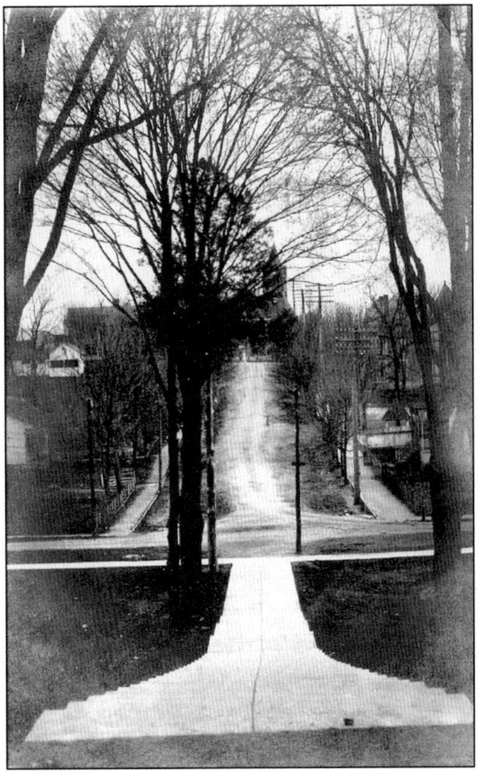

With students coming to McMinnville from various parts of the country to study at the Southern School of Photography, important alliances were often formed among the student body. One such alliance was between Anna Taylor from Connecticut and Coyd B. Yost from West Virginia, who met while studying at the school and were married in 1917. Written on the back of this unusual image by Coyd Yost was, "first photograph with my camera." It is a view from the entrance of the school facing south, down the long flight of steps, down College Street toward the courthouse. The old school building (page 81) can be seen at top right. Yost took this photograph, below, of Anna Taylor, his future wife, while studying at the school.

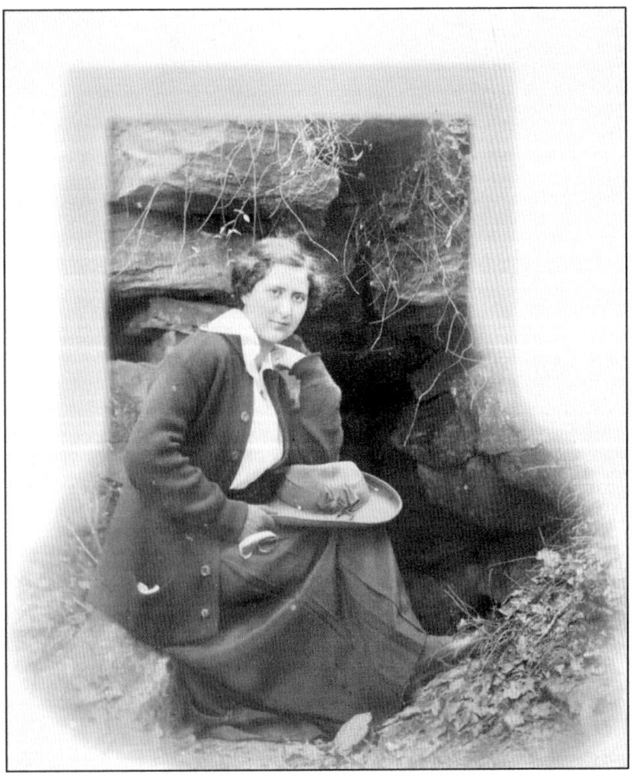

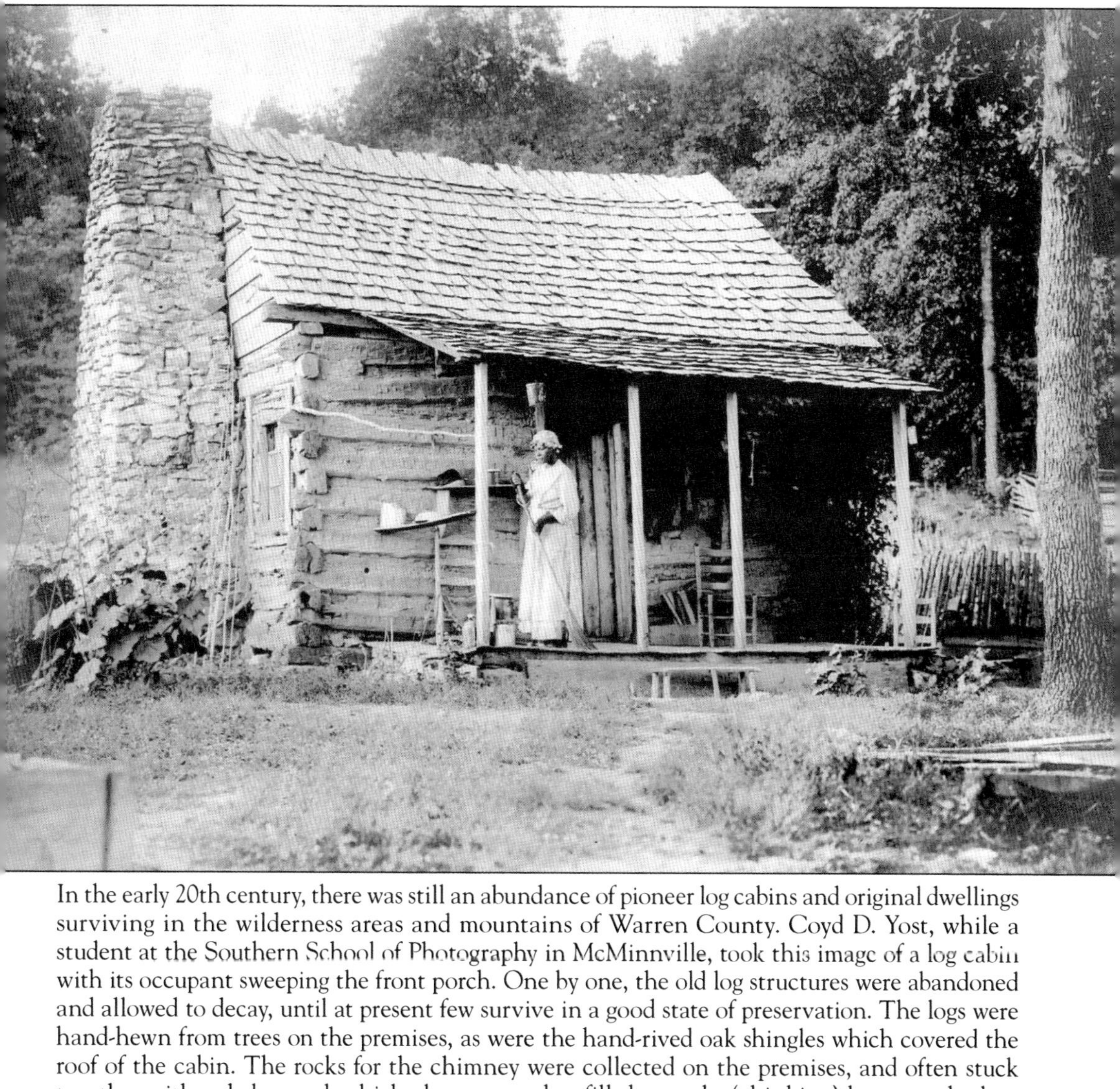

In the early 20th century, there was still an abundance of pioneer log cabins and original dwellings surviving in the wilderness areas and mountains of Warren County. Coyd D. Yost, while a student at the Southern School of Photography in McMinnville, took this image of a log cabin with its occupant sweeping the front porch. One by one, the old log structures were abandoned and allowed to decay, until at present few survive in a good state of preservation. The logs were hand-hewn from trees on the premises, as were the hand-rived oak shingles which covered the roof of the cabin. The rocks for the chimney were collected on the premises, and often stuck together with red clay mud, which also was used to fill the cracks (chinking) between the logs which formed the rooms. Usually the only source of heat was the large fireplace in which a fire was often kept continually burning.

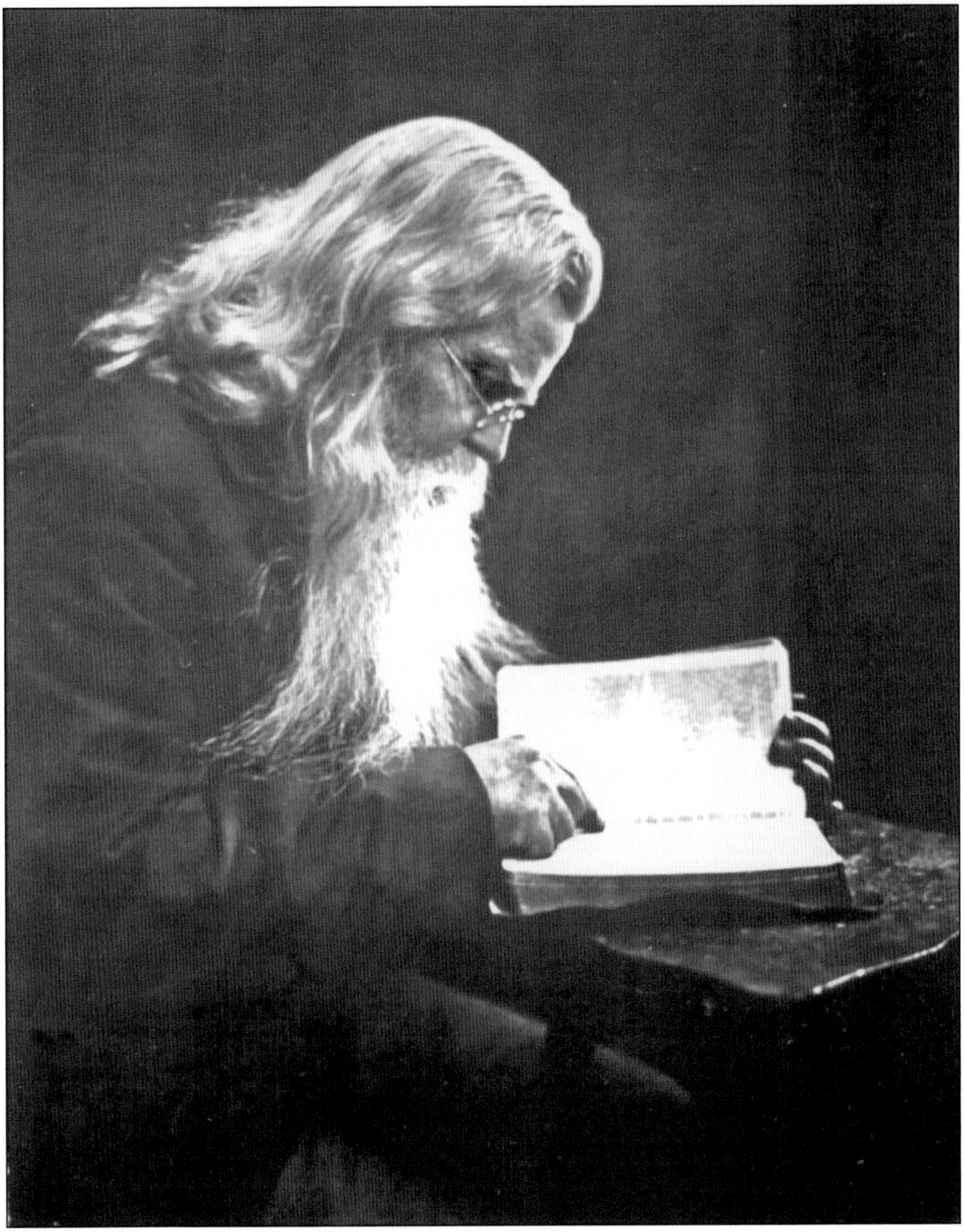

Considered a masterpiece of photographic art, and said by his son William Lively Jr. to be his father's favorite picture of his career, this study titled "If by Reason of Strength" captures William Spencer Lively's friend and McMinnville jeweler, William H. Meadows, reading the Bible. Lively had asked Meadows to grow his hair and beard for two years in order to achieve the desired results captured with his camera in 1909. The original 16-by-20-inch glass-plate negative and an original contact print have been acquired by The Southern Museum and Galleries of Photography, Culture and History in McMinnville, where they will be placed on permanent display.

This photographic portrait of young Thomas Edwin Bostick by William Spencer Lively was exhibited at the Paris World's Fair in the year 1900. Thomas Edwin Boasick (1897–1954) was the son of McMinnville pharmacist, Thomas King Bostick. Throughout his illustrious career, the innovative photographer won numerous prestigious awards, and numbered among his colleagues and admirers George Eastman, the camera manufacturer.

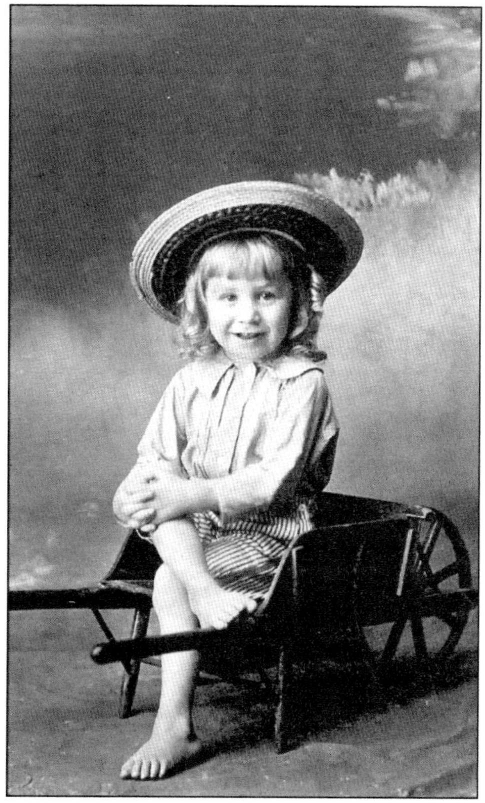

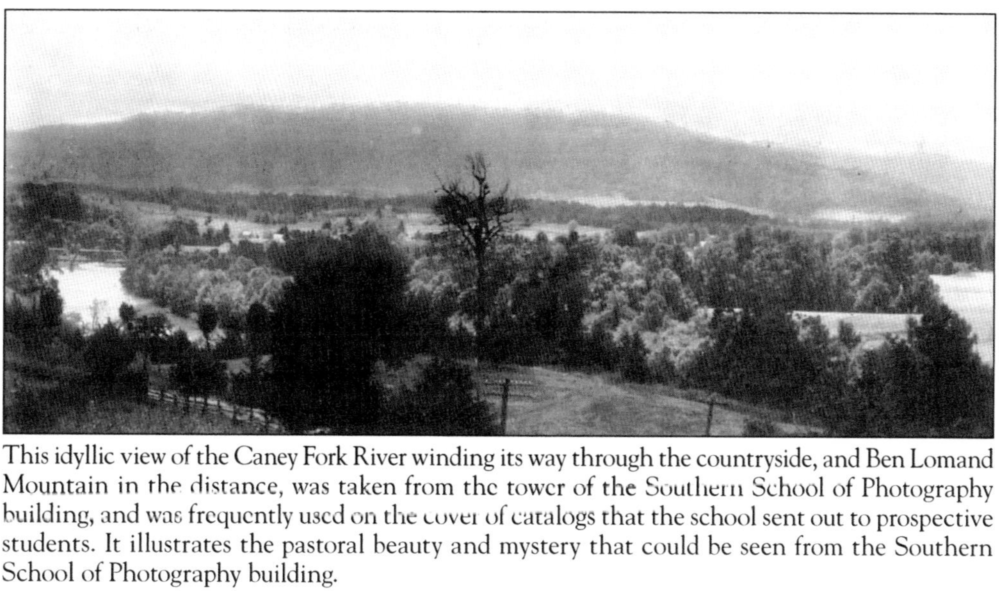

This idyllic view of the Caney Fork River winding its way through the countryside, and Ben Lomand Mountain in the distance, was taken from the tower of the Southern School of Photography building, and was frequently used on the cover of catalogs that the school sent out to prospective students. It illustrates the pastoral beauty and mystery that could be seen from the Southern School of Photography building.

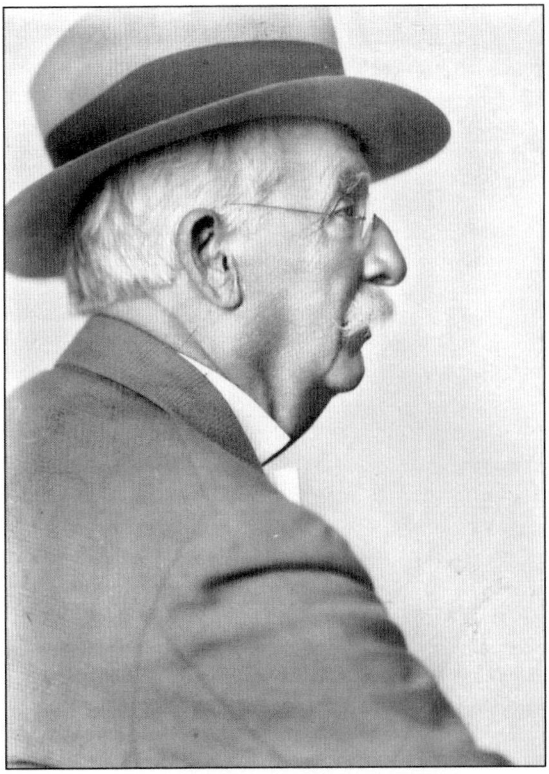

In his later years, Dad Lively was often photographed in profile, as shown in this photograph taken sometime in the late 1930s. He continued to receive awards, even after he retired in 1931. He received the greatest honor in August 1936, at the 50th Annual Convention of the Photographer's Association of America in Chicago, when he was awarded the first master of photography honorary degree. In this image taken by Earl Burnell of Sarasota, Florida, in 1936, Lively is receiving a loving cup from some former students and his son, Lee. Standing left to right are the following: unidentified, Joe Nappel, unidentified, and Lee Lively. Written on the back of the photograph in pencil is, "To Dad. We miss you. From Earl." When he died in 1944, an obituary appeared in *Time* magazine.

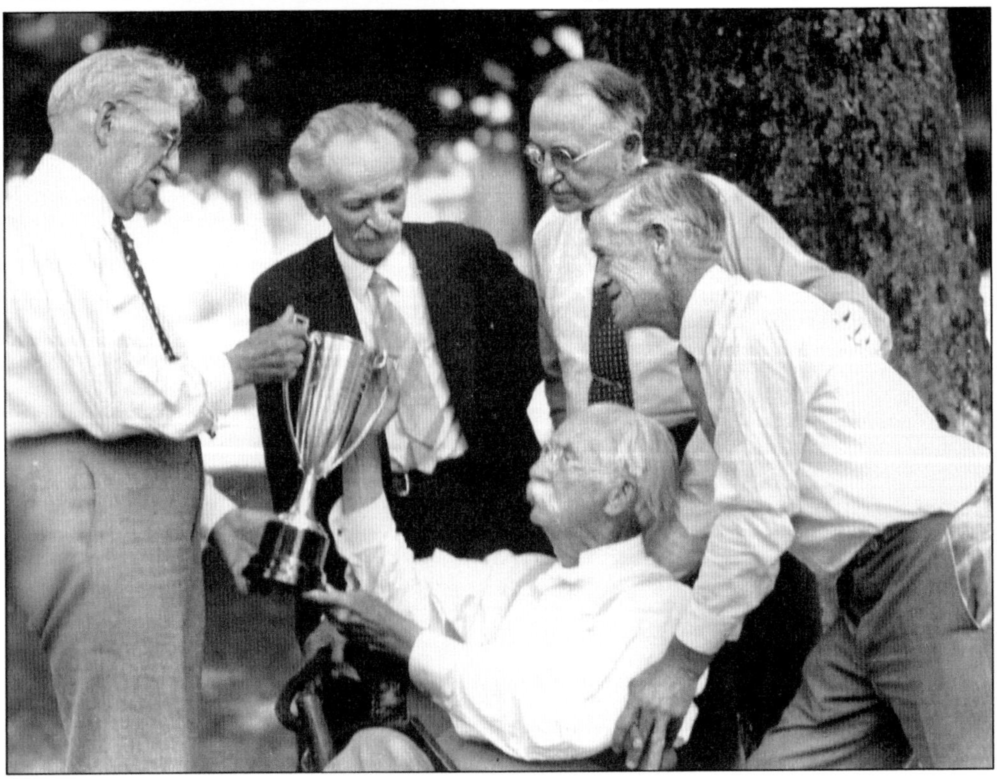

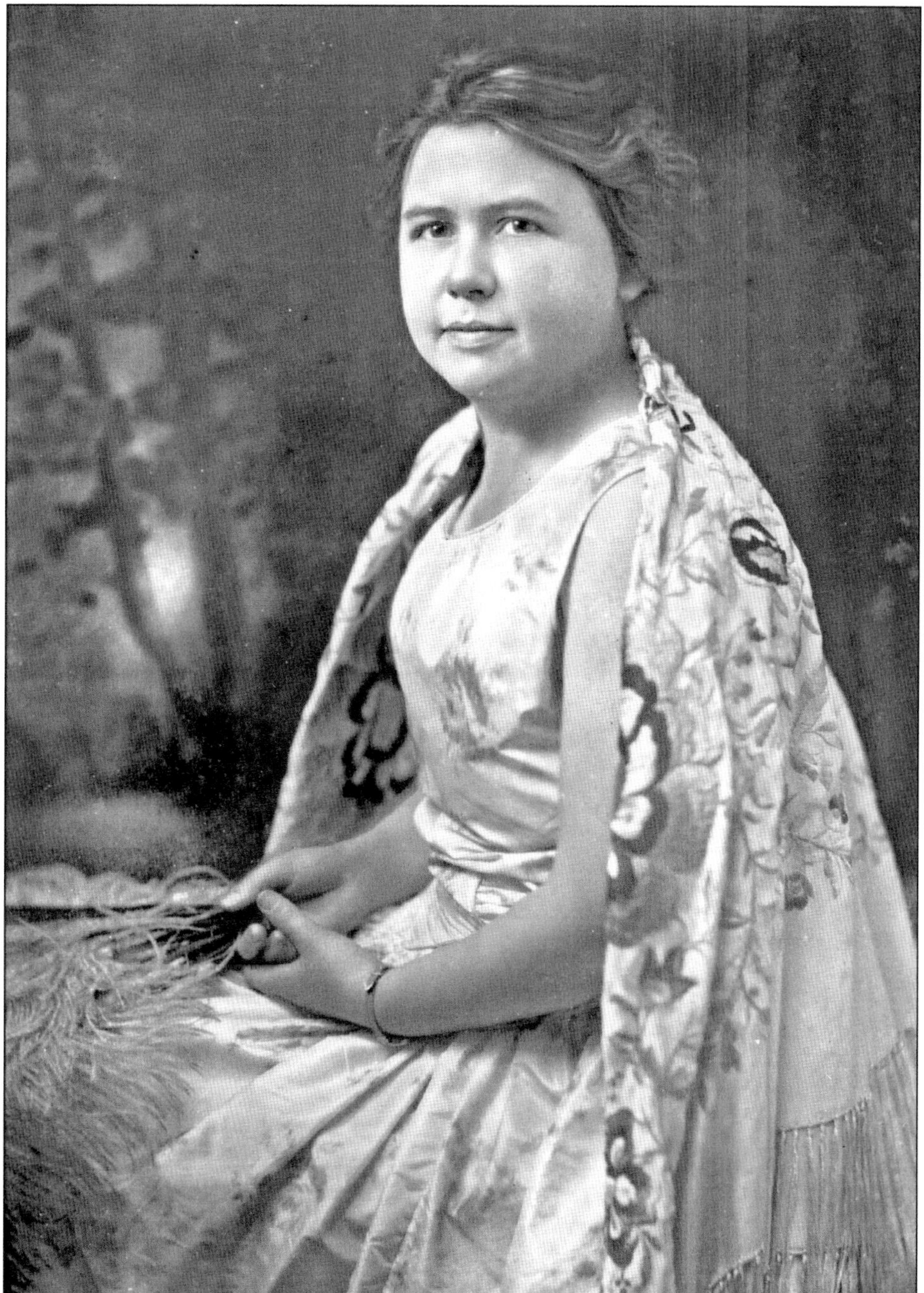

This portrait of Ethel Cook Lively, Dad Lively's second wife, was made about 1922 by the photographer's daughter, Nancy Pearl (Lively) Austin, who was also a photographer and maintained a photography studio in North Carolina. Nancy had attended the Southern School of Photography, beginning in 1904. Those in McMinnville who knew Ethel Cook spoke of her deep compassion and humanity, and relate the story of how Lela Lively, on her deathbed, admonished Ethel Cook to marry Dad Lively after she died, which she did and remained his wife and companion for the remainder of his life.

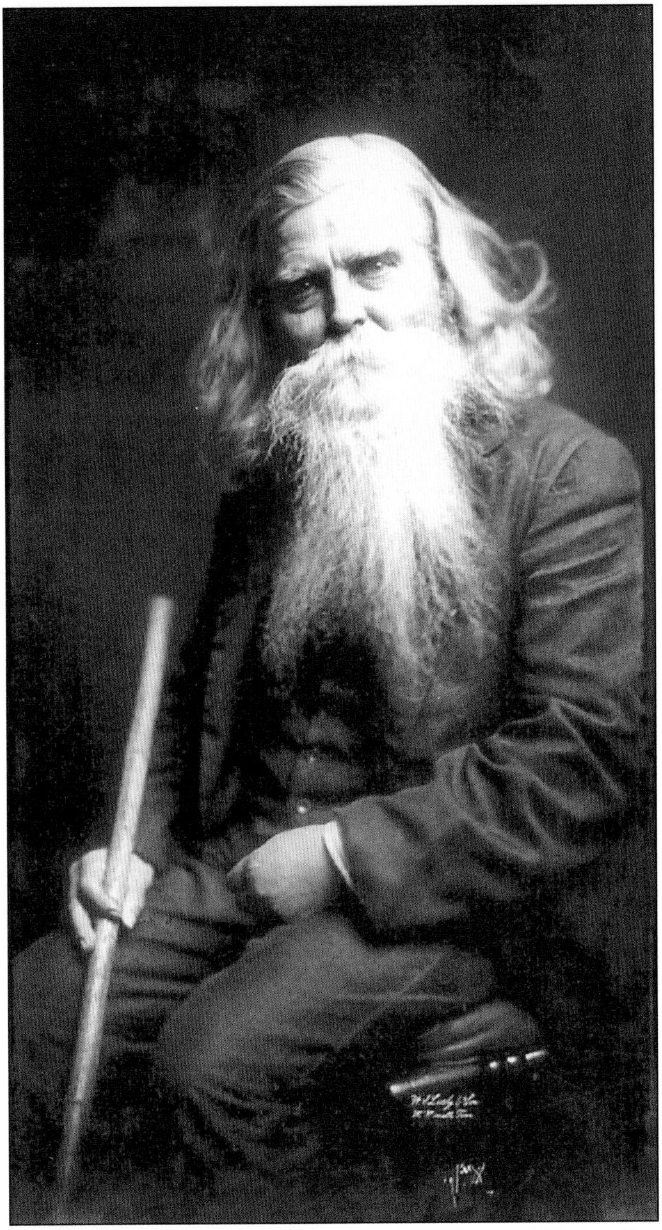

When photographer Dad Lively was asked by camera manufacturer George Eastman to produce the entire exhibit for display at the National Photography Convention in 1909, Lively proposed that he would produce three large, exceptional pictures for the event instead of a large number. He produced three 30-by-60-inch portraits from glass-plate negatives and a camera he and his furniture-making brother Sam designed and made, which measured 11 feet long, 6 feet high, and 5 and one half feet wide. One of the three sensational pictures produced for the 1909 convention was this study of Lively's longtime friend William Meadows, who had let his hair and beard grow for the shooting. Nothing had ever been seen to compare with Lively's three pictures, which were actually one-third larger than life and received nothing but astonishment and praise from the professionals assembled at the convention. Unfortunately, the camera was destroyed in the fire of 1928.

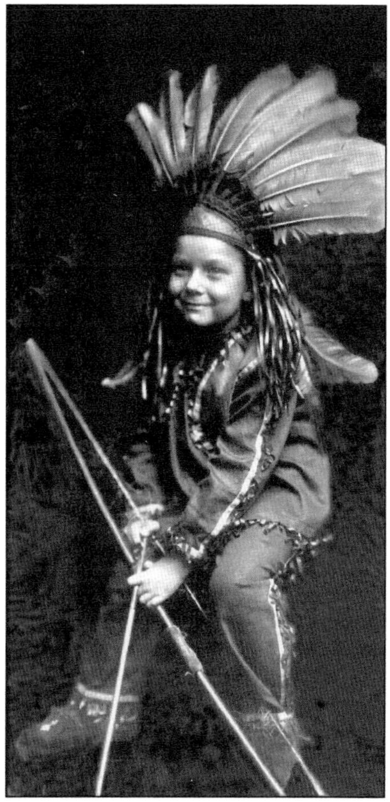

The second 30-by-60-inch sensational portrait created for the 1909 convention was that of photographer Lively's young grandson, William, who had long been a favorite subject, and had become one of the most photographed children in America by the time this study was made. The third portrait was that of 17-year-old Rose Taliferro, proclaimed at the time to be the most beautiful woman in McMinnville. The three large photographs were proclaimed an outstanding achievement and attracted greater attention than any display ever exhibited at the national convention. The three 30-by-60-inch glass-plate negatives are housed in the Smithsonian Institution in Washington, D.C. A set of original contact prints are a part of the Smithsonian collection as well. The Southern Museum and Galleries of Photography, Culture, and History has on permanent display a set of 30-by-60-inch digitally produced prints of the famous pictures.

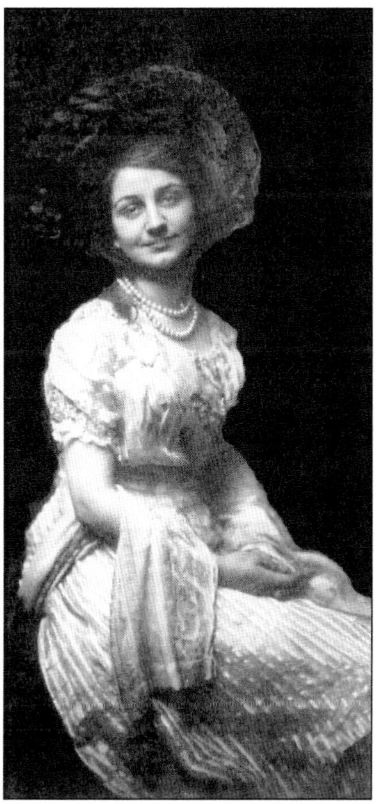